LIBRARY OF NEW TESTAMENT STUDIES

611

Formerly the Journal for the Study of the New Testament Supplement Series

Editor
Chris Keith

Editorial Board
Dale C. Allison, John M.G. Barclay, Lynn H. Cohick, R. Alan Culpepper,
Craig A. Evans, Robert Fowler, Simon J. Gathercole, Juan Hernandez Jr.,
John S. Kloppenborg, Michael Labahn, Love L. Sechrest, Robert Wall,
Catrin H. Williams, Britanny Wilson

THE CONTEST FOR TIME AND SPACE IN THE ROMAN IMPERIAL CULTS AND 1 PETER

Reconfiguring the Universe

Wei Hsien Wan

LONDON • NEW YORK • OXFORD • NEW DELHI • SYDNEY

T&T CLARK
Bloomsbury Publishing Plc
50 Bedford Square, London, WC1B 3DP, UK
1385 Broadway, New York, NY 10018, USA

BLOOMSBURY, T&T CLARK and the T&T Clark logo
are trademarks of Bloomsbury Publishing Plc

First published in Great Britain 2020
Paperback edition first published 2021

Copyright © Wei Hsien Wan, 2020

Wei Hsien Wan has asserted his right under the Copyright,
Designs and Patents Act, 1988, to be identified as Author of this work.

For legal purposes the Acknowledgements on pp. x–xi constitute
an extension of this copyright page.

Cover design: Tjaša Krivec

All rights reserved. No part of this publication may be reproduced or
transmitted in any form or by any means, electronic or mechanical,
including photocopying, recording, or any information storage or retrieval
system, without prior permission in writing from the publishers.

Bloomsbury Publishing Plc does not have any control over, or responsibility for,
any third-party websites referred to or in this book. All internet addresses given
in this book were correct at the time of going to press. The author and publisher
regret any inconvenience caused if addresses have changed or sites have
ceased to exist, but can accept no responsibility for any such changes.

A catalogue record for this book is available from the British Library.

Library of Congress Cataloging-in-Publication Data
Names: Wan, Wei Hsien, author.
Title: The contest for time and space in the Roman imperial cults and 1
Peter: reconfiguring the universe / by Wei Hsien Wan.
Description: London; New York, NY, USA: T&T Clark, 2019. |
Includes bibliographical references and index.
Identifiers: LCCN 2019016136 | ISBN 9780567684431 (hb) |
ISBN 9780567684479 (epub) | ISBN 9780567684448 (ePDF)
Subjects: LCSH: Bible. Peter, 1st–Criticism, interpretation, etc. |
Space–Biblical teaching. | Time–Biblical teaching. | Rome–Religion.
Classification: LCC BS2795.52.W36 2019 | DDC 227/.9206–dc23
LC record available at https://lccn.loc.gov/2019016136

ISBN: HB: 978-0-5676-8443-1
PB: 978-0-5677-0144-2
ePDF: 978-0-5676-8444-8
eBook: 978-0-5676-8447-9

Series: Library of New Testament Studies, 2513-8790, volume 611

Typeset by RefineCatch Limited, Bungay, Suffolk

To find out more about our authors and books visit
www.bloomsbury.com and sign up for our newsletters.

In memory of the victims of the Batang Kali massacre
&
for those who resist empire everywhere

CONTENTS

Acknowledgments	x
Abbreviations	xii
INTRODUCTION	1

Chapter 1
CONTEXTUALIZING THE PRESENT STUDY — 3

- 1.1 Paul, 1 Peter, and Empire — 4
  - 1.1.1 Insights from the Pauline Discussion — 4
  - 1.1.2 First Peter and Empire — 11
  - 1.1.3 Furthering the Work on 1 Peter — 17
- 1.2 Domination, Resistance, and Ideology — 19
  - 1.2.1 The Contributions of James Scott — 19
  - 1.2.2 Applications to the Present Study — 23
- 1.3 Time, Space, and the Social Order — 25
  - 1.3.1 The Ideological Nature of "Time" — 27
  - 1.3.2 The Ideological Nature of "Space" — 35
- 1.4 Converging Lines of Inquiry: The Present Study — 40

Chapter 2
THE SOCIO-HISTORICAL CONTEXT — 43

- 2.1 The Imperial Cults: An Overview — 43
  - 2.1.1 Historical Development in Anatolia — 43
  - 2.1.2 Ritual and Infrastructure — 48
  - 2.1.3 Their Remarkable Diversity — 52
  - 2.1.4 Indigenous Initiatives or Imperial Impositions?: Hybridity — 55
  - 2.1.5 Representing Roman Power — 59
- 2.2 First Peter: Establishing Parameters for Ideological Analysis — 62
  - 2.2.1 Authorship and Date of Composition — 62
  - 2.2.2 Provenance and Destination — 67
  - 2.2.3 Formulating a Working Hypothesis for 1 Peter — 70

Chapter 3
TIME IN THE IMPERIAL CULTS — 73

- 3.1 A New Calendar for Asia and the Reinterpretation of Time — 74
- 3.2 Imperial Festivals: Shaping the Rhythm of Time — 83
- 3.3 "Imperium Sine Fine": The Future of an Empire without End — 89
- 3.4 Conclusion — 96

Chapter 4
TIME IN 1 PETER — 97

- 4.1 From "Before the Foundation" to "the Last of the Ages" (1:20): A Primopetrine Thesis of Time — 97
- 4.2 The Power of Now: The Present as a State of Eschatological Urgency — 100
  - 4.2.1 The Ethical Imperative of the Present — 101
  - 4.2.2 Valorizing Estrangement and Suffering in the Present — 107
- 4.3 The Past in 1 Peter: Writing Empire Out of History — 111
  - 4.3.1 The Present in the Past: Reinterpreting Scripture, Reinterpreting History (1:10–12) — 111
  - 4.3.2 The Contest for History and the Politics of Identity — 115
- 4.4 The Future in 1 Peter: Complicating the Things to Come — 119
  - 4.4.1 Hiddenness, Revelation, and Reserve: De-Colonizing the Future — 121
  - 4.4.2 Judgment and Vindication: Relativizing Roman Justice in Anatolia — 123
  - 4.4.3 The Rhetoric of Impermanence: Circumscribing Empire — 124
- 4.5 Conclusion — 127

Chapter 5
SPACE IN THE IMPERIAL CULTS — 131

- 5.1 The Location and Prominence of Imperial Cultic Sites — 133
- 5.2 Imperial Temples: Ideology in Marble and Stone — 135
  - 5.2.1 Ephesus — 135
  - 5.2.2 Aphrodisias — 138
    - 5.2.2.1 Allegorical Figures — 139
    - 5.2.2.2 Idealized Ethnic Personifications — 139
    - 5.2.2.3 Emperors and Captives — 141
    - 5.2.2.4 Scenes from Greek Mythology — 142
  - 5.2.3 Ankara — 143
    - 5.2.3.1 The Spatial Ideology of the *Res Gestae* — 143
    - 5.2.3.2 Text as Monument — 147
- 5.3 The Imperial Cults and Sanctuaries of Traditional and Local Gods — 149
- 5.4 The Imperial Cults and the Transformation of Civic Spaces — 151
- 5.5 Conclusion — 154

Chapter 6
SPACE IN 1 PETER — 157

- 6.1 The Spatial Production of Non-Belonging — 158
  - 6.1.1 Exile: παρεπίδημος, πάροικος, παροικία — 159
  - 6.1.2 To the Diaspora, from Babylon — 164
- 6.2 The Spatial Production of Belonging — 169

	6.2.1	The οἶκος πνευματικός (2:5): Household or Temple?	169
	6.2.2	The Locus of Belonging: οἶκος πνευματικός (2:5) as Spatial Production	173
6.3	Spatial Imagination, Belonging, Resistance		175
6.4	Conclusion		177

CONCLUSION: (RE)PLACING THE EMPEROR, (RE)CONFIGURING THE UNIVERSE 179

Bibliography 183
Index of Biblical References 195
Index of Modern Authors 199

ACKNOWLEDGMENTS

"It takes a village," the saying goes, "to raise a child." Though it is labor of a far lesser order, this book would not have been possible without a village of my own. I say this mindful that I owe too many people too much to thank them all in any kind of stipulated space. That being said, I would like to mention those who've played a special role in helping me bring this work to completion.

To David Horrell I owe thanks for his inspiring synthesis of gentle wisdom, patient humility, and encyclopedic knowledge that's made him the best mentor I could've asked for. Thanks, Dave, for the friendship, many cups of coffee, lunches, and hours of encouraging conversation that have kept me going, especially in the last few months of this manuscript's completion, when I needed them most.

While I knew that writing something like this would be an intellectual endeavor, I didn't realize that it would also be—even more so!—a matter of psychological endurance and existential stamina. To the friends I met in Exeter I owe my very survival in this marathon—especially to Helen John, Francesca Stavrakopoulou, James Dyche, Sharanya Murali, Ryan Sweet, Evelyn O'Malley, Brad Arnold, Nora Williams, Kai Kidston, and Nick Humphreys. For the happy years in Manchester, a city that will forever be precious to me, I want to thank in particular Hassan "Eeyore" Ahmed, Tom Stevens, David Perkins, Charlie Pemberton, and my colleagues at The Federal Café for vivifying doses of northern spirit. Thank you all for being not only the best company a stranger to England could have found, but also for helping me find my heart and my voice as this work came into being, and for making everything brighter with laughter, drinks, and animal videos along the way. My gratitude belongs also to friends made during an earlier stint in Leuven: Emmanuel Nathan, Dorin Cerbu, Bradford Manderfield, Brano Kuljovksy, and Viorel Coman.

Without my father and my sister none of this would have been possible. Thanks, Erinn, for being my trusty sidekick in life. I think we both know that I've kept my hair and my health because of you. Mom would have loved to hold this book in her hands, I imagine.

Thank you also to colleagues who, along with Dave, meticulously read and commented on earlier drafts: John Barclay, Morwenna Ludlow, Louise Lawrence, Siam Bhayro, Esther Reed, and Kelly Liebengood. The strengths of this work I share with you all; its weaknesses are entirely my own.

And to everyone else in the village, I hope you know that, in so many ways, this work is truly yours too. My inadequate but heartfelt thanks to all who have left their mark on this work, knowingly or unknowingly.

Some of the material in Chapters 3 and 4 appeared earlier in Wei Hsien Wan, "Whose Time? Which Rationality? Reflections on Empire, 1 Peter, and the 'Common Era,'" in *Postscripts* 7, no. 3 (2011), 279–94; as well as David Horrell and Wei Hsien Wan, "Christology, Eschatology and the Politics of Time in 1 Peter," in *Journal for the Study of the New Testament* 38, no. 3 (2016), 263–76.

Some of the material in Chapters 5 and 6 first appeared in Wei Hsien Wan, "Repairing Social Vertigo: Spatial Production and Belonging in 1 Peter," in *The Urban World and the First Christians*, ed. Steve Walton, Paul Trebilco, and David W. J. Gill (Grand Rapids, MI: Eerdmans, 2017), 287–303.

ABBREVIATIONS

Unless otherwise stated, citations from classical sources and their translations are taken from the Loeb Classical Library (LCL) editions; these have not been listed again in the Bibliography.

AGRW	Ascough, Richard S., Philip A. Harland, and John S. Kloppenborg, *Associations in the Greco-Roman World: A Sourcebook* Berlin and Waco. TX: de Gruyter/Baylor University Press, 2012.
AvP	*Die Altertümer von Pergamon (1895–).*
BCH	*Bulletin de correspondance hellénique.*
Bosch, *Quellen Ankara*	Bosch, Emin. *Quellen zur Geschichte der Stadt Ankara im Altertum.* Türk Tarih kurumu yayainlarindan, Series 7, no. 46. Ankara: Türk Tarih Kurumu Basimevi, 1967.
FGrH	Jacoby, Felix, ed. *Die Fragmente der griechischen Historiker.* 15 vols. Berlin: Weidmann, 1923–58.
IAssos	Merkelbach, Reinhold. *Die Inschriften von Assos.* IGSK 4. Bonn: Rudolf Habelt, 1976.
IEph	Engelmann, H., H. Wankel, and R. Merkelbach. *Die Inschriften von Ephesos.* IGSK 11–17. Bonn: Rudolf Habelt, 1979–84.
IG II^2	Kirchner, Johannes, ed. *Inscriptiones Atticae Euclidis anno anteriores.* 4 vols. Berlin: Walter de Gruyter, 1913–40.
IG XII, Suppl.	Hiller von Gaertringen, Friedrich F., ed. *Supplementum.* Berlin: Walter de Gruyter, 1939.
IGladiateurs	Robert, Louis. *Les gladiateurs dans l'orient grec.* Bibliothèque de l'École des Hautes Études IVe section, Sciences historique et philologiques. Amsterdam: Adolf M. Hakkert, 1971 [1940].
IGR	Cagnat, R.L., J.F. Toutain, V. Henry, and G. L. Lafaye, eds. *Inscriptiones graecae ad res romanas pertinentes.* 4 vols. Paris: E. Leroux, 1911–27. Vol. 1: (nos. 1–1518) ed. R.L. Cagnat, J.F. Toutain, and P. Jouguet (1911); Vol. 2: never published; Vol. 3: R. Cagnat and G. Lafaye (1906); Vol. 4: Asia (nos. 1–1764) ed. G. L. Lafaye (1927).
IOlympia	Dittenberger, Wilhelm. *Die Inschriften von Olympia.* Berlin: Asher, 1896.
MAMA	Calder, W. M., E. Herzfeld, S. Guyer and C.W.M. Cox, eds. *Monumenta Asiae Minoris antiqua.* 10 vols. American Society for Archaeological Research in Asia Minor. Publications 1–10. London: Manchester University Press, 1928–93.
OGIS	Dittenberger, Wilhelm, ed. *Orientis graeci inscriptiones selectae. Supplementum Sylloge inscriptionum graecarum.* 2 vols. Leipzig: S. Hirzel, 1903–5. Repr. Hildesheim: G. Olms, 1970.

REG	*Revue des études grecques.*
SEG	*Supplementum epigraphicum graecum.* Leiden: Brill, 1923– .
TAM V	Peter Herrmann, *Tituli Lydiae linguis graeca et latina conscripti* (1981, 1989).

INTRODUCTION

Sometime in April 2015, groups of homeless people began setting up tent camps in various locations throughout Manchester's city center, triggering an open conflict between the city's rough sleepers and its authorities. As highly visible clusters of tents formed in busy places—including the historic St. Ann's Square and Market Street, the main artery of the city's shopping area—they created unease with the city authorities, who soon responded with court orders for eviction, seizure of tents, and arrests of those charged as instigators of the movement.

Though this series of events later came to be known in media channels and to the general public as "the Manchester homeless protests," there was a dispute as to its nature. Its supporters insisted that they were not in fact protesting anything (including the city council's efforts to help the homeless), but rather creating conditions in which people who were sleeping on the streets could do so more comfortably and safely. "First of all I was sleeping in a cardboard box, then I started to build walls around us like windbreakers," said Ryan McFee, one of those charged with violating the ban. "What I was trying to do was create a homeless shelter of the kind that's not currently available in Manchester. Normally they kick you out during the day. Here, people are welcome to rock up and chill, 24/7. Where does it state anything about Manchester city council's homelessness policy? I'm not protesting against no homeless policy." Another rough sleeper later said of a disbanded homeless settlement termed "The Ark" by its inhabitants: "We were trying to create a space where people could come and feel safe. We gave tents away, toiletries, food, anything to help people on the streets."[1] Nevertheless, for city center chief councilor Pat Karney, these camps were an affront to the city council's efforts: "From day one our town hall team [has] offered and spoken to every homeless person in the city centre. They [the homeless] are now in danger of losing public support for the cause by turning it into some sort of pantomime all around the city centre."[2] During a court hearing some months after the camps began,

1. Helen Pidd and Aidan Balfe, "Manchester Homeless People Face Jail Over City Centre Tent Camps," *The Guardian*, September 30, 2015.
2. Katie Butler, "Homeless Protesters Set Up New Camp on Market Street in Manchester City Centre," *Manchester Evening News*, October 22, 2015.

prosecutor for Manchester City Council Arron Walthall insisted that these settlements were "a challenge to the homeless policy of the local authority" that incurred "a very substantial and significant expenditure to the public purse," and requested that the district judge put an end to what amounted to "a trespass or unauthorised use of land."[3] The council won its case.

It is often the case that conflict and transgression reveal the boundaries of our thinking. Our habitual and tacit assumptions about what a square or a street is for, for example, can be disclosed by embodied practices that violate them. Likewise, one community's implicit values about clock time and punctuality (e.g., "It is disrespectful to be late") are exposed when it encounters another group that keeps time differently and construes social obligations in a different way. In these instances, conflict and transgression become revelatory, for they uncover the lines and borders by which particular cultural patterns of living and thinking—and thus identities—are delineated.

This work is an attempt to probe the relationship between two different ways of construing the world, two ideologies, by examining them side by side. By exploring and interrogating difference, I hope to bring to the foreground the distinctive ways in which each side configures—or reconfigures—that shared world. Cults to the Roman emperor and his family were a unique development in the imperial period, as was the movement to which the author of 1 Peter belonged—a phenomenon we now know as early Christianity. In studying them alongside each other, we can, I think, come to a better understanding of the distinctiveness of each, as well as the relationship between them—an ambivalent affair that would later take hold of the Christian imagination in a variety of ways, from graphic accounts of saintly deaths in martyrdom literature to the hopeful elaborations of Byzantine *symphonia* between the Church and the imperial state.

This work is laid out in six chapters. Chapter 1 sets the study in its scholarly context, tracing a trajectory from investigations in Pauline studies to developments in 1 Peter, and articulating important theoretical principles that will be elaborated in subsequent chapters. Chapter 2 provides a socio-historical context, and looks at orienting aspects of the Roman imperial cults as well as 1 Peter that will facilitate our considerations of them as "sources" of ideology and ideological conflict. Chapter 3 studies the ways in which time is construed in the practices of the imperial cults of Anatolia. The patterns that emerge then serve as the backdrop against which I examine temporal imagination in 1 Peter in Chapter 4. Whereas these two chapters consider the axis of time, the next two consider space. In Chapter 5, I return to the imperial cults, this time looking at its practices (architecture in particular) as acts of spatial construction—attempts to define, appropriate, and even dominate space. Chapter 6 then examines 1 Peter under the same light. These comparisons, I hope, will give us further insight into how Roman imperialism and 1 Peter were drawn into a contest of imaginations as they each sought to construct time and space according to distinct—and rivaling—criteria.

---

3. Jennifer Williams, "Manchester's Homeless Protest Camp Banned from City Centre," *Manchester Evening News*, July 20, 2015.

Chapter 1

CONTEXTUALIZING THE PRESENT STUDY

Recent decades have undoubtedly witnessed a surge of interest in the relationship between New Testament texts and the Roman Empire. Much of the focus has revolved around the Pauline corpus, though scholars in Revelation and Gospel studies have likewise brought their expertise and tools to the table, along with those taking approaches more marginal to the traditional canons of modern biblical studies—feminist and liberationist readings, decolonial and postcolonial perspectives, and perhaps most broadly, cultural studies and critical theory. The result has been something akin to a polyphonic scholarly motet, with diverse voices sometimes coming together in unison, sometimes parting ways in dissonance, and at other times playing off each other in clusters of intriguing, if more ambiguous, tensions.

Since there is, at this time, no book-length treatment on the subject of 1 Peter and the Roman Empire, it is ultimately within the context of this broader discussion that the present project finds its place. To situate this investigation in its academic context, I begin by tracing a path leading from the study of Paul and the Roman Empire to similar developments in the study of 1 Peter (Section 1.1). This trajectory not only reflects my own encounter with what has been called "empire criticism" of New Testament literature, but—more importantly—serves to highlight some of the key themes that I will both underscore and push against in subsequent chapters. The aim, therefore, is not to provide a comprehensive review of the secondary literature but a focused one, making use of transferable insights from recent studies. The task has of course been facilitated by the shared epistolary character of both the Pauline corpus and 1 Peter. Following this, the chapter moves on to examine some conceptual frameworks that will inform my reading of 1 Peter. These will draw from studies in domination, resistance, and ideology, particularly the work of James Scott (Section 1.2). Next, I introduce a foundational assumption adopted in this study, namely, that the ways in which we think of and experience time and space are culturally conditioned or constructed; as such, they are ideological and political (Section 1.3). I will return to these theoretical aspects in later chapters as they become relevant. The goal in this chapter is to identify the lines of inquiry that converge on the formulation of a thesis statement, as well as establish the boundaries of my current endeavor.

1.1 Paul, 1 Peter, and Empire

1.1.1 Insights from the Pauline Discussion

As with so many questions and themes in New Testament studies, questions about the Roman Empire have, not surprisingly, found their epicenter in the writings of the Pauline tradition. This is not, of course, to downplay the attention rightly deserved by other texts, such as the canonical Gospels or the book of Revelation—an inevitable contender in the arena of critical scholarship, given its staunch critique of Rome. The course that I will trace here, however, takes as its reference point the scholarly attention on Paul, that figure who looms so large in New Testament studies. I have chosen this line of inquiry for two reasons: (1) it was through Paul's letters that I first "cut my teeth" on the relationship between the New Testament and imperial discourse; and (2) the special relevance of the Pauline corpus for 1 Peter due to their shared epistolary genre as well as the traditional links that have been identified between them.[1]

As far as studies on Paul and empire are concerned, the work of Adolf Deissmann at the beginning of the twentieth century can be regarded as a predecessor to later lines of inquiry.[2] Deissmann began with observations regarding shared vocabulary between the New Testament and imperial terminology—words such as κύριος, θεοῦ υἱός, εὐαγγέλιον, σωτήρ, and παρουσία used by New Testament writers that found corresponding resonances in Roman usage. Although Deissmann concluded that the early Christian uses of these terms were primarily rooted in the Jewish Septuagintal tradition, and as such did not originate in attempts to refute the Caesars' claims to divinity, he nevertheless raised the possibility of polysemy: in applying these terms to Christ and his kingdom, Christians triggered a "polemical parallelism between the cult of the emperor and the cult of Christ."[3] For Deissmann, this "polemical parallelism" would inevitably have been activated whenever and wherever Christians used theological and cultic terminology that "happen[ed] to coincide with solemn concepts of the Imperial cult which sounded the same or similar," thus arousing "sensations of contrast" between Christ and Caesar, God's kingdom and the Roman Empire.[4] As John Barclay notes, in Deissmann's work we already see an outline of the key issues driving more current investigations into the New Testament and empire, namely: (1) the overlap between early Christian and imperial vocabulary; (2) explanations for this overlap; (3) its

---

1. On the relationship between 1 Peter and Paul's letters, see, for example, M. E. Boring, "First Peter in Recent Study," *Word and World* 24.4 (2004): 358–67 (361–4).

2. Adolf Deissmann, *Light from the Ancient East: The New Testament Illustrated by Recently Discovered Texts of the Graeco-Roman World*, trans. Lionel R. M. Strachan (London: Hodder & Stoughton, 1910).

3. Deissmann, *Light from the Ancient East*, 346, 381.

4. Deissmann, *Light from the Ancient East*, 346.

significance for the first Christians; and (4) the extent to which anti-imperial intent can be ascribed to Paul.[5]

Nonetheless, the question of the imperial context of the New Testament fell into relative neglect ("relative," that is, to the proliferation of interest we see now), and only gained significant scholarly attention in the closing decades of the twentieth century.[6] This development cannot be separated from at least two other concurrent developments that received much attention in academic guilds: the emergence of liberation theologies in postcolonial Latin America, as well as the genesis of what has been termed "postcolonial studies," inaugurated, as is generally acknowledged, by the beachhead publication of Edward Said's *Orientalism* in 1978.[7]

One primary stimulus for this revival came in the form of a now well-known collection of essays edited by Richard Horsley, *Paul and Empire: Religion and Power in Roman Imperial Society*.[8] Its fourteen essays, twelve of which had been previously published in some form between 1978 and 1994, come together as a cross-disciplinary anthology of sorts, collating insights from a diverse team of scholars ranging from classicists like S. R. F. Price and Paul Zanker to liberationist and feminist interpreters such as Neil Elliott and Elisabeth Schüssler Fiorenza. By means of Horsley's judicious editorial hand, the collection represents an earnest effort to consider the pervasive and incisive power of Rome in the lives of both Paul and the first recipients of his letters, as well as the political nature of texts in the Pauline tradition.[9]

As a whole, *Paul and Empire* drew attention not only to the pervasive imperial context under which Christianity's earliest documents were produced and read, but also to the kerygma and praxis of Pauline communities as counter-imperial

---

5. John M. G. Barclay, "Why the Roman Empire Was Insignificant to Paul," in *Pauline Churches and Diaspora Jews*, WUNT 275 (Tübingen: Mohr Siebeck, 2011), 364. Justin Meggitt ("Taking the Emperor's Clothes Seriously: The New Testament and the Roman Emperor," in *The Quest for Wisdom: Essays in Honor of Philip Budd* [Cambridge: Orchard Academic, 2002], 157–8) believes that "polemical parallelism" remains the best model for understanding the interactions between imperial ideology and the development of Christology in the New Testament.

6. On some relevant developments in intervening decades, see Meggitt, "Taking the Emperor's Clothes Seriously," 143; Barclay, "The Roman Empire," 2011, 364 n. 4.

7. On the development of postcolonial studies vis-à-vis biblical studies, see R. S. Sugirtharajah, "Charting the Aftermath: A Review of Postcolonial Criticism," in *The Postcolonial Biblical Reader*, ed. R. S. Sugirtharajah (Oxford: Blackwell, 2006), 7–32 as well as other essays in the collection. See also Stephen D. Moore, *Empire and Apocalypse: Postcolonialism and the New Testament*, The Bible in the Modern World 12 (Sheffield: Sheffield Phoenix Press, 2006).

8. Richard A. Horsley, ed., *Paul and Empire: Religion and Power in Roman Imperial Society* (Harrisburg, PA: Trinity Press International, 1997).

9. This is expressly stated in Horsley's general introduction to the collection (*Paul and Empire*, 3).

forces—as means by which Christians of the first century resisted Roman domination. These thrusts—that is, the overarching reality of empire in early Christianity and the ways in which its disciples pushed back against imperial rule—received sustained attention from an increasing number of scholars in the ensuing years, and continue to generate similar studies in New Testament texts beyond the Pauline corpus, as a sampling of publications after *Paul and Empire* will show.[10] The imperial context of Christian origins has, it would seem, become indelibly stamped into the consciousness of modern biblical scholars.

Though scholarly voices in this discussion have by no means been monolithic—diverse as they are both in the methods they employ and the conclusions they draw—there has been a recurrent tendency among scholars to see early Christianity as a movement poised against Roman power. Driving this perspective is the idea that early Christian proclamation of Christ's lordship, wherever and whenever it was made, constituted an antithesis, a challenge, to imperial authority—and, indeed, oppressive forces everywhere. Christian practices informed by that kerygma are subsequently understood as acts of resistance formulated as alternatives to practices in wider Roman society, particularly that of cultic veneration of the emperor himself.[11] Taking as it does Deissmann's earlier conclusions from the realm of conjecture into that of historical paradigm, such an approach already formed the basis of several essays in the pioneering *Paul and Empire*.[12]

---

10. Bearing in mind that the following are by no means uniform in their methods or conclusions, see, e.g., Wes Howard-Brook and Anthony Gwyther, *Unveiling Empire: Reading Revelation Then and Now*, The Bible & Liberation Series (Maryknoll, NY: Orbis Books, 1999); Warren Carter, *Matthew and Empire: Initial Explorations* (Harrisburg, PA: Trinity, 2001); Richard A. Horsley, *Jesus and Empire: The Kingdom of God and the New World Disorder* (Minneapolis, MN: Fortress Press, 2002); John K. Riches and David C. Sim, eds., *The Gospel of Matthew in Its Roman Imperial Context* (New York, NY: T&T Clark, 2005); Seyoon Kim, *Christ and Caesar: The Gospel and the Roman Empire in the Writings of Paul and Luke* (Grand Rapids, MI: Eerdmans, 2008); Warren Carter, *John and Empire: Initial Explorations* (New York, NY: Bloomsbury T&T Clark, 2008); Justin K. Hardin, *Galatians and the Imperial Cult: A Critical Analysis of the First-Century Social Context of Paul's Letter* (Tübingen: Mohr Siebeck, 2008); Kavin C. Rowe, *World Upside Down: Reading Acts in the Graeco-Roman Age* (New York, NY: Oxford University Press, 2009); Tom Thatcher, *Greater Than Caesar: Christology and Empire in the Fourth Gospel* (Minneapolis, MN: Fortress Press, 2009); James R. Harrison, *Paul and the Imperial Authorities at Thessalonica and Rome: A Study in the Conflict of Ideology* (Tübingen: Mohr Siebeck, 2011); Jason A. Whitlark, *Resisting Empire: Rethinking the Purpose of the Letter to "the Hebrews"* (London/New York, NY: Bloomsbury, 2014).

11. A notable example of this is John Dominic Crossan and Jonathan L. Reed, *In Search of Paul: How Jesus' Apostle Opposed Rome's Empire with God's Kingdom* (New York, NY: HarperCollins, 2004). Deissmann's influence can be clearly seen in the authors' prologue (1–12).

12. See especially the essays in Part III (140–204).

Within this paradigm, the New Testament writers' declarations concerning Jesus' Messiahship, God's righteousness/justice, and peace, along with practices such as habitual assembly and assistance of the poor and disadvantaged, can all be seen as part of a broader Christian program of opposition to the imperial agenda. The first Christians thus embraced the gospel with its promises of salvation and peace instead of Caesar's counterfeits of the same, and lived so as to form counter-cultural groups within a wider society firmly in the grip of Roman domination. So, for example, in Horsley's reading of 1 Corinthians, Paul's "adamant opposition to Roman imperial society" led him to found communities of discipleship that functioned as cells of "an exclusive alternative community to the dominant society and its social networks."[13] More broadly, the Pauline letters are "Paul's instruments to shore up the assemblies' [i.e. local churches'] group discipline and solidarity over against the imperial society, 'the present evil age' (Gal. 1:4), 'the present form of this world [that is] passing away' (1 Cor. 7:31)."[14]

Indeed, in an iconic lecture, N. T. Wright, one of the most prolific proponents of this school of thought, goes so far as to say that "Paul's answer to Caesar's empire is the empire of Jesus," "[a] new empire, living under the rule of its new Lord."

> [T]he scattered and often muddled cells of women, men and children loyal to Jesus as Lord form colonial outposts of the empire that is to be: subversive little groups when seen from Caesar's point of view, but when seen Jewishly an advance foretaste of the time when the earth shall be filled with the glory of the God of Abraham and the nations will join Israel in singing God's praises (cf. Rom. 15.7–13). From this point of view, therefore, this counter-empire can never be merely critical, never merely subversive. It claims to be the reality of which Caesar's empire is the parody; it claims to be modelling the genuine humanness, not least the justice and peace, and the unity across traditional racial and cultural barriers, of which Caesar's empire boasted.[15]

Wright's words here exemplify what Margaret Aymer has called "a rhetoric of alter-empire"—that is, "a rhetoric that presupposes a parallel, more powerful imperial structure and presence to that which is being made manifest in the world."[16]

---

13. "1 Corinthians: A Case Study of Paul's Assembly as an Alternative Society," in *Paul and Empire*, 242–52 (242, 248–9). This reading is anticipated in his general introduction to the volume: "in his mission Paul was building an international alternative society (the 'assembly') based in local egalitarian communities ('assemblies')" (8).

14. Horsley, "1 Corinthians," 252. For more work along similar lines, see Richard A. Horsley, ed., *Paul and Politics: Ekklesia, Israel, Imperium, Interpretation: Essays in Honour of Krister Stendahl* (Harrisburg, PA: Trinity Press International, 2000); Richard A. Horsley, ed., *Paul and the Roman Imperial Order* (Harrisburg, PA: Bloomsbury T&T Clark, 2004).

15. N. T. Wright, "Paul's Gospel and Caesar's Empire," in Horsley, *Paul and Politics*, 182–3.

16. Margaret P. Aymer, "Empire, Alter-Empire and the Twenty-First Century," *Union Seminary Quarterly Review* 59 (2005): 141.

Despite his use of the term "counter-empire" to designate "the empire of Jesus," Wright nevertheless envisions a Paul who opposes Roman imperialism, not, in fact, with that which is contrary to imperialism *per se* ("anti-empire"), but with imperialism of a different agency ("*alter*-empire").[17] His Paul rejects Rome not because it was an empire, but because it belonged to Caesar rather than to God.[18] The kingdom of God, on the other hand, is the true and ultimate alter-empire, superior to Rome and destined to supplant it. The latter is only a parody, a pale imitation of a greater reality that promises genuine human belonging, justice, and peace.[19]

But can such counter-imperial readings of Paul be justified? As one might expect, their emphasis on the dogged anti-imperial stance of Paul's letters has not gone without criticism. In his 2007 debate with Wright at the San Diego meeting of the Society of Biblical Literature, John Barclay argued that the heightened significance which Horsley, Wright, and others have ascribed to Rome in Pauline theology "misconstrue[s] the terms with which Paul addressed the political (and other) dimensions of human life."[20] Rome itself, Barclay points out, does not figure in Paul's letters as often as Wright thinks. It is telling that Paul never explicitly identifies the worldly powers he criticizes as being specifically *Roman* (e.g., Rom. 8:35–39; 1 Cor. 2:6–8; 15:24–28; 2 Cor. 11:25–26; Phil. 1:13; 1 Thess. 5:1–5).[21] Such a conspicuous "missing link" is not merely curious, but quite detrimental to the decidedly anti-imperialist Paul whom Wright constructs. It is a powerful indication that Paul inhabited a cosmos larger than the Empire itself—something greater than Caesar. For Barclay, Paul takes Jesus' death and resurrection, not the Roman Empire, as his starting point and center. Consequently, his stance toward Rome was characterized by flexible and differentiated evaluations that cannot be painted with a single stroke. Political authorities can, in the eyes of the apostle, both oppose

---

17. Jeremy Punt, "Empire and New Testament Texts: Theorising the Imperial, in Subversion and Attraction," *Hervormde Teologiese Studies/Theological Studies* 68, no. 1 (2012): 7–8, http://dx.doi.org/10.4102/hts.v68i1.1182.

18. Wright, "Paul's Gospel and Caesar's Empire," 164.

19. The Paul whom Wright champions is, quite obviously, an imperialist ideologue of sorts. Whether or not his portrait is correct, it is evident from Wright's writings that he does not regard this as a problem. Those reading the Bible in societies caught in the aftermath of modern colonialisms, however, might see things differently. On the Bible as a problematically imperialist text that legitimizes the exploitation of foreign peoples and lands, see, e.g., Musa Dube, "Toward a Post-Colonial Feminist Interpretation of the Bible," in *An Eerdmans Reader in Contemporary Political Theology*, ed. William T. Cavanaugh, Jeffrey W. Bailey, and Craig Hovey (Cambridge: Eerdmans, 2012), 585–99; eadem, *Postcolonial Feminist Interpretation of the Bible* (St. Louis, MO: Chalice Press, 2000), esp. 57–83.

20. Barclay, "The Roman Empire," 2011, 363. This essay is the reworked version of his contribution at the debate.

21. Barclay, "The Roman Empire," 2011, 374–5.

God and serve his purposes: it is the gospel, not the Empire as such, that forms the criterion of discernment. While passages such as Rom. 8:31–39, 1 Thess. 5:1–11, and Phil. 1:27–30 indicate Paul's critical, arm's-length approach to earthly powers, the more affable tone of Rom. 13:1–7 suggests that he was, after all, quite capable of recognizing aspects of Roman rule that were compatible with God's kingdom.[22] The careful reader cannot, in the end, reduce Paul to either a vehement opponent or an accommodating supporter of empire.

Rather than seeing the Roman Empire as the anvil against which Paul hammered out his theology (political in scope though it be), Barclay argues that Paul's most subversive act against Rome was in fact "not to oppose or upstage it, but to relegate it to the rank of a dependent and derivative entity, denied a distinguishable name or significant role in the story of the world."[23] The import of this move lies precisely in its denying the imperial project a role on the stage of world history:

> Where we divide the world into historical periods and ethno-political units (the Hellenistic or Roman eras; the Seleucid kingdom or the Roman empire), Paul sees no significant differences between Romans and Greeks, only a categorical distinction between κόσμος and καινὴ κτίσις which was created by the cross (Gal. 6.14–15): in shattering other classifications of culture and power, the world is divided anew around the event of Christ.[24]

By reframing reality on the basis of the gospel, Paul effectively blurs Rome into the background, into the scrapyard of empires of old. "We thus reach the paradoxical conclusion that Paul's theology is political precisely in rendering the Roman Empire theologically insignificant."[25]

A similar case is made by Peter Oakes in his earlier study of 1 Thessalonians and Philippians with relation to the imperial cults.[26] After examining passages often posited as directly antithetical to the worship of the Roman emperor (1 Thess. 4:15–17, 5:3; Phil. 2:6–11, 3:20), Oakes concludes that in them, Paul was neither engaging in anti-Roman polemics as such nor writing to forbid Christian participation in these cults.[27] What we in fact find in these passages is an articulation of Christology and a Christocentric eschatology first and foremost, but one which, by virtue of its narrative, indirectly—yet no less *decisively*—de-centers the Empire and all for which it stands. Paul is not pushing back against Rome *qua* Rome, but rather articulating a Christian way of living in and seeing the world. He is, as Oakes

---

22. Barclay, "The Roman Empire," 385.
23. Barclay, "The Roman Empire," 383–4.
24. Barclay, "The Roman Empire," 384.
25. Barclay, "The Roman Empire," 387.
26. Peter Oakes, "Re-Mapping the Universe: Paul and the Emperor in 1 Thessalonians and Philippians," *Journal for the Study of the New Testament* 27, no. 3 (2005): 301–22.
27. Oakes, "Re-Mapping the Universe," 321.

puts it, "redrawing the map of the universe."[28] In this redrawn cosmos, Christ, himself alienated by the Empire through the criminal death of crucifixion, is placed at the center, and his followers around him. By reconfiguring space and time (history) around the revelation of God in Christ, Paul de-centers Rome and the earthly power and security it offers. This logic of displacement undoubtedly undermines the veneration of the Roman emperor, premised as it is on his importance, but Oakes emphasizes that there is little in these letters to suggest that doing so was a *primary* concern for Paul. Like Barclay, Oakes conceives of Paul as one for whom the Christ-event lay at the heart of Christian theological imagination. The dismissal of Rome—rendering the Empire insignificant—is a highly consequential *effect* of that endeavor but not its principal, animating force.

In a very real and crucial way, the approaches taken by Barclay and Oakes cede greater agency both to Paul and the early Christian movement as a whole. What I mean by this is that, from their perspective, Christians were not gridlocked into an enclosed, colonized-colonizer dyad with Rome, as if all they said and did were defined by, and therefore can only be understood within, the terms of Roman imperialism. Rather, the readings of both scholars deliberately (and necessarily!) complicate the encounter between Paul and the Empire, allowing the apostle to develop a theological axis that is not simply forged within a Christ-vs-Caesar dialectic. This axis thus emerges as something simultaneously more independent and more innovative, for it is principally defined not by opposition to the Roman imperial order but rather by the Christ-event, in turn interpreted through the scriptures of Israel (cf. 1 Cor. 15:3–4). Granted, the development of Pauline theology did not occur in a vacuum, since early Christianity and the traditions from which it drew (Jewish and Hellenistic, among others) evolved and were situated within the historico-geographical context of Roman conquest of the Mediterranean world. Yet Rome *qua* Rome, as Barclay has pointed out, perspicuously takes the backseat in Paul's thought. This does not mean that his theology is apolitical, but rather that the political realm is, in the Pauline vision, subsumed into a greater cosmic struggle, a grander narrative of contest between sin and grace, between "the world" and God's "new creation" in Christ (Gal. 6:14–15; cf. Rom. 3:23–24; 2 Cor. 5:17).[29]

On the basis of Barclay's and Oakes' points, we ought to remain open to seeing Paul and other New Testament authors as creative theologians who were not simply defined by a polemical relationship with Rome. This is not merely another way of saying that the New Testament texts evidence differentiated stances toward the Roman Empire, but also a plea to think of the theological vision of the early Christians in wider and more complex terms than are often allowed by biblical scholars who engage in empire criticism. While Rome may

---

28. Oakes, "Re-Mapping the Universe," 321.

29. Barclay, "The Roman Empire," 2011, 384. See also Barclay's preceding essay in the same collection, "Paul, Roman Religion and the Emperor: Mapping the Point of Conflict" (pages 345–62).

have in fact dominated their everyday realities, they were not *merely* subjects of the Empire faced with only two options: to be "for" or "against" it.[30] The nuclear core of their identity and worldview was not, after all, opposition to worldly power *per se*, but rather the momentous event of God's revelation in Jesus of Nazareth.

1.1.2 First Peter and Empire

Scholarship on the New Testament and its relationship to Roman domination has, by comparison to Paul's letters and other texts in the canon, only marginally engaged 1 Peter. Tellingly, a recent collection of essays "evaluating empire in New Testament Studies," as its subtitle announces, passes over 1 Peter entirely.[31]

When scholars *have* evaluated 1 Peter in terms of its stance toward Rome, they have tended to conclude that the epistle shows no signs of resistance toward the Empire but rather endorses submission to it. The *locus classicus* of this position is 1 Pet. 2:13–17:

> For the Lord's sake accept the authority of every human institution, whether of the emperor as supreme, or of governors, as sent by him to punish those who do wrong and to praise those who do right. For it is God's will that by doing right you should silence the ignorance of the foolish. As servants of God, live as free people, yet do not use your freedom as a pretext for evil. Honor everyone. Love the family of believers. Fear God. Honor the emperor. (NRSV)

The conciliatory tone of this passage has, quite understandably, led most interpreters to conclude that 1 Peter adopts an accommodative stance toward Rome. Ramsey Michaels characterizes 1 Peter as urging a "compliant attitude" toward Caesar and his magistrates, and commends the author for his optimistic

---

30. So Karl Galinsky ("In the Shadow [or Not] of the Imperial Cult: A Cooperative Agenda," in *Rome and Religion: A Cross-Disciplinary Dialogue on the Imperial Cult*, ed. Jeffrey Brodd and Jonathan L. Reed [Atlanta, GA: Society of Biblical Literature, 2011], 217):

> There was a broad spectrum of interactions [between the Roman Empire and early Christianity], by no means limited to anti and pro. Similarly those of us who don't buy into the construction of early Christianity as a single-minded anti imperial movement are not *ipso facto* singing *laudes imperii*. Instead, we are seeking to do justice—and that is an aspect of justice, too—to the many faces, and facets, both of the Roman Empire and the various, and varied, Christian communities. It is a task we need to pursue and that, in fact, is what a small but increasing number of New Testament scholars are doing.

31. Scot McKnight and Joseph B. Modica, eds., *Jesus Is Lord, Caesar Is Not: Evaluating Empire in New Testament Studies* (Downers Grove, IL: IVP Academic, 2013).

vision of a (largely) harmonious relationship between church and state.³² Steven Bechtler states that the above passage "enjoins fear of God and honor of the emperor in a single breath and commands subjection to the emperor in recognition of his status as ὑπερέχων," noting that nowhere does the Petrine author show caution or open animosity toward the Empire such as we find, for example, in Revelation.³³ John Elliott likewise considers these verses politically inert: they "explicate no theory of the state, nor do they present any critique of Roman or local political power"—as can be said of the epistle as a whole.³⁴

Studies based on passages beyond 2:13–17 have arrived at similar conclusions. For David Balch, 1 Peter enjoins a household ethic that "encouraged Christians, as a new, Eastern religious community, to acculturate to Roman society."³⁵ Elisabeth Schüssler Fiorenza is more critical: the repeated injunctions to "submit" (2:13, 18; 3:1; 5:5) in 1 Peter exemplify an overall "rhetoric of subordination" by which the author "theologizes and moralizes the dominant kyriarchal ethos of Roman imperialism," thus justifying his readers' capitulation to the structures of domination.³⁶ Jennifer Bird's study of the letter's injunction to wives has similarly led her to adopt the position that "1 Peter is one of many texts in the Christian canon that perpetuate imperial ideology."³⁷ These readings reinforce the view of 1 Peter as an invariably submissive voice in the face of imperial domination.

In response to this line of thinking, others have called for more nuanced readings of the letter's stance toward Rome. Warren Carter offers an innovative argument that attempts to hold together the Petrine author's subtle critique of

---

32. J. Ramsey Michaels, *1 Peter*, WBC 49 (Dallas, TX: Word, 1988), lxiii, 132. The Petrine author, Michaels posits, assumes that "[u]nder normal circumstances loyalty to God and loyalty to the empire will not come into conflict," though of course the latter must be circumscribed by the former (132).

33. Steven R. Bechtler, *Following in His Steps: Suffering, Community and Christology in 1 Peter*, SBL Dissertation Series 162 (Atlanta, GA: Scholars, 1998), 50.

34. John H. Elliott, *1 Peter: A New Translation with Introduction and Commentary* (New York, NY: Doubleday, 2000), 502, 132.

35. David L. Balch, *Let Wives Be Submissive: The Domestic Code in 1 Peter*, SBL Monograph Series 26 (Atlanta, GA: Scholars Press, 1981), 119.

36. Elisabeth Schüssler Fiorenza, "The First Letter of Peter," in *A Postcolonial Commentary on the New Testament Writings*, ed. Fernando F. Segovia and R. S. Sugirtharajah, The Bible and Postcolonialism 13 (London and New York, NY: T&T Clark, 2009), 380–403 (394–5). See also Betsy Bauman-Martin, "Speaking Jewish: Postcolonial Aliens and Strangers in First Peter," in *Reading First Peter with New Eyes: Methodological Reassessments of the Letter of First Peter*, ed. Robert L. Webb and Betsy Bauman-Martin, LNTS 364 (New York, NY: T&T Clark, 2007), 144–77.

37. Jennifer G. Bird, *Abuse, Power and Fearful Obedience: Reconsidering 1 Peter's Commands to Wives*, LNTS 442 (London and New York, NY: T&T Clark International, 2011), 3.

empire and his conformist stance.[38] Noting the critical barb indicated in the letter's qualified injunction to submit to imperial authorities διὰ τὸν κύριον (2:13), Carter nevertheless understands the order "honor the emperor" in 2:17 as an outright endorsement of participation in the imperial cults.[39] As long as they sanctify Christ in their hearts (3:15)—that is, secretly and privately—Christians can "engage in the publicly conformist and submissive behavior of cultic participation without compromising loyalty to God."[40] For believers trapped in oppressive structures they cannot change, this strategy of combining (false) outward compliance with inner loyalty "offers a protest not designed to topple the structures of power, but to enable *hopeful* survival."[41] This proposal, however, is plagued by serious difficulties. For one, the argument that 2:17 directly enjoins worship of the emperor is unconvincing, especially in light of David Horrell's detailed treatment of this passage (see below), but also because he seems to have grossly overestimated the pressure exerted on Christians to participate in the imperial cults.[42] It also does not take into consideration the ontological critique of the emperor as a "human creature" in 2:13 (for which Travis Williams has argued so cogently; see below)—a text that may well have tarred as idolatrous the worship of the emperor.[43] Finally, it

---

38. Warren Carter, "Going All the Way? Honoring the Emperor and Sacrificing Wives and Slaves in 1 Peter 2:13–3:6," in *A Feminist Companion to the Catholic Epistles and Hebrews*, ed. Amy-Jill Levine, Feminist Companion to the New Testament and Early Christian Writings 8 (Cleveland, OH: Pilgrim, 2004), 14–33.

39. Carter, "Going All the Way?" 24.

40. Carter, "Going All the Way?" 28.

41. Carter, "Going All the Way?" 32 (emphasis in original).

42. In relation to this, see Fergus Millar, "The Imperial Cult and the Persecutions," in *Le culte des souverains dans l'Empire romain*, ed. Willem den Boer, Entretiens sur l'Antiquité classique 19 (Geneva: Fondation Hardt, 1973), 145–75, whose examination of the historical evidence leads him to conclude that the imperial cults *per se* played "only a modest role" (164) in the Empire's persecution of Christians. The greater point of conflict, Millar argues, was Christians' rejection of the cults of the gods as a whole (of which the imperial cults were but one form). I think Millar is more or less correct in his assessment, even if he may have been too hasty in assuming that the accounts which only mention "the gods" or "idols" in general would have excluded the imperial gods. The fact that the emperor and his family were incorporated into local cults and sometimes identified with traditional gods (see Chapter 2 below) warrants more caution. For the specific context of Roman Asia Minor and the possible role played by the imperial cults in the persecution and harassment of Christians, see Travis B. Williams, *Persecution in 1 Peter: Differentiating and Contextualizing Early Christian Suffering*, Supplements to Novum Testamentum 145 (Leiden: Brill, 2012), 245–54.

43. This flaw is aggravated by Carter's attempt to explain away the denunciation of idolatry (εἰδωλολατρία) in 4:3, under which worship of a human being would certainly have been included from a Jewish perspective. He ends up arguing that the modifier ἀθέμιτος here ("lawless," NRSV) restricts the condemnation to the "mode" of idolatry—that is, its immoderation and social disruptiveness—and not idolatry *per se* ("Going All the Way?" 28–9)!

is difficult to see how a letter that tells its readers to abandon "all deceit and hypocrisies" (πάντα δόλον καὶ ὑποκρίσεις, 2:1; cf. 2:22)[44] and to courageously suffer for the good (3:17; 4:15–16) can at the same time so blatantly advocate dissimulation for the sake of survival. Carter's attempt to depict 1 Peter as a voice of resistance cloaked in the guise of conformity ultimately falters.

David Horrell maintains that "the fact of empire" was the overwhelming reality that shaped the lives of 1 Peter's first readers, but insists that the letter's response to the imperial order cannot be so easily branded as one of total acquiescence.[45] While the letter does indeed prescribe submission to Roman structures of governance and social conventions, Horrell points out that its conciliatory tenor is circumscribed by an unmistakable call to higher allegiances to God and the believing community: "Love the family of believers. Fear God. Honor the emperor" (2:17b–c, NRSV). In this text, the Petrine author "draw[s] a line in the sand marking the limits of Christian obedience to Rome" by deliberately distinguishing honor (τιμή) due to the emperor (as it is to all humans) from fear (φόβος) due to God alone, making it clear that "only (the one) God is to be worshipped, so the emperor may (only) be honoured."[46] Elsewhere in 1 Peter, the author demonstrates a more critical stance toward Rome by, for example, identifying it as "Babylon" (5:13) and showing keen awareness of the suffering inflicted by local and imperial authorities on believers (4:12–19).[47] In light of these observations, the hard-lined distinction between conformity and resistance to Rome in 1 Peter, for Horrell, becomes more porous than is often conceived. He characterizes the author's stance as one of "measured but conscious resistance to imperial demands"—that is, a "polite resistance."[48]

---

44. On these vices, see Michaels, *1 Peter*, 85–6.

45. David G. Horrell, "Between Conformity and Resistance: Beyond the Balch-Elliott Debate Towards a Postcolonial Reading of 1 Peter," in *Becoming Christian: Essays on 1 Peter and the Making of Christian Identity* (London and New York, NY: Bloomsbury T&T Clark, 2013), 211–38 (see esp. 229–38). As the title of this essay indicates, Horrell takes as his launching point an earlier debate between David Balch and John Elliott regarding 1 Peter's attitude toward wider Roman society. For the Balch–Elliott debate, see their respective essays in Charles H. Talbert, ed., *Perspectives on First Peter* (Macon, GA: Mercer University Press, 1986), chs 4 and 5.

46. David G. Horrell, "'Honour Everyone . . .' (1 Pet. 2.17): The Social Strategy of 1 Peter and Its Significance for the Development of Christianity," in *To Set at Liberty: Essays on Early Christianity and Its Social World in Honor of John H. Elliott*, ed. Stephen K. Black (Sheffield: Phoenix, 2014), 192–210 (205).

47. Horrell, "Between Conformity and Resistance," 234–5. See also David G. Horrell, "The Label Χριστιανός (1 Pet. 4.16): Suffering, Conflict, and the Making of Christian Identity," in *Becoming Christian: Essays on 1 Peter and the Making of Christian Identity*, LNTS 394 (London and New York, NY: Bloomsbury T&T Clark, 2013), 361–81.

48. Horrell, "Between Conformity and Resistance," 234, 238.

Along similar lines, Travis Williams finds in 1 Pet. 2:13 an endorsement of submission to Roman power coupled with subtle critique.⁴⁹ While the text does in fact call for obedience to the emperor and his delegates, Williams observes that it simultaneously undercuts Roman authority. By couching this as submission to a "human creature" (Ὑποτάγητε πάσῃ ἀνθρωπίνῃ κτίσει), the author introduces an ontological cleft between God the Creator and the created emperor. In this way, "popular claims about Caesar's divinity are surreptitiously subverted beneath a thin veneer of compliance."⁵⁰ Moreover, this surreptitious subversion is reinforced by the reason given for submission: Christians are to yield to imperial authority "on account of the Lord" (διὰ τὸν κύριον). It is thus ultimately God's authority, not the emperor's, which legitimates their obedience.⁵¹ For Williams, the theological strategy in 2:13 reflects the author's attempt to negotiate the pervasive realities of the imperial cults, and no less counts for "an act of subtle yet calculated resistance."⁵²

Does 1 Peter, then, "accommodate" or "resist" Roman rule? Horrell and Williams show that the question is itself inadequate and reductionistic, impoverishing our ability to appreciate the wider spectrum of possible responses to the Roman Empire—an entity that was itself multifarious. Horrell, drawing from the work of political scientist James Scott, cautions scholars against equating "resistance" only with overt or open forms of rebellion:

> More usual, but no less forms of resistance, are modes of communication and action that subtly and changeably weave resistance into what is in various other respects a discourse of conformity and obedience. Indeed, an appreciation of the variable, complex, ambiguous, even compromised, relations between resistance and complicity is a crucial methodological key....⁵³

---

49. Travis B. Williams, "The Divinity and Humanity of Caesar in 1 Peter 2,13: Early Christian Resistance to the Emperor and His Cult," *ZNW* 105 (2014): 131–47.

50. Williams, "The Divinity and Humanity of Caesar," 145. It should be noted that Williams is careful to state that this ontological critique was made from the Petrine author's Christian perspective of the divine–human distinction, and did not necessarily reflect what other Greek-speakers might have meant when they addressed the emperor as θεός (*idem*, 141). On the semantic range of θεός as it is used in the imperial cults, see S. R. F. Price, "Gods and Emperors: The Greek Language of the Roman Imperial Cult," *The Journal of Hellenic Studies* 104 (January 1, 1984): 79–95. For a similar reading of 2:13, see Paul J. Achtemeier, *1 Peter*, Hermeneia (Minneapolis, MN: Augsburg/Fortress, 1996), 182–3.

51. Williams traces this point to Leonhard Goppelt, *A Commentary on 1 Peter*, ed. Ferdinand Hahn, trans. John E. Alsup (Grand Rapids, MI: Eerdmans, 1993), 184–5, who remarks that the qualifier διὰ τὸν κύριον "removes from the βασιλεύς, the 'king,' the sacral and ideological splendor with which both the continuation of the ancient oriental cult of the ruler and political philosophy and poetry had surrounded him."

52. Williams, "The Divinity and Humanity of Caesar," 147.

53. Horrell, "Between Conformity and Resistance," 218. For James Scott's work, see the discussion below.

Williams likewise emphasizes that 1 Peter's response to Rome, though falling far short of a call to open rebellion, must nevertheless be understood as a prudential pushback against Roman power:[54]

> If we are content to employ traditional resistance models and their monolithic tendencies, we will most certainly end up with an oversimplification.... With the Petrine audience belonging to a subaltern group in Roman Anatolia, this would have involved accommodating certain societal norms; at the same time, it also appears to include an effort to undercut and subvert—when practically feasible—those values which were contrary to the author's Christian ideology.[55]

In sum, both Horrell and Williams refuse the "for-or-against empire" binary that has come to characterize discussions of the topic with respect to 1 Peter and other New Testament texts. They offer much-needed nuance to scholarly analyses by adopting a more theoretically sensitive and differentiated notion of "resistance" that encompasses a broader range of acts of negotiation with power. In doing so, they underscore the complexity of Christian engagement with the imperial context—"the fact of empire," as Horrell calls it—in the first century AD.[56]

Despite these more perceptive readings offered by Horrell and Williams, however, it is quite clear that current discussions of 1 Peter's attitude toward the Empire remain largely focused on the letter's direct treatment of Roman political and social institutions (the emperor, imperial cults, the household, etc.), with particular attention to the *locus classicus*, 2:13–17. Some recent work that bucks this trend comes to us from Kelly Liebengood.[57] Noting that "confrontation or subversion is often best discerned at the level of competing narratives,"[58] Liebengood asks whether 1 Peter might confront imperial claims by offering an alternative narrative, another way of reading the world. He discerns in 1 Peter just such a story—that of the eschatological Davidic shepherd-king from Zech. 9–14. For Liebengood, shared motifs between 1 Peter and Zech. 9–14, such as the "house" of God's elect, a messianic agent who is cast as a slain shepherd, and the

---

54. Williams, "The Divinity and Humanity of Caesar," 146.
55. Williams, "The Divinity and Humanity of Caesar," 145–6.
56. Throughout this work, I will use the designations "BC" and "AD" rather than "BCE" and "CE." This usage more clearly reflects the Christian and European legacy of the Gregorian calendar, and thus its religious, social, and political roots, which the "Common Era" terminology obscures.
57. Kelly D. Liebengood, "Confronting Roman Imperial Claims: Following the Footsteps (and the Narrative) of 1 Peter's Eschatological Davidic Shepherd," in *An Introduction to Empire in the New Testament*, ed. Adam Winn (Atlanta, GA: SBL Press, 2016), 255–72. This piece builds on the more extensive work in his monograph, *The Eschatology of 1 Peter: Considering the Influence of Zechariah 9–14*, Society for New Testament Studies Monograph Series (Cambridge: Cambridge University Press, 2014).
58. Liebengood, "Confronting," 265.

eschatological trial of the faithful,[59] point to an implicit narrative in the letter that is "Davidic at its core"—"a narrative about a different king and a different empire" that ultimately serves to "confront, contradict, and subvert the notion that the golden age has dawned and is sustained through loyalty to Rome."[60]

As some have pointed out, this Zecharian, Davidic substructure Liebengood posits for 1 Peter is rather difficult to defend.[61] This is chiefly because the letter, despite the density of its scriptural quotations, contains no direct quotations from Zech. 9–14. It would be peculiar for the Petrine author to have worked primarily with a Zecharian framework without citing the source text directly, though he elsewhere quotes generously from his other sources, such as Isaiah and the Psalms. In the stark absence of any direct references, moreover, it is not clear that the allegedly Zecharian allusions detected by Liebengood ought to be traced to Zech. 9–14 rather than to a larger body of shared prophetic and/or eschatological traditions, from which even Zechariah may have drawn. Nevertheless, even if Liebengood's work here remains ultimately unpersuasive, it takes an important step by inviting us to consider broader ways in which 1 Peter can be said to challenge Rome—in this case, that of presenting an alternative story to Rome's story.

Working along similar lines, I propose that adopting a more "wide-angle" perspective of 1 Peter can in fact yield a more holistic sense of the letter's stance towards Rome. This book is precisely an endeavor to expand the ongoing scholarly conversation beyond what has been considered up to this point. I will outline my approach below, building on insights from earlier scholarship.

1.1.3 Furthering the Work on 1 Peter

Taking a cue from the work of Barclay and Oakes on Paul, I think it is quite evident that the principal concern of the Petrine author was not so much to oppose Rome and her Empire as it was to articulate a distinctly Christian way of being in the world. (This may, in fact, be why so many exegetes have failed to see any critique of Rome in 1 Peter at all.) His worldview is resolutely theocentric and Christological from start to finish,[62] as the opening benediction (1:3–12) and conclusion

---

59. For the full list of these shared motifs, see Liebengood, "Confronting," 268–9, as well as the detailed analysis in his *Eschatology*, 23–52.

60. Liebengood, "Confronting," 265, 270, 271.

61. On the following points, see Christopher Beetham, review of *The Eschatology of 1 Peter: Considering the Influence of Zechariah 9–14*, by Kelly D. Liebengood, *Journal of the Evangelical Theological Society* 58.1 (2015): 197–9; and John H. Elliott, review of *The Eschatology of 1 Peter: Considering the Influence of Zechariah 9–14*, by Kelly D. Liebengood, *Review of Biblical Literature* (2018), http://www.bookreviews.org.

62. For the theological themes of 1 Peter, see Ralph P. Martin, "The Theology of Jude, 1 Peter, and 2 Peter," in *The Theology of the Letters of James, Peter, and Jude*, by Andrew Chester and Ralph P. Martin (Cambridge: Cambridge University Press, 1994), 104–30. "Probably no document in the New Testament is so theologically oriented as 1 Peter, if the description is taken in the strict sense of teaching about God. The epistle is theocentric through and through . . ." (104).

(5:12–14) make clear. The letter focuses on what God has accomplished and will accomplish in his readers through Christ and the Spirit (e.g., 1:2–12, 18–23; 2:21–25; 3:18–22; 4:14), and its express purpose is "to encourage [them], and to testify that this is the true grace of God" (5:12a). Christians are called to set all their hope on the grace that will be revealed at Christ's return (1:13)[63] and, in the meantime, to realize their identity as God's elect (2:1–10), bearing suffering in patient endurance (1:6–7; 3:13–17; 4:12–19; 5:9–10). Authentic discipleship is set in contrast, not against Roman imperial ways as such, but rather against the immorality of "the Gentiles" (2:12; 4:3; cf. 1:18), just as the explicitly-named adversary is not Rome but "the devil" (5:8).

Nevertheless, the Petrine author is by no means oblivious to the looming shadow of Rome over the lives of his readers; neither does he gloss over its potential threats to Christians. He possesses firm awareness of the Roman structures of governance (2:13–17) and a reserved, though far from absolute, confidence in the imperial mechanisms of justice, whose failures led to the death of an innocent Christ and leave Christians vulnerable to suffering under false charges (2:14; 3:17–18; 4:15–16). He exhorts his readers to submit to the emperor "as supreme," but classifies him as a "human creature" and subordinates this to the more general imperative to "honor everyone" (2:13, 17).[64] He realizes, too, that the term "Christian" could lead to open hostility and persecution, most likely at both local and imperial levels (4:15–16).[65] The imperial city is tarred by the designation "Babylon" (5:13), the icon of self-aggrandizement against God and aggression toward God's people in Israel's scriptures (cf. Isaiah 13). The author is attentive to the precarious existence of Anatolian Christians, and carefully embeds his subtle critique of imperial power into the letter's ostensibly irenic tone. Comparing 2:13–17 and Rom. 13:1–7, Horrell rightly concludes that 1 Peter's stance toward Roman imperial rule is one that is "a good deal more reserved, even implicitly critical, than Paul's."[66]

The decidedly theological character of the letter, along with its lucid ambivalence toward imperial realities, strongly suggests the author must have been aware that his theological vision of the world *ipso facto* implicated the Roman Empire and its claims over that same world. With one (critical) eye toward Rome, he places his

---

63. E. G. Selwyn ("Eschatology in 1 Peter," in *The Background of the New Testament and Its Eschatology*, ed. William David Davies and David Daube [Cambridge: Cambridge University Press, 1956], 396): "[T]he grace they enjoy is regarded as in a sense thrown backwards from the world to come (1.13): it is a foretaste of the final revelation and the eternal glory."

64. On the subordination of these injunctions by means of grammatical form, see Horrell, "Honour Everyone."

65. See Horrell, "The Label Χριστιανός," esp. 176–97. On the need to dispense with the binary opposition between "official" state persecution and "unofficial" local hostility, see Williams, *Persecution in 1 Peter*.

66. Horrell, "The Label Χριστιανός," 187.

readers in a cosmos theocentrically imagined, in which their suffering acquires both a Christological rationale (2:21; 3:16–17) and pneumatic efficacy (4:14). In that world, those who follow Christ take center-stage in history (1:12) and the Empire, to whom they are subservient if only "for the Lord's sake" (2:13), is relegated to the status of marginalia.

The present study is an exploration of that world. More precisely, it is an exploration of that world and the ways in which it denied the Roman Empire that significance it claimed for itself. Earlier exegetes, as I have shown, have sought to discern if 1 Peter advocates accommodation or resistance to Rome. Horrell and Williams have convincingly demonstrated that, while 1 Peter lacks a "snarling, fang-baring hostility toward the Roman state,"[67] it yet evinces an unmistakably critical stance toward the Empire's structures of power. The author's strategy cannot, therefore, be contained by a binary model of accommodation-or-resistance. Still, discussions of 1 Peter and empire have for the most part been confined to 2:13–17. I would argue, however, that if we take a step back and look at the world which the author imagines in the letter, particularly in terms of its constructions of time and space, we will see that 1 Peter pushes against Rome in another, more holistic sense. In order to do this, we must first expand our notion of "resistance."

1.2 Domination, Resistance, and Ideology

1.2.1 The Contributions of James Scott

Perhaps more than any political theorist of the twentieth century, it is James Scott who has contributed most richly to our understanding of the complex ways in which subjugated peoples resist domination and oppression. Drawing from his extensive fieldwork among agrarian communities in rural Malaysia, Scott draws our attention to more subtle strategies of resistance that have too often escaped the analytical eye of modern social scientists.[68] Open, organized activity against ruling powers, he observes, has historically been a luxury of the middle class and intelligentsia, and is rarely afforded to most subordinate classes. For the weakest of classes, he contends, explicit defiance of oppressors would often only expose them to greater risk of harm and further endanger what little well-being they did possess, if not ultimately prove suicidal—as the vast majority of peasant revolutions throughout history attest.[69] This being the case, Scott argues that we ought not limit the study of resistance only to its overt manifestations, but rather take

---

67. The phrase comes from the pen of Moore, *Empire and Apocalypse*, 32.
68. James C. Scott, *Weapons of the Weak: Everyday Forms of Peasant Resistance* (New Haven: Yale University Press, 1987). Scott's analysis is developed and extended to other historical and cultural contexts in *Domination and the Arts of Resistance: Hidden Transcripts* (New Haven, CT and London: Yale, 1990).
69. Scott, *Weapons of the Weak*, xv–xvi.

seriously also what he calls "everyday forms of resistance"—"the prosaic but constant struggle" of the oppressed against their oppressors that often stops short of outright defiance.[70] Such resistance can consist in clandestine strategies such as foot-dragging, dissimulation, desertion, feigned ignorance, jokes and rumors, arson, poaching, and sabotage, among others. These strategies work precisely because they routinely evade detection under the guise of apparent conformity to formal operations of hierarchy and power.[71] Moreover, they are not simply a disparate collection of behaviors performed for the sake of survival under oppressive conditions. Rather, they reveal a somewhat coherent set of beliefs in those who resist—beliefs about the social order, the meaning of justice, how things ought to be, and so forth. These beliefs in turn condition their actions—as they do human action in general—and assign to them meaning, value, and purpose.[72]

In making this connection between acts and thought in resistance, Scott provides an important corrective to an ongoing discussion of domination that has often neglected the fuller range of responses on the part of the oppressed. Especially in Marxist analyses of the social order, ruling elites have often been said to secure and maintain power in two ways: by coercion and by consent. The chief exponent of this idea is Antonio Gramsci, for whom domination is accomplished not only through the use of force, but also by holding captive the minds of the subordinated so that they submit "willingly." The latter process, aimed at manufacturing consent in the ruled, Gramsci calls "hegemony."[73] It involves the reproduction of the dominant group's views and values in the minds of the subjugated, principally by representing the social order in ways that favor the dominant. This is accomplished through institutions of social-symbolic production that are controlled by ruling elites, such as schools, media, and the Church. By manipulating how their subjects see the world and their place in it, those in power effectively create an order in which their own authority is legitimated and exercised rightfully, as a given. The subjugated thus come to accept the conditions of their subordination as inevitable, and perhaps even necessary. In the "thicker" version of this theory, they are said to actively believe in the dominant group's self-representation and so see their subjugation as "natural" or "normal." In its "thinner" variant, even without accepting the elites' ideas, subjects nevertheless acquiesce because they are persuaded that their subjugation is an unavoidable state of affairs.[74]

For Scott, however, this model of hegemony is unsatisfactory because it cannot fully explain known histories of conflict. As evidence, he points especially to the

---

70. Scott, *Weapons of the Weak*, 29.
71. Scott, *Weapons of the Weak*, 33.
72. Scott, *Weapons of the Weak*, 38.
73. Gramsci's thoughts on the subject are not systematically presented, but rather scattered throughout his *Prison Notebooks*. See, e.g., Antonio Gramsci, *Selections from the Prison Notebooks*, ed. Quintin Hoare and Geoffrey Nowell-Smith (London: ElecBook, 1999), 144–6, 285, 404–6, 526–7, 542, 570–1, 641–2, 697, 809–10.
74. Scott, *Domination and the Arts of Resistance*, 72.

numerous instances when revolutions have occurred from within or "below" systems of totalizing oppression, as in the case of peasant or slave uprisings. In these instances, change occurs even when dominant groups have allegedly imposed, with great success, their views on the dominated. Such precipitations of conflict are not abrupt events without a history. They are instead eruptions of subterranean discontent that have been flowing beneath a landscape of apparent quiescence. Whether in the German Peasant Wars, the French Revolution, or slave revolts in North America, it is clear that oppressed populations appear at times quite capable of either denaturalizing their domination, or even rejecting their oppressors' social schema entirely.[75] Hegemony, as it turns out, is rarely if ever airtight.[76]

To further this argument, Scott points to two other kinds of responses to power.[77] First, there are instances when oppressed classes show the ability to imagine a reversal of the social order. For many millennialist and folk utopian movements, the world as it exists, with its social and economic hierarchies, is turned upside down. He cites as an example this Vietnamese folksong:

The son of the king becomes king.
The son of the pagoda caretaker knows only how to sweep with the leaves of
    the banyan tree.
When the people rise up,
The son of the king, defeated, will go sweep the pagoda.[78]

Closer to the historical period that is our concern in this book, of course, we may call on this signature Lukan text of reversal:

[God] has shown strength with his arm;
he has scattered the proud in the thoughts of their hearts.
He has brought down the powerful from their thrones,
and lifted up the lowly;
he has filled the hungry with good things,
and sent the rich away empty.

Lk. 1:51–53, NRSV

---

75. Scott, *Domination and the Arts of Resistance*, 77–9.

76. The disagreement between Gramsci and Scott can perhaps be explained by historical context. Gramsci developed his theory of hegemony in an effort to understand why it was that the Marxist revolution never materialized in Western Europe even though the economic conditions were ripe for it (Ania Loomba, *Colonialism/Postcolonialism* [London: Routledge, 1998], 28). As such, he was far more concerned with why revolutions do *not* occur. Scott, on the other hand, is focused on why they do.

77. Scott, *Domination and the Arts of Resistance*, 80–1.

78. Nguyen Hong Giap, *La condition des paysans au Viet-Nam à travers les chansons populaires* (Paris: Sorbonne, 1971), 183, as quoted in Scott, *Domination and the Arts of Resistance*, 80.

A second way in which the oppressed have responded to domination is by imagining the outright negation of the existing social order. Scott cites the case of the fifteenth-century Taborites, who, while living under the exploitative conditions of serfdom, nevertheless declared: "Princes, ecclesiastical and secular alike, and counts and knights should only possess as much as common folk, then everyone would have enough. The time will come when princes and lords will work for their daily bread."[79] Despite living within a highly stratified sociopolitical structure, this group was able to anticipate a future marked by radical egalitarianism. For Scott, imagined inversions and negations of the social order indicate that hegemony is not total, and that a measure of agency and creativity is retained in the mind of the subjugated, who are yet capable of imagining other possibilities and worlds of liberation. This is the case even when their bodies are regulated and their physical freedom constrained by rigorous controls of power.[80]

The very existence of everyday acts of resistance, along with imaginative reversals and inversion of the social order, betrays the fact that subjugated groups do not always accept in full (if at all!) the world as it is told by the ruling elites—that they operate under the influence of alternative interpretations and constructions of the social order and, indeed, of the world itself. This being the case, the study of resistance cannot be limited to analysis of open confrontations. Public political action is, in most instances, a luxury: for many underprivileged and powerless populations, it is too costly an option. For a more comprehensive view of resistance, we must therefore pay attention also to more covert, "everyday" acts of resistance and subtle forms of critique (e.g., jokes, parodies, coded speech) by which these groups navigate the conditions of their oppression. To focus only on open retaliations is "to miss the immense political terrain that lies between quiescence and revolt."[81]

More important for the purposes of this study, however, is Scott's insight that it is not only domination but also *resistance* that operates on the level of ideas and beliefs—that is, on the level of ideology. (Though he nowhere defines the term with any precision, Scott uses the term "ideology" in the generic sense, to mean "a set of ideas or beliefs"—not merely about political or social matters, but about the world as a whole.)[82] Ideas and beliefs are implicated in the processes of domination and

---

79. Norman Cohn, *The Pursuit of the Millennium* (London: Secker and Warburg, 1957), 245, as quoted in Scott, *Domination and the Arts of Resistance*, 81.

80. Scott, *Domination and the Arts of Resistance*, 91.

81. Scott, *Domination and the Arts of Resistance*, 199.

82. The very word "ideology" is, of course, a loaded and contested word with a complicated pedigree in political theory (a lucid account of which is given in Loomba, *Colonialism/Postcolonialism*, 25–43). In the Marxist tradition this term is typically used in a negative sense, i.e., to refer to misrepresentations or distortions about the world (false consciousness) propagated by the bourgeoisie to perpetuate their hold over the working class. Scott, however, consistently uses "ideology" in its neutral sense to mean *any* set of beliefs or ideas, whether held by dominant elites or the dominated. His reason for doing so is hinted at as

resistance by virtue of our character as thinking actors. Even when they are not expressed verbally, thoughts about resistance are implied in acts of resistance. Ideology both shapes and is shaped by action in a kind of "mutual feedback loop":

> Acts born of intentions circle back, as it were, to influence consciousness and hence subsequent intentions and acts. Thus acts of resistance and thoughts about (or the meaning of) resistance are in *constant* communication—in constant dialogue.[83]

Whereas the role of ideology in domination has been given sustained attention in Marxist analyses, Scott's work counterbalances this overemphasis by emphasizing its role in resistance as well. For him, ideology is at work both "in the rationalization of exploitation and in the resistance to that rationalization."[84] In fact, given that embodied acts of resistance are often dangerous and costly to the survival of any subjugated group, Scott suggests that subordinate classes "are likely to be more radical at the level of ideology than at the level of behavior, where they are more constrained by the daily exercise of power."[85] The inclusion of ideology in the dynamics of domination and resistance constitutes a crucial starting point for my argument in this book.

1.2.2 Applications to the Present Study

As I have shown earlier, discussions of resistance to empire in 1 Peter have tended to focus on how the letter treats particular Roman institutions such as the emperor, governors, local authorities, household structures, and the imperial cults. Conclusions about the Petrine author's stance toward the imperial order are then drawn on the basis of whether the text as a whole seems positive or critical towards these entities. At the close of Section 1.1, I suggested that these evaluations can be enriched by a broader notion of "resistance." Scott's work provides us with two helpful insights to this end by (1) expanding the concept of "resistance" to include

---

passage in *Domination and Resistance* (72), where he points out that any use of "ideology" to refer to the misrepresentation of social reality "must, by definition, claim some superior knowledge of what that social reality is." Using ideology in the neutral sense, therefore, allows for analysis of the views of both the oppressor and the oppressed without judgment about the truth of each. For this reason, I adopt Scott's use of "ideology" throughout this work.

83. Scott, *Weapons of the Weak*, 38 (emphasis in original). Scott's care in preserving the connection between thought and action here renders mystifying Anathea Portier-Young's criticism: "Scott does not allow for the ways in which practices shape consciousness" (*Apocalypse Against Empire: Theologies of Resistance in Early Judaism* [Grand Rapids, MI; Cambridge: Eerdmans, 2011], 36).

84. Scott, *Weapons of the Weak*, 204.

85. Scott, *Weapons of the Weak*, 331.

not only its more explosive, openly revolutionary episodes, but also subtler, quotidian manifestations that nevertheless defy authority just the same; and (2) drawing attention to the role of ideology in resistance as well as domination. For the purposes of this study, it is the latter insight that interests me more.

I suggest that we take a step back and look at the ways in which Rome and 1 Peter offered different—and ultimately incompatible—ideological constructions of the world. The existence of Rome's empire depended not only on the use of force but also on the engineering of consent in its subjects, achieved by the propagation of a distinctly Roman perspective of the social order.[86] First Peter likewise advanced a tangibly Christian way of thinking about the same. If we are to gain a more comprehensive view of the letter's stance toward the Empire, we need to look at how these different worlds, Roman and Christian, bumped up against each other. It is in this sense that 1 Peter manifests an early Christian counter-ideology in the face of Roman hegemony.

To be clear, we need not equate incompatibility with complete, binary opposition—or imagine that "counter-ideology" means that Petrine and Roman perceptions of the world were hostile to each other on every single point. What we can do, rather, is think of these ideologies as overlapping entities, each of which possesses its own distinctive contours. Because of these contours, certain "zones" of one worldview press against the other in some places more than others, creating different pressure points of varying intensity, while other "zones" overlap or coexist more comfortably.[87] This might explain the conflicting reports we have seen regarding 1 Peter's stance toward the Roman Empire: while some scholars have detected a conformist stance, others have posited an antagonistic one. First Peter might be distinctly Christian, but it need not for this reason be monolithically or uniformly anti-Roman. Instead, our Petrine author may well have had a nuanced, differentiated approach to Roman-ness, sharing its ideals in one instance and pushing back in another. As scholars in the fields of postcolonial and decolonial studies often point out, the historical dynamics of domination and subordination have consistently troubled earlier, binary models of colonizer–colonized.[88] There is no need, in short, to suppose that indications of conformity or resistance in any one aspect can be generalized to the entire letter.

Any study of ideology, especially ideological conflict between two groups, will require some focal points if it is not to become unmanageable. Following Scott, in this work I use "ideology" in its broad, non-pejorative sense to refer to a complex of ideas and beliefs. In this sense, a group's ideology can include its vision of what the world is, how it works, as well as how it *ought* to work. In communities both ancient and modern, ideas about the social order (e.g., descriptions and prescriptions for the fabric of human relations) are often modulated by a

---

86. This is the thesis of Clifford Ando's masterful *Imperial Ideology and Provincial Loyalty in the Roman Empire* (Berkeley and Los Angeles, CA: University of California Press, 2000).

87. As, for example, when a person lies flat on an even surface. The difference in contours will mean that the person will feel more pressure in some parts of the body than in others.

88. See, for example, the discussion in Loomba, *Colonialism/Postcolonialism*, 60–2.

correspondent cosmology, i.e. what one means when one refers to "the world" (*kosmos, ha-eretz, bumi*, etc), its origins, its constitution, its destiny, and hence its very meaning.

I have chosen for my analysis two intersecting axes of ideology—time and space, since they are the basic constituents of any cosmology and foundational matrices through which we perceive the world. The French anthropologist Pierre Bourdieu argued that the ways in which a particular group of people construe time and space "structure not only the group's representation of the world but the group itself, which orders itself in accordance with this representation."[89] This is not to say, however, that time and space are objective grids onto which human experience can be so straightforwardly mapped. The ways in which people think about and experience time and space are culturally conditioned and subject to a whole range of social forces (see Section 1.3 below). Nevertheless, time and space do provide pragmatic entry points into studying how some very powerful social actors in imperial Rome as well as the early Christian author of 1 Peter saw the world and their place in it.

1.3 Time, Space, and the Social Order

In *The Condition of Postmodernity*, David Harvey observes:

> The history of social change is in part captured by the history of the conceptions of space and time, and the ideological uses to which those conceptions might be put.[90]

We can quite helpfully think about an ideology or worldview in terms of how it represents time and space. For example, does a particular belief system differentiate time by dividing history into distinct epochs, as did various millennialist movements, or Joachim of Fiore in the twelfth century? What event, if any, constitutes the apex of time? Does time have a destination—is it "going somewhere" as the outworking of some divine plan such as we find referred to in Jer. 29:11 or Eph: 1.10, or does time repeat itself in an unending series of circular progressions (as Qoheleth seems to suggest)? Similarly, we can ask how an ideology represents and differentiates space, such as the *Bhagavad Gita*'s representation of worlds as emanations from Krishna's body and how it situates people and objects within the cosmos, or the prominence of Jerusalem in the Psalms. In the Synoptics' accounts of Jesus' baptism, to use a New Testament example, the voice of God speaks from the divine space of "heaven" above (Mt. 3:17; Mk 1:11; Lk. 3:21), and it is to this space that Jesus returns after his resurrection (Mk 16:19; Lk. 24:51; cf. Jn 20:17).

---

89. Pierre Bourdieu, *Outline of a Theory of Practice*, trans. Richard Nice, Cambridge Studies in Social Anthropology 16 (Cambridge: Cambridge University Press, 1977), 163.

90. David Harvey, *The Condition of Postmodernity: An Enquiry into the Origins of Cultural Change* (Oxford/Cambridge, MA: Blackwell, 1989), 218.

Prompted by questions such as these, other studies in Second Temple literature and New Testament have focused on how time and space are constructed within narrative and apocalyptic visions.[91] These are nothing short of analyses of the constitutive elements of cosmology—and thus ideology—engendered within texts.

The aim of this section is to demonstrate that how different groups think about the social order is, in turn, inflected by variations in how they think about space and time. By taking into consideration the realm of social relations, we can see how conflicting ideas about space and time might play themselves out in embodied life. Harvey writes:

> Beneath the veneer of common-sense and seemingly 'natural' ideas about space and time, there lie hidden terrains of ambiguity, contradiction, and struggle. Conflicts arise not merely out of admittedly diverse subjective appreciations, but because different objective material qualities of time and space are deemed relevant to social life in different situations. . . . How we represent space and time in theory matters, because it affects how we and others interpret them and then act with respect to the world.[92]

Ideological conflict is not only a matter of opposing abstractions in the minds of people who disagree. They have a visceral aspect.

Before moving to more detailed discussions of temporal and spatial ideologies, it is worth noting two working assumptions I have adopted in this book:

1. *The relationship between ideas about cosmology (time–space) and ideas about the social order is not unidirectional but reciprocal.* In the core chapters of this work (Chapters 3–6), I will argue that imperial Rome and 1 Peter imagined time and space in distinct ways, and in so doing posited incompatible visions of the social order. It is difficult to say, however, which particular set of ideas—the cosmological or the social—came first, or if it even makes sense to

---

91. Some important studies include: Steven J. Friesen, *Imperial Cults and the Apocalypse of John: Reading Revelation in the Ruins* (New York, NY: Oxford University Press, 2001); Harry O. Maier, "From Material Place to Imagined Space: Emergent Christian Community as Thirdspace in the Shepherd of Hermas," in *Early Christian Communities between Ideal and Reality*, ed. Mark Grundeken and Joseph Verheyden, WUNT 342 (Tübingen: Mohr Siebeck, 2015), 143–60; Matthew Sleeman, *Geography and the Ascension Narrative in Acts* (Cambridge: Cambridge University Press, 2009); Portier-Young, *Apocalypse Against Empire*; R. Alan Culpepper, *Anatomy of the Fourth Gospel: A Study in Literary Design* (Philadelphia, PA: Fortress, 1987); and Elizabeth Struthers Malbon, *Narrative Space and Mythic Meaning in Mark* (San Francisco, CA: Harper & Row, 1986). Of these, the most important for me—as will be evident in the footnotes of this work—has been Steven Friesen's book, which has served as a standard and an inspiration for my own work. I am also indebted to Harry Maier and Matthew Sleeman for our helpful conversations at conferences.

92. Harvey, *The Condition of Postmodernity*, 205.

ask if one in fact preceded or caused the other. What we can only discern is that they reflect and reinforce each other in coherent ways.

2. *To talk about time and space separately is to invoke an entirely artificial separation.* By virtue of our bodies, humans always experience them together[93] and, as will become evident in the following chapters, ideas about time and space likewise constitute an inseparable matrix. For example, the depictions of Roman triumph in art discussed in Chapter 4 represent particular moments in time, but their expression in material form inherently and significantly transformed the spaces in which they were erected, and as such also exert a spatial effect. Working on a different level, we have in 1 Peter the promise of an inheritance that is kept in a particular space ("in heaven"; 1:4) but will be revealed in an appropriate time, such that eschatology acquires spatial dimensions. Teasing apart constructions of time and space merely serves convenience in this study. It allows us to focus on one of these dimensions "at a time", but it is no less aberrational.

With these caveats in mind, we can now take a closer look at the ideological nature of constructions of time and space, and the relationship of these to imaginations of the social order.

1.3.1 *The Ideological Nature of "Time"*

While in the physical sciences a mathematical, objective concept of time (i.e. time as something that is simply "there" and measurable) more or less holds sway, the

---

93. The artificiality of this separation can be keenly felt when one ponders Doreen Massey's moving reflection on one of her visits home:

> For the truth is that you can never simply "go back", to home or to anywhere else. When you get 'there' the place will have moved on just as you yourself will have changed. And this of course is the point. For to open up 'space' to this kind of imagination means thinking time and space as mutually imbricated and thinking both of them as the product of interrelations. You can't go back in space-time. To think that you can is to deprive others of their ongoing independent stories. It may be "going back home", or imagining regions as backward, as needing to catch up, or just taking that holiday in some "unspoilt, timeless" spot. The point is the same. You can't go back.... You can't hold places still. What you can do is meet up with others, catch up with where another's history has got to 'now', but where that 'now' (more rigorously, that "here" and "now", that *hic et nunc*) is itself constituted by nothing more than—precisely—that meeting-up (again) (Doreen B. Massey, *For Space* [London: SAGE, 2005], 124–5).

In the course of writing this book I have been repeatedly haunted by the ominous warning delivered by the wise Gandalf the Grey to his friend Saruman in J. R. R. Tolkien's *The Fellowship of the Ring*: "He who breaks a thing to find out what it is, has left the path of wisdom." (One might also recall that Saruman gave no heed to these words, to his own detriment.)

human sciences have, at least since Émile Durkheim, been concerned with notions of time as subjective constructions. For Durkheim, our understandings of time are socially-derived "collective representations" (*représentations collectives*)—that is, they are inherited from society and reflect its shared categories of knowledge and experience of the world.[94] Following Durkheim, we can think of each of these articulations of time as an imaginative system that carries within it a specific set of ideas or ideology—that is, it envisions and "diagnoses" the world, including social relations, in a certain way. How we keep and segment ("periodize") time, along with the value we attached to these segments, are already culturally-specific expressions of ideology.

We can begin looking at the ideological nature of temporal constructions using a relevant discussion of ethnography in Johannes Fabian's *Time and the Other*.[95] Although Fabian is primarily concerned with rhetoric in the anthropological method, his work is helpful because it shows us how relations of power condition our notions of time. Moreover, Fabian takes as his starting point a confrontation that took place under conditions not entirely dissimilar to those in the present study, i.e. the encounter between (European) empires and colonized peoples. Under European expansionism, cross-cultural differences in ideology and practice became entangled in an array of power differentials and social transformations generated by colonial engagements with the non-European Other. It is within these inequalities in power that thinking about time played into social realities.[96]

The Enlightenment, Fabian argues, set in motion a new framework of time that was markedly distinct from an earlier, medieval understanding that was fundamentally Christian (or Judeo-Christian). This transformation was marked not only by the shift from a "sacred" or theological conception of time to a secular

---

94. On the contribution of Durkheim along with critical evaluations, see Alfred Gell, *The Anthropology of Time: Cultural Constructions of Temporal Maps and Images* (Oxford: Berg, 1992), 1–14; Nancy D. Munn, "The Cultural Anthropology of Time: A Critical Essay," *Annual Review of Anthropology* 21 (1992): 93–123 (esp. 94–8). See also Barbara Adam, *Timewatch: The Social Analysis of Time* (Cambridge: Polity Press, 1995).

95. Johannes Fabian, *Time and the Other: How Anthropology Makes Its Object* (New York, NY and Chichester: Columbia University Press, 1983).

96. The production of European knowledge under the conditions of colonialism has been a key area of reflection in decolonial thought. See the seminal essays of Enrique Dussel, "Eurocentrism and Modernity (Introduction to the Frankfurt Lectures)," *Boundary 2* 20, no. 3 (October 1, 1993): 65–76; and Aníbal Quijano, "Coloniality and Modernity/Rationality," *Cultural Studies* 21, no. 2–3 (March 1, 2007): 168–78. On the implications of this relationship for biblical studies, see Gregory Allen Banazak and Luis Reyes Ceja, "The Challenge and Promise of Decolonial Thought to Biblical Interpretation," *Postscripts: The Journal of Sacred Texts and Contemporary Worlds* 4, no. 1 (March 27, 2010): 113–27. For a study on the effects of European domination on the development of Christian theology in particular, see Willie James Jennings, *The Christian Imagination: Theology and the Origins of Race* (New Haven, CT and London: Yale University Press, 2010).

one, but it also engendered a new set of temporal relations. In the earlier medieval framework, the non-European Other was distanced in time from the European center by their status as "pagans" and "infidels" who had yet to experience conversion. As such, they were "backwards," not having "caught up" with the revelation of the gospel, but were ripe for evangelization. With the Enlightenment, this temporal distance was transposed to the more secular key of "civilization": the Other were now seen no longer as the unconverted but as primitive savages to be civilized. Despite their differences, the medieval and Enlightenment conceptions shared a common understanding of European time as a "natural" or objective given. They also expressed the expansion of Europe in social-temporal terms, i.e. as either the conversion or the civilization of non-European peoples that would bring these outmoded societies into the European present. Time was thus invoked to explain—or rather, create—social difference: pagans and savages who were not yet converted or civilized were both temporally "behind" Christianized or Enlightened Europe. This time-lag served as the justification for "mission" (whether of evangelization or civilization) and was deeply embedded in the practice and ideology of European colonialism.[97]

In the nascent days of anthropology, European anthropologists working in the era of colonial occupations of African peoples drew their subjects into the regnant Enlightenment discourse of "civilization,"[98] the benchmark of which was, of course, Europe itself. By situating these societies along a spectrum of maturation (e.g., describing them as "primitive" or "civilized"), they imposed onto a host of non-European societies what was in fact a European schema of time.[99] This, along with the exoticization of these societies (using descriptions like "mythical," "tribal," etc.), served to create a temporal distance between ethnographer and subject. Although they in fact existed in the same time (and place), the referents of ethnography

---

97. Fabian, *Time and the Other*, 26–7. Fabian makes it clear that the spatial dimension is implicated here as well, i.e. both medieval and Enlightenment models invoke a temporal as well as spatial gap between the European and the Other. Peoples became more backwards as one moved further away from an assumed European center.

98. Throughout the book, I will use the term "discourse" to refer to the way in which language is used to talk about or construct a particular domain of knowledge. Discourse in this sense involves verbal language as well as non-verbal forms of communication that are embedded in a whole range of material and social practices and institutions. The colonial discourse of "civilization," for example, would involve not only how people spoke or wrote about the colonized, but also how they represented colonized bodies in visual art and music. Similarly, the Roman imperial discourse of the emperor is to be discerned not only in historical writings or inscriptions, but also in ritual, numismatic, and architectural representations of him. Cf. Loomba, *Colonialism/Postcolonialism*, 38–9.

99. For an account of contesting notions of time in French Algeria, see William Gallois, "The War for Time in Colonial Algeria," in *Breaking up Time: Negotiating the Borders between Present, Past and Future*, ed. Chris Lorenz and Berber Bevernage, Schriftenreihe der FRIAS School of History 7 (Göttingen: Vandenhoeck & Ruprecht, 2013), 252–73.

became rhetorically and existentially Other-ed, pushed into the past. In Fabian's terms, they were denied "coevalness" or synchronicity with those who studied them, being repeatedly forced into a different time.[100] This denial of coevalness was fed by colonial dynamics between the anthropologist's society and the society that was studied; it cannot therefore be thought of as accidental. The discourses produced by these ethnographers were "not mistakes, but *devices* (existential, rhetorical, political)"[101] by which indigenous groups became caricatured as backwards or primitive, more proximate to humanity in its original state. The use of a particular temporal schema to deny coevalness to an out-group, to situate them in a different (often inferior) time, Fabian calls "allochronism." The referents in allochronistic–ethnographic accounts are constituted not only as objects (of study and spectacle); they are simultaneously placed in a relationship of unequal power with the observer-ethnographer, who inevitably holds the upper hand as a more evolved superior. In this way, power relations become inscribed into the anthropological method by means of something which, on the surface, appears to be an innocent temporal model, but which turns out to be ideologically laden and insidious.

Though Fabian does not use the term in this sense, we can think of allochronism not only as an ethnographic device but also as a strategy of social critique. For the colonial anthropologists and their successors, this social critique was already at least implicit in the ethnographies they produced. Yet the practice of creating temporal distance as a means of evaluating the social order is, in fact, older than the medieval period, the Enlightenment, or modern anthropology itself.

In antiquity, the Romans already engaged in allochronism of a similar kind in their imagination of the barbarian Other. The barbarian was marked by entrapment in the primal conditions of life, animal-like unrefinement, and perpetual war,[102] and so had to be civilized.[103] Seneca's words offer a telling example:

> Consider all the tribes whom Roman civilization does not reach—I mean the Germans and all the nomad tribes that assail us along the Danube. They are oppressed by eternal winter and a gloomy sky, the barren soil grudges them support, they keep off the rain with thatch or leaves, they range over ice-bound marshes, and hunt wild beasts for food.[104]

The African-born Roman historian Florus (second century AD) remarked of the Sarmatians whom Rome had subjugated in 12 BC: "They have nothing except

---

100. Fabian, *Time and the Other*, 31–3.
101. Fabian, *Time and the Other*, 32 (emphasis in original).
102. See, e.g., Livy, *Ab urbe condita* 23.24.11; Caes., *B. gall.* 1.2.
103. On the Roman discourse of barbarism, see Jane Webster, "Ethnographic Barbarity: Colonial Discourse and 'Celtic Warrior Societies,'" in *Roman Imperialism: Post-Colonial Perspectives*, ed. Jane Webster and Nicholas J. Cooper, Leicester Archaeological Monographs 3, 1996, 111–24.
104. Seneca, *Dial.* 1.4.14.

snow, frost, and trees. Their barbarism is such that they don't even understand peace."[105]

The process of bringing these barbarians out of the past involved training in Roman ways, as Benjamin Rubin writes:

> All nations had once lived as savages before the discovery of culture and thus were all equally capable of civility and barbarity (Vitr. *De Arch* 2.5 and 1.6). What separated the humans from the savages was a set of customs and values known as civilization or *humanitas*. This included the practice of sedentary settlement, agriculture, urbanism, bathing, proper dress (i.e., the toga), proper table manners, the study of liberal arts, as well as the possession of certain abstract virtues such as industry, frugality, courage, chastity, and respect for authority (Tac. *Agricola* 21). The Romans, of course, imagined themselves to be in possession of *humanitas* while all other nations in one respect or another all fell short of the mark.[106]

This doctrine of the backwardness of the Other was in fact a vital component of the Empire's self-representation as the harbinger of peace. Earlier, Julius Caesar had justified the "pacification" of Gaul on the basis of the incessant warring among its natives: "In Gaul, not only every tribe, canton, and subdivision of a canton, but almost every family, is divided into rival factions."[107]

Similarly, Rome's conquest of Hellenic populations was frequently rehearsed as the quelling of a long history of internecine strife. Herodian of Antioch was not alone when he wrote that the propensity to mutual destruction was "an ancient failing of the Greeks; the constant organizing of factions against each other and their eagerness to bring about the downfall of those who seem superior to them."[108] Plutarch captures in one sweep the arrival of peace with Roman rule:

> [W]hile the mightiest powers and dominions among men were being driven about as Fortune willed, and were continuing to collide one with another because no one held the supreme power, but all wished to hold it, the continuous movement, drift, and change of all peoples remained without remedy, until such time as Rome acquired strength and growth, and had attached to herself not only the nations and peoples within her own borders, but also royal dominions of foreign peoples beyond the seas, and thus the affairs of this vast empire gained stability and security, since the supreme government, which never knew reverse, was brought within an orderly and single cycle of peace.[109]

---

105. Florus 2.29, as quoted in Ando, *Imperial Ideology*, 326.

106. Benjamin B. Rubin, "(Re)presenting Empire: The Roman Imperial Cult in Asia Minor, 31 BC–AD 68" (PhD diss., University of Michigan, 2008), 17–18.

107. *B. gall.* 6.11. See, however, Webster, "Ethnographic Barbarity," 118–20.

108. Herodian 3.2.8 (Echols trans.). For other Roman authors who thought the same, see Ando, *Imperial Ideology*, 55 (esp. n. 30).

109. *De Fort. Rom.* 2 (Babbitt trans.).

Recountings like the above show how temporalization can be used to polarize and politicize the social order: the past is embroiled in chaos, the present distinguished by imperial peace. History thus becomes a narrative of progress—at least for those taken up into the outstretched arms of Rome's rule.

But the past need not necessarily be constructed as inferior. It is equally possible to "canonize" a particular period in history as normative for the present. To take an example further removed from European civilization, we can look to the sixth-century BC Chinese political philosopher, Confucius, who lived in the last days of long decline of the Chou (Zhou) dynasty (c. 1050–256 BC). In his day, the Chou dynasty had become reduced to rivaling fiefdoms, and so for Confucius, it seemed, things were hurtling toward anarchy and lawless violence. Living amid social disorder, Confucius saw as the antidote a return to the virtues of earlier Chou kings and their predecessors. For him, society's continued existence was predicated on faithful observance of rites handed down from one generation to the next:[110]

> [A disciple] asked: "Can ten generations hence be known?"
> The Master said: "The Yin built on the rites of the Hsia. What was added and what was omitted can be known. The Chou built on the rites of the Yin. What was added and what was omitted can be known. Should there be a successor to the Chou, even a hundred generations hence can be known."[111]

For Confucius, social stability was a function of the extent to which rulers in each generation preserved ritual, from the Yin clan to the Hsia clan, and then to Chou.[112] The now-lost peace of Chou rule was once attained precisely because its kings looked to past dynasties: "The Chou is resplendent in culture, having before it the examples of the two previous dynasties."[113] Correspondingly, the age of upheaval in which Confucius lived was to be explained in terms of rupture and infidelity in the transmission of ritual. As a social reformer, he regarded himself as one commissioned by Heaven to restore the political order by reinstating the ancient ritual of preceding kingdoms.

---

110. The Confucian use of the word 禮 (lǐ; rite/ritual) encompasses not only what we might today call "religious" practices (e.g., sacrifice to ancestors), but an entire range of prescriptions for social order.

111. *Analects* 2.23. Translations, unless otherwise noted, are from *The Analects: Translation with an Introduction*, trans. D. C. Lau (London: Penguin, 1979). For comparison, I have used *The Analects of Confucius: Translation and Notes*, trans. Simon Leys (New York, NY: W. W. Norton, 1997). The notes and commentary from both have been exceedingly helpful and inform my discussion here.

112. In the *Analects*, these former dynasties are enshrined as ideal states in which rulers were archetypal kings (see 2.23; 3.14, 21; 7.5; 8.20; 15.11; 17.5; 18.11; 20.1).

113. *Analects* 3.14a.

Decide on standard weights and measures after careful consideration, and re-establish official posts fallen into disuse, and government measures will be enforced everywhere. Restore states that have been annexed, revive [dynastic] lines that have become extinct, raise men who have withdrawn from society [i.e. exiles] and the hearts of all the common people in the Empire will turn to you.[114]

In his program for reform, Confucius created temporal distance between himself and his contemporaries not by accusing them of being stuck in the past, but precisely by aligning himself with it as a follower of Chou.[115] What is also important to note is that, in looking back, Confucius prescribed as a sure guide an ethical code, a system of "oughts" for social relations which, he believed, characterized that past. This code was a staunchly hierarchical one in which inferiors related to their superiors (children to parents, subjects to kings) with self-sacrificing loyalty and deference.[116] In the Confucian schema, the past extends into the present like the rope that joins a lifeboat to its ship: to abandon it is to drift toward pandemonium.

A final and much more contemporary form of allochronism may be found in recent denunciations of terrorist groups such as the Islamic State (ISIS/ISIL) as "medieval."[117] This term of opprobrium creates temporal distance by casting the group as backward and is based on an implicit moral evolutionism. In a recent essay on ISIS, Graeme Wood attempts to vindicate the label, citing Bernard Haykel, Professor of Near Eastern Studies at Princeton University:

> In Haykel's estimation, the fighters of the Islamic State are authentic throwbacks to early Islam and are faithfully reproducing its norms of war.... "Slavery, crucifixion, and beheadings are not something that freakish [jihadists] are cherry-picking from the medieval tradition," Haykel said. Islamic State fighters "are smack in the middle of the medieval tradition and are bringing it wholesale into the present day."[118]

While the reliability of this account has been rendered suspect,[119] the rhetoric here is no less interesting. The descriptors "throwback" and "medieval" (used seven

---

114. *Analects* 20.1. On the origin of this passage, see Lau, *Analects*, 158 n. 1.
115. *Analects* 3.14b.
116. This hierarchical ordering pervades the *Analects*, but the following text is iconic: "A man who respects his parents and his elders would hardly be inclined to defy his superiors. A man who is not inclined to defy his superiors will never foment a rebellion. A gentleman works at the root. Once the root is secured, the Way unfolds. To respect parents and elders is the root of humanity" (1.2; Leys' translation).
117. See, e.g., Anoosh Chakelian, "Nick Clegg: 'It's Not Obvious' What the UK Can Do Legally on New Terror Powers," *The New Statesman*, September 2, 2014.
118. Graeme Wood, "What ISIS Really Wants," *The Atlantic*, March 2015.
119. See Jack Jenkins, "What *The Atlantic* Left Out About ISIS According To Their Own Expert," *ThinkProgress*, accessed December 11, 2015, http://thinkprogress.org/world/2015/02/20/3625446/atlantic-left-isis-conversation-bernard-haykel/.

times in the entire article) are employed to indicate just exactly what the reader is supposed to find wrong with ISIS: it is a regressive phenomenon that is attempting to intrude into "the present day," and must be kept in the past. What is denied here, to use Fabian's term, is coevalness between the more evolved "us" and the more primitive—in this case, medieval—"them." The tendency to consign violence to a specific period in the past is, I note, profoundly ironic in a generation for whom the bloodiest century of human history is a matter of recent memory. Is it in fact true that aggression and brutality are characteristic of the "medieval" and "medieval-minded" groups like ISIS, but not "us"? To answer "Yes" is to not only embrace an ideology of time as progress (rather than, say, moral regress) but also to blot out from "modernity" the Armenian genocide, two World Wars, the Holocaust, the calculated decimations of Hiroshima and Nagasaki, and the staggering number of civilian deaths caused by drone bombings in Pakistan. Describing ISIS as "medieval" functions precisely to eject a group of people from the present century so as to save the idea that we now live in what is perhaps the most civilized of ages.[120] An ideology of time can be highly selective in what it accents and underplays as much as human memory does the same.[121]

No set of beliefs, no ideology, about time is in the end truly neutral or "innocent." The examples above furnish three principles integral to temporal ideologies. First, constructions of time function as truth claims: they assert something. They envision the world in a particular way—how things were, are, will be, and ought to be—and categorize it in some way (e.g., pagans and believers). Second, as a corollary to the first principle, temporal ideologies engender, at least implicitly, both descriptions of social relations as well as *prescriptions* for their proper ordering; in this sense they acquire a moral hue. Finally, as Fabian's critique of ethnography shows, they are caught up in historical relations of power and thus acquire political force, especially when different ideologies of time come into contact with one another.

---

120. Historian John Terry comments insightfully: "The danger of calling ISIS 'medieval' is not that it hurts medievalists' feelings; it is that it tempts us to define the group's special barbarism as something from the past that should be eradicated because, by God, we've progressed and are therefore advanced as a people. This . . . is dangerous thinking induced by the assumption that the Enlightenment fixed everything. (It didn't.)" ("Why ISIS Isn't Medieval," *Slate*, February 19, 2015).

121. In modern cognitive psychology, our tendency to selectively recall data that correspond to pre-held conceptions and ignore contravening information has been amply demonstrated in studies on what is called "confirmation bias." For a rudimentary introduction and relevant literature, see E. B. Goldstein, *Cognitive Psychology: Connecting Mind, Research and Everyday Experience* (Belmont, CA: Thomson Wadsworth, 2008), 462–3.

1.3.2 The Ideological Nature of "Space"

In an interview on the subject of space, Michel Foucault opined:

> I think it is somewhat arbitrary to try to disassociate the effective practice of freedom by people, the practice of social relations, and the spatial distribution in which they find themselves. If they are separated, they become impossible to understand. Each can only be understood through the other.[122]

Since what has been termed "the spatial turn" in the social sciences and humanities, it is no longer possible to speak of space simply as an objective grid of reality which we can measure and thus pin down, or a bounded area in which things happen. The groundbreaking re-conceptualization of space found expression in Henri Lefebvre's *The Production of Space* (1974), and has since been taken up by scholars such as Edward Soja, Doreen Massey, and David Harvey, among others.[123] These thinkers have challenged what had been, for so long, taken for granted—namely, the objective facticity and "given-ness" of space as something that "simply is." They have instead underscored its constructed and symbolic nature, drawing our attention to the diverse ways in which space is experienced, conceived, and imagined in human practice. Rather than being the passive stage on which human activity takes place, it is transformed into a dynamic element of social life itself—caught up in, forming, and being formed by our interactions with one another.

In the Western intellectual tradition, none has asserted the sociality of space more strongly than Henri Lefebvre. "To speak of 'producing space'," he wrote in 1974, "sounds bizarre, so great is the sway still held by the idea that empty space is prior to whatever ends up filling it."[124] Lefebvre's revolutionary contribution to the spatial turn is precisely the notion that space does not exist as a universal "thing-in-itself"; it is always and everywhere the product of social relations: "(Social) space is a (social) product."[125] In what sense is this the case? Lefebvre states that

---

122. Michel Foucault, "Space, Knowledge, and Power," interview by Paul Rabinow, trans. Christian Hubert, n.d., in Paul Rabinow, ed., *The Foucault Reader* (New York, NY: Pantheon Books, 1984), 246.

123. See Henri Lefebvre, *The Production of Space*, trans. Donald Nicholson-Smith (Oxford: Blackwell, 1991), French original: *La production de l'espace* (Paris: Éditions Anthropos, 1974); Edward W. Soja, *Thirdspace: Journeys to Los Angeles and Other Real-and-Imagined Places* (Cambridge, MA: Blackwell, 1996); Harvey, *The Condition of Postmodernity*; Massey, *For Space*. Useful summaries of the contributions of these and other thinkers to the renewed study of spatiality are given in Rob Kitchin and Phil Hubbard, eds., *Key Thinkers on Space and Place*, 2nd ed. (London: SAGE, 2010). For a brief but very helpful survey of the spatial turn and its relevance for biblical studies, see Sleeman, *Geography and the Ascension Narrative in Acts*, 22–56.

124. Lefebvre, *The Production of Space*, 15.

125. Lefebvre, *The Production of Space*, 26.

what we call "space" is produced by social interactions occurring on three dimensions:[126]

1. *spatial practice* (perceived space): the sum total of material interactions (inclusive of persons and goods) occurring in and across space;
2. *representations of space* (conceived space): the signs, codes, and knowledge by which we speak about and understand spatial practices—e.g., descriptions, terminology, scientific theories, maps, plans, etc.; and
3. *spaces of representation* (imagined or lived space): the complex symbols (conceptual and material) "linked to the clandestine or underground side of social life"[127] that propose new meanings and possibilities for spatial practices, often by inverting existing conceptions of space (representations of space)—e.g., utopias, imaginary landscapes, paintings, street art and graffiti, etc.

In Lefebvre's schema, therefore, a space can be said to be three-dimensional: it is made up of "not only a concrete materiality but a thought concept and a feeling—an 'experience.'"[128] A space is "produced" by the complex interactions of these three dimensions, which cannot be separated from one another.

The cumulative force of this new phase of investigation, of analyzing space, has not only compelled various disciplines to leave behind the notion of space as a fixed or stable "container" in favor of far more fluid, dynamic views, but has also given rise to multiple interrogations of what Harvey termed the "hidden terrains of ambiguity, contradiction, and struggle" that in fact operate beneath what were once thought to be commonsensical or "plain" understandings of space. Once we think of space as something socially produced rather than as a static "area," it emerges as an arena of contest for different ways of thinking and living, shaped and reshaped by both power and responses to power within the complex web of human relations. It is not only the site of thought and action, but also of power, and thus of control and domination. People can think of the same space differently, move in it differently, appropriate it differently, and thus *experience* it differently. Powerful individuals or groups can seek to control and appropriate spaces, and in

---

126. Lefebvre, *The Production of Space*, 33. Due to the absence of a systematic exposition of these processes on Lefebvre's part, various scholars have interpreted them differently. Although Soja has perhaps been most influential in Anglophone scholarship, I am here following the (broadly) concordant interpretations of Harvey (*The Conditions of Postmodernity*, 218–20) and Christian Schmid, "Henri Lefebvre's Theory of the Production of Space: Towards a Three-Dimensional Dialectic," in *Space, Difference, Everyday Life: Reading Henri Lefebvre*, ed. Kanishka Goonewardena et al. (New York, NY: Routledge, 2008), 27–45. For criticisms of Soja's reading of Lefebvre, see Schmid, "Henri Lefebvre's Theory," 42.

127. Lefebvre, *The Production of Space*, 33. For Lefebvre, "the clandestine and underground side of social life" is of great significance since space always "escapes in part from those who would make use of it" (26).

128. Schmid, "Henri Lefebvre's Theory," 41.

so doing regulate or limit how others relate to that space and to each other.[129] The good news, from Lefebvre's standpoint at least, is that space always leaks out from the clutched hands of those who attempt to master it, and so always remains open to the counter-forces of resistance.[130]

Contests of spatial imagination are of pivotal importance because symbolic orderings (and re-orderings) of space form an essential part of how we interpret and move in that world. Ideologies of space—we would do better to say "of time-space"—are not merely inert ways of construing the world; they in fact shape our patterns of behavior and practices. (In Lefebvre's terms, what I understand as spatial ideologies would encompass not only representations of space, but also spaces of representation.) As such, they are truly constitutive of a community's social and political life. When political leadership in the United Kingdom calls citizens to live in accordance with "British values," for example, its message can only be meaningful if one first presupposes a specific idea of "Britain" as the sovereign nation-state (itself a concept consolidated in the nineteenth century) defined by its present-day, fixed boundaries. In other words, the inculcation of "British values" in education, domestic policy, and so forth is premised on a shared set of concepts and beliefs about territory—that is to say, a spatial ideology. We cannot speak of "Britishness" as a cultural concept without evoking, at least implicitly, what "Britain" is (i.e. a territory and/or the people inhabiting that territory). To show that what constitutes "Britain"—and thus British identity and values—can be disputed by alternative spatial ideologies, one needs only to look to the long—and electric—traditions of separatism in its constituent countries, not least in Northern Ireland and, most recently, Scotland. "Drawing boundaries in space," as Doreen Massey notes, "is always a social act."[131] The material, representational, and experienced dimensions of space are contestable and/or unstable in the face of social change. Differing constructions of space are, like differing constructions of time, potentially volatile: they can, as they have historically, give rise to discontent, referendums, riots, and intense violence.[132]

---

129. Harvey, *The Condition of Postmodernity*, 222.

130. Lefebvre, *The Production of Space*, 26.

131. "The Conceptualization of Place," in *A Place in the World?: Places, Cultures and Globalization*, ed. Doreen B. Massey and Pat Jess (Oxford: Oxford University Press/Open University, 1995), 61.

132. In this example, what constitutes "Britain" is also dependent on a specific interpretation of the history of territories that now make up the United Kingdom. Jonathan Boyarin ("Space, Time, and the Politics of Memory," in *Remapping Memory: The Politics of Timespace*, ed. Jonathan Boyarin [Minneapolis, MN: University of Minnesota Press, 1994], 15–16), insightfully observes that "statist ideologies involve a particularly potent manipulation of the dimensionalities of space and time, invoking rhetorically fixed national identities to legitimate their monopoly on administrative control.... States may be said to map history onto territory."

To further consider how ideologies of space and the social order are mutually implicated, I return again to the Roman Empire. We have already seen how the Roman discourses of "civilizing" the barbarian Other and the pacification of internecine strife served the Empire's image as an instrument of peace. We live in an age in which such claims tend to inspire deep skepticism shaped, no doubt, by colonialism and the totalitarian regimes of more recent decades. Clifford Ando has warned, nonetheless, that this suspicion toward power may well be anachronistic when applied to antiquity, and that we must be vigilant of the ways in which it shapes our view of how Rome's self-representation was received by those whom it ruled. He directs us to documentary evidence that there were those among Rome's subjects who did in fact express an authentic sense of belonging and loyalty to the Empire—that though its claims may qualify for what we pejoratively call today "propaganda," they genuinely found resonance in the experience of those under imperial rule.[133] In rejoicing over the rebirth of classical rhetoric in his day, Dionysius of Halicarnassus (late first century BC) remarked:

> the cause and origin of this great revolution has been the conquest of the world by Rome, who has thus made every city focus its attention upon her. Her leaders are chosen on merit and administer the state according to the highest principles. They are thoroughly cultured and in the highest degree discerning, so that under their ordering influence the sensible section of the population has increased its power and the foolish have been compelled to behave sensibly.[134]

Likewise, we have little reason to doubt the sincerity of Aelius Aristides (second century AD) when he spoke of Rome as a "common republic of the world under the single best ruler and governor, in which everyone comes, as it were, into a common agora"[135]—or when he praises the Romans for being "most eager to promote the political interests of their friends,"[136] since cooperation between Greeks and their Roman occupiers were after all for the common good. From among Jewish thinkers we have Rabbi Shimon ben Lakish (third century AD), whom the tradition records as declaring the Roman Empire "very good," because "it exacts justice for human beings."[137]

The cases adduced above show that the vision of *Pax Romana* held currency among at least some, if not many, of Rome's provincial subjects, for whom the promise rang as true. For these individuals and groups, Ando writes, "the manifest success of Rome in and of itself gave that propaganda considerable empirical

---

133. Ando, *Imperial Ideology*, 49–70.
134. *Orat. vett.* 1.3 (Usher trans.), quoted in Ando, *Imperial Ideology*, 52.
135. *Or.* 26.60, quoted in Ando, *Imperial Ideology*, 57.
136. *Prae. ger. reip.* 814C, quoted in Ando, *Imperial Ideology*, 58.
137. *Sefer Ha-Aggadah* 5.91 (trans. Braude).

validity."¹³⁸ The establishment of stability and order cultivated a sense of belonging as well as loyalty to the Empire. To lean on Lefebvre's nomenclature, we can think of the imperial production of space as one in which intentional, material *spatial practices* (e.g., conquest, reorganization of occupied territory into provinces, legal reforms, new and safe roads to facilitate movement and commerce, etc.) interacted with particular *representations* of space (e.g., provinces as peripheries of the imperial metropolis, boundaries of the Empire, Aristides' notion of "a common agora") to yield the *lived (experienced) space* of an Empire of peace. This can be concretely shown in the case of Asia Minor, which Rome organized (or rather, reorganized) into provinces that only loosely corresponded to its pre-Roman political and ethnic divisions—by combining Pontus and Bithynia into a single joint province and, later, incorporating Cappadocia into Galatia, for example. Despite these changes, the provincial council of Asia, to whom we shall return later in this book, did not see Roman occupation as a violent incursion, but rather celebrated it as something that Providence accomplished "for the benefaction of all people" (εἰς εὐεργεσίαν ἀνθρώπων).¹³⁹ Within these re-imaginations of space, subjects of the Empire were gradually persuaded to shift their identity and belonging from a more local to a global one,¹⁴⁰ from specific localities (individual *poleis* and regions) to the expansive *oikoumenē* with its single center. Gradually, "Rome became to her empire what another city was to its surrounding territory[,] ... the *communis patria* of the world."¹⁴¹ The imperial ideology of space worked in tandem with Rome's reconfigurations of social relations in its territories.

It will become clear in due course that not everyone accepted the imperial way of imagining space. Lefebvre's chief insight that space is socially produced means that different groups, unequal in power though they be, have a hand in spatial production. Every assertion of control over space is, at least in theory, vulnerable to being challenged. Differences in spatial ideologies become tangible not only when the boundaries of an established territory are questioned (as in the discussion of "British values" above), but also when the *meaning* of a space is disputed. I will reserve analysis of an early Christian example of this for later, but for now, a more recent example can serve to illustrate this point.

---

138. Ando, *Imperial Ideology*, 67. One could, of course, explain this willingness to be ruled in terms of Rome's total ideological hegemony, i.e. the subjugated had entirely bought into the Empire's legitimation of its own domination (see Section 1.2.1 above). Nevertheless, Ando argues that Rome's ascent to power was in these cases interpreted *within* the ancient religious worldviews of its subjects, according to which gods were responsible for human victory and defeat (*idem*, 65–6).

139. *OGIS* 458.34. See the discussion of this inscription in Chapter 3.

140. See Gillian Rose, "Place and Identity: A Sense of Place," in *A Place in the World?: Places, Cultures and Globalization*, ed. Doreen B. Massey and Pat Jess (Oxford: Oxford University Press/Open University, 1995), 87–132.

141. Ando, *Imperial Ideology*, 69.

On Sunday, April 1, 1990, toward the close of a chapel service attended by some 309 prisoners at Strangeways Prison in Manchester, one inmate, Paul Taylor, seized the microphone from the chaplain and began a rousing speech about inhumane practices in the prison, calling for reform. A riot ensued among the congregation, some of whom had smuggled weapons and hoods into the service. Prison staff, overwhelmed by the uprising, were instructed to evacuate. Within an hour, the entire prison had been taken over by the rioters.[142] Over the course of a twenty-five-day siege that inspired copycat riots in other prisons throughout the UK, Strangeways' inmates visibly protested from the prison's rooftop and used the media attention they received to demand reforms to the intolerable conditions of their incarceration. This episode left a crucial mark in British history, triggering an overhaul of the penal system. No more would inmates have to defecate and urinate in buckets inside their own cells; ombudsmen were appointed to represent the grievances of prisoners, and telephone access was made easier so inmates could stay in touch more easily with their families.[143] This riot shows that, even in environments marked by dramatically asymmetrical structures of power and stringent mechanisms of control, disenfranchised groups can still contest the meaning of spaces. For twenty-five days, a space of incarceration was transformed into one of protest that reverberated throughout the penal system. Here is evidence for Lefebvre's contention that space, even when produced in such a way as to exert control, nevertheless "escapes in part from those who would make use of it."[144]

We find, then, that space is something more than the passive stage on which life unfolds. It is "alive," shaping and being shaped by human practice. The principles that apply to ideologies of time apply to ideologies of space too: (1) the ways in which we think of space amount to truth claims—they are statements about the "reality," including social reality (e.g., what a nation is, or that criminals can be reformed in prisons); (2) as such, they are morally prescriptive (i.e. they propose an "ought" for social relations); and (3) they are permeated by relations of power.

1.4 Converging Lines of Inquiry: The Present Study

From the preceding sections, we can now identify three trajectories that converge on my project in this book.

1. After "overhearing" the debate on Paul and empire, we can likewise say that the author of 1 Peter was first and foremost concerned with the Christ event,

---

142. For the account of the committee of public inquiry formed to investigate this incident, see *The Woolf Report: A Summary of the Main Findings and Recommendations of the Inquiry into Prison Disturbances* (London: Prison Reform Trust, 1991), 3–5.

143. Eric Allison, "The Strangeways Riot: 20 Years On," *The Guardian*, March 30, 2010, sec. Society.

144. Lefebvre, *The Production of Space*, 26.

not resisting Rome, as the epicenter of Christian identity and practice. However, he also demonstrates clear awareness of the mechanisms and scope of imperial power, and exhibits a cautious stance toward the Empire that is marked by strategic, measured resistance. His caution indicates that he knew that his vision of the world was not entirely compatible with the established Roman order, and his readers would have to negotiate this difference carefully.
2. As James Scott has shown, resistance among marginalized groups cannot be contained to instances of open conflict, but also includes more covert practices and alternative ideologies that subvert the forces of domination.
3. In the interest of studying ideological conflict, we can look at how different ideologies construct the world or "reality" by imagining time and space in incompatible ways. These differences in temporal and spatial imagination are correlated to different construals of the social order.

The present investigation lies at the intersection of these three lines of inquiry. Its overarching purpose here is twofold: to explore the ways in which imperial Rome and the Petrine author each constructed their own understandings of time and space; and, by placing these constructions alongside each other, assess the extent to which 1 Peter offered ideological resistance to the Empire.

Some further points regarding method are necessary at this juncture. Studying the temporal–spatial ideology of 1 Peter is more straightforward given our access to the text, but what can we take as the source or gauge of temporal–spatial representations in something as nebulous as "Roman imperial ideology"? For this, I turn to the Roman imperial cults. Though I do not regard these as by any means comprehensive sources for imperial ideology, there are at least two advantages to this decision. First, in considering the imperial cults, we have a more concrete sense of that ideology, since we rely not only on historical documents that address imperial ambitions, but also on epigraphic, numismatic, and archeological evidence that embodies it in ritual and popular practice. Attention to these forms of embodiment is crucial since, as Ittai Gradel reminds us, in Roman religion, ritual not only reflects but also *constructs* theology, worldview, and social order.[145] Second, as I hope my handling of the evidence will make clear, examining the imperial cults of Anatolia gives us a localized understanding of their workings *in Anatolia*, the region to which 1 Peter was originally addressed. Adapted to local religious piety, veneration of the imperial family took different forms in different parts of the Empire and was thus legitimated in a variety of ways. By looking specifically at Anatolian imperial cults, I hope to avoid overgeneralizations derived from studies based on other parts of the Empire, though these may nonetheless prove helpful at points.

There is, of course, a stark asymmetry to the evidence. On one level, there is the matter of volume: the sheer amount of evidence for the Anatolian imperial cults

---

145. Ittai Gradel, *Emperor Worship and Roman Religion* (Clarendon Press, 2004), 3–4.

far outweighs the text of 1 Peter, which is relatively short even as far as New Testament letters go. This disparity does not detract from the importance of the letter, however, given that we hope to arrive at a fuller appreciation for this pivotal early Christian text. The second asymmetry might be disconcerting for some—that is, the asymmetry of kind. On the side of the Roman ideology and the imperial cults, I will be reconstructing an ideology from a range of textual as well as non-textual evidence—dedicatory inscriptions, festal calendars, numismatics, archeology, etc. On the side of 1 Peter there is only the text as basis for my analysis. This asymmetry, however, is strictly speaking not a problem so much as a limitation. The aim—and it is a narrow aim—of this study is to examine the ideology of 1 Peter in terms of space and time, setting it against Roman imperial ideology on similar matters. For a different project, one could equally, for example, reconstruct the temporal–spatial ideology of 1 Peter within the context of broader Christian practices in Anatolia in the first century AD, without any particular focus on the imperial cults. Nevertheless, it is the conflict between the Petrine and imperial imaginations that lies at the heart of this investigation, which is but one aspect of a much larger line of inquiry. As I hope will be clear, I have tried here to be as careful as possible when drawing inferences from the imperial evidence, and not to make claims that exceed the limits. The actors in the ideological production of the imperial cults are relatively more numerous and complex when compared to that of 1 Peter. Throughout the course of my research I have become acutely aware of this, and have attempted to be as mindful of this as possible.

We move forward, then, with care. To anchor this study in a concrete socio-historical setting, the next chapter provides orienting data for both the imperial cults of Anatolia and 1 Peter. Subsequent chapters will then tease out the contrasting ways in which each construed time and space.

Chapter 2

THE SOCIO-HISTORICAL CONTEXT

To lay some groundwork for the comparative study of temporal and spatial ideologies that follows, the present chapter offers some preliminary considerations regarding the Roman imperial cults of Anatolia as well as 1 Peter. The overview of the historical development, forms, and ideological contours of the imperial cults in Section 2.1 aims to give a general sense of the dominant discursive forces operative in the author's world. (The relatively greater volume and complexity of the evidence in this case necessitates more navigation, and the cults have thus been given slightly more attention here.) Considerations regarding the authorship, dating, provenance, and destination of 1 Peter (Section 2.2) serve to establish parameters for reading the text as an instantiation of early Christian ideology—in particular, as a response to Roman domination.

2.1 *The Imperial Cults: An Overview*

2.1.1 *Historical Development in Anatolia*

By the time of the spread of Christianity in the first century AD, the cultic veneration of rulers was already a well-established practice among the Hellenized communities of Asia Minor.[1] Ruler cults in the region date to as early as the fifth century BC, when the Greek island of Samos offered cult to the Spartan general Lysander after the Peloponnesian War. Alexander the Great received cult even in

---

1. On the subject of imperial cults in Asia Minor, no work is more important than Simon Price's magisterial *Rituals and Power: The Roman Imperial Cult in Asia Minor* (Cambridge: Cambridge University Press, 1984). See also *idem*, "Gods and Emperors"; Steven Friesen, *Twice Neokoros: Ephesus, Asia, and the Cult of the Flavian Imperial Family* (Leiden: Brill, 1993); Rubin, "(Re)presenting Empire." On Hellenistic ruler cults in Asia Minor leading up to the imperial period, see Price, *Rituals and Power*, 23–52; Jon D. Mikalson, "Greek Religion: Continuity and Change in the Hellenistic Period," in *The Cambridge Companion to the Hellenistic World*, ed. Glenn R. Bugh (Cambridge: Cambridge University Press, 2006), 208–22 (esp. 213–15).

his lifetime, as did his Seleucid successor Antiochus III and his queen Laodice.² As Roman presence in the Greek world increased throughout the second century BC, there emerged corresponding cults to Roman power. At Chios we find a cult to the goddess Roma, marked by a procession, sacrifice, and games. Elsewhere in the Hellenistic world there emerged cults collectively dedicated to "the Hearth of the Romans,"³ "the People of the Romans," "the universal Roman benefactors," and even individual Roman officials.⁴

The accession of Octavian in the late first century BC marked a transformative moment not only for the Roman Empire, but also the evolution of ruler cults in Roman-occupied Anatolia. Although we find in Asia Minor a long tradition of the cultic veneration of rulers that predates Roman presence, in the time of Augustus these cults developed a palpable focus on the emperor, his family, and the imperial center.⁵ By 29 BC, he had already granted sanctuaries to Roma and Julius Caesar at Nicea and Ephesus, and was himself the recipient of divine honors at Pergamum and Nicomedia. Dio Cassius records:

> Caesar, meanwhile, besides attending to the general business, gave permission for the dedication of sacred precincts in Ephesus and in Nicaea to Rome and to Caesar, his father, whom he named the hero Julius. These cities had at that time attained chief place in Asia and in Bithynia respectively. He commanded that the Romans resident in these cities should pay honour to these two divinities; but he permitted the aliens, whom he styled Hellenes, to consecrate precincts to himself, the Asians to have theirs in Pergamum and the Bithynians theirs in Nicomedia. This practice, beginning under him, has been continued under other emperors, not only in the case of the Hellenic nations but also in that of all the others, in so far as they are subject to the Romans.⁶

The novelty of what happened in Pergamum and Nicomedia—that is, the establishment of cult to a living emperor—is duly noted by Dio, who adds that no

---

2. Price, *Rituals and Power*, 26, 37.
3. *IG* II² 5102.
4. For documentation and discussion of the last three cults in this list, see Price, *Rituals and Power*, 41–2.
5. "There is nothing anywhere to suggest that the scale of the cult-acts for Hellenistic kings had ever approached that which immediately appears for Augustus. Few cults of the deceased Hellenistic kings lingered on, and only a modest range of evidence attest cults or games or shrines for even the major Roman figures of the late Republic. The sudden outburst of the celebration of Octavian/Augustus was a new phenomenon" (Fergus Millar, "The Impact of Monarchy," in *Caesar Augustus: Seven Aspects*, ed. Fergus Millar and Erich Segal [Oxford: Clarendon Press, 1984], 53, quoted in Meggitt, "Taking the Emperor's Clothes Seriously," 152).
6. Dio Cassius, 51.20.6–7. For a discussion of the developments in Pergamum, see Friesen, *Imperial Cults*, 25–32.

such thing had ever occurred in Rome or elsewhere in Italy, where emperors received cultic veneration only after their death.[7]

In 27 BC, upon Octavian's taking the name *Sebastos* (the Greek equivalent of "Augustus"), the number of temples and sacrifices in his honor escalated, accompanied by a proliferation of cults to his successors and other members of the imperial family in subsequent years. By that same year, Macedonia already had a cult dedicated to Augustus, an imperial priesthood, and imperial games.[8] Within only one year after Augustus took the title, as the epigraphic evidence shows, there was erected in Ephesus a statue of the *Sebastos* along with a sacred precinct (*temenos*). By that same year, the city of Philadelphia in Lydia had already consecrated a priest dedicated to the cult of Roma and Augustus.[9] A contemporary of Augustus, Nicolaus of Damascus, reporting from the eastern part of the Empire, could thus say:

> Because men call him by this name as a mark of esteem for his honour, they revere him with temples and sacrifices, organized by islands and continents, and as cities and provinces they match the greatness of his virtue and the scale of his benefactions towards them.[10]

The above claim is supported by the fact that priests of the cult to Augustus are attested to in 34 cities in Asia Minor—"doubtless," Stephen Mitchell argues, "only a fraction of the original total."[11]

The imperial cults also extended into more remote areas of Anatolia quite speedily. Within three years of the annexation of Paphlagonia to the province of Galatia, there existed in 3 BC multiple *Sebasteia* throughout the region in which oaths of loyalty could be sworn to Augustus and other members of the imperial family. By 20 AD, three years after the annexation of Cappadocia, a provincial council (*koinon*) had been founded and organized imperial games. Within months after Lycia became a province in 43 AD, a provincial Caesareum was established in Xanthos at the initiative of the reigning emperor, Claudius.[12] The establishment of imperial cults appears to have been a reliable index of Roman occupation in Anatolian territories.

This unprecedented focus on the Roman emperor was not simply a matter of increase in the number of cultic sites. It was accompanied by a corresponding transformation in how both emperor and empire were constructed. In its well-known decree promulgating Augustus' birthday as the new beginning of its provincial

---

7. Dio Cassius, 51.20.8.

8. Stephen Mitchell, *Anatolia: Land, Men, and Gods in Asia Minor, Volume I: The Celts and the Impact of Roman Rule* (Oxford: Clarendon, 1993), 102.

9. Mitchell, *Anatolia, Vol. I*, 100.

10. FGrh 90 F. 125.1, translated and quoted in Mitchell, *Anatolia, Vol. I*, 100.

11. *Anatolia, Vol. I*, 100. Cf. Price, *Rituals and Power*, 58.

12. Mitchell, *Anatolia, Vol. I*, 102.

calendar, the provincial council (*koinon*) of Asia in 9 BC described his birth as the apex of history. The council hailed Augustus as "a savior who put an end to war and brought order to all things," whose birth marked "the beginning of good tidings to the world through him."[13] It also mandated that this inscription be displayed in all imperial sanctuaries of the major cities in the province. A contemporaneous Mytilene decree compared Augustus to "those who have attained heavenly glory and possess the eminence and power of gods,"[14] and yet another inscription declared that Augustus, "son of god, god Sebastos," by his benefactions had "surpassed even the Olympian gods" (ὑπερτεθεικὼς καὶ τοὺς Ὀλυμπίους θεούς).[15]

These explicit comparisons of Augustus to the Olympian gods signaled a decisive turn in the history of ruler cults in Asia Minor. Until then, the cults seem to have restricted themselves to speaking of the rulers only in terms of benefactions to the city, not the cosmos. These inscriptions, on the other hand, no longer confine themselves to gratitude for political benefactions to the city, but go significantly further by comparing the accomplishments of Augustus to those of the gods. Furthermore, whereas previous cults were offered on the basis of benefaction to a particular city (even if the benefactors were based outside the city, as in the case of Antiochus III and Laodice), these decrees acknowledge a much broader notion of authority. So it was that the Asian *koinon*, seeing Augustus' birth as good tidings "for the world," thought it fitting that a new calendar dated from this event be adopted not just in any one city, but throughout the entire province. Beginning with Augustus, the extant (and more Hellenistic) model of ruler cults based in particular cities enlarged into regional—that is, provincial—festivals and sacrifices of the emperor-god, whose power reached far beyond the city walls.[16] Gradually, traditional democratic institutions in Anatolian cities, such as councils and assemblies, were transformed into mechanisms for bestowing divine honors to the emperor.[17] For the inhabitants of the region, the cult of the emperor "defined

---

13. *OGIS* 458. Throughout this work, I have used Steven Friesen's translation of this inscription given in his *Imperial Cults*, 33–5. The Greek and Latin recensions of the text, along with commentary, can be found in Robert K. Sherk, *Roman Documents from the Greek East: Senatus Consulta and Epistulae to the Age of Augustus* (Baltimore, MD: Johns Hopkins University Press, 1969), 328–37.

This important inscription will be discussed in greater detail in the following chapter as it represents, I will argue, a distinctly imperial construction of the temporal order.

14. *OGIS* 456 (= *IGR* IV.39). For text, translation, and discussion of the historical setting of this inscription, see Greg Rowe, *Princes and Political Cultures: The New Tiberian Senatorial Decrees* (Ann Arbor, MI: University of Michigan Press, 2002), 124–53, esp. 133–5, 150–1.

15. *IOlympia* 53.

16. Price, *Rituals and Power*, 55–6. This spatial expansion of the emperor's influence via cultic practice will be the chief subject of Chapter 5.

17. Rowe, *Princes and Political Cultures*, 127. "The change was irreversible because Rome became the sole and permanent power. Unlike the old Hellenistic empires, Rome had no effective counterweight in the Greek world" (*idem*).

their own relationship with a new political phenomenon, an emperor whose powers and charisma were so transcendent that he appeared to them as both man and god."[18]

It must be observed, however, that the lavish honors of the Augustan period do seem to have been particularly acute, and were not fully sustained beyond the reigns of his immediate successors. The cults of later emperors, for one, were typified by more modest expressions of adulation. A decree by the demos and the boule of Ephesus proclaiming celebrations of Titus' birthday makes reference to "the kingdom which he received from his divine father" but noticeably lacks the effusive language of earlier pronouncements in the time of Augustus.[19] Simon Price observes that this phenomenon was accompanied by a decline in cults dedicated to specific emperors and members of the imperial family toward the end of the first century AD. Whereas even relatively unimportant figures such as Augustus' adopted son, Agrippa Postumus, and Claudius' daughter, Antonia, had priests dedicated to their cults in the mid first century AD, there existed only four known cults for members of the imperial family from that time onwards. Prominent consorts such as Plotina and Sabina, the wives of Trajan and Hadrian respectively, conspicuously lacked their own priesthoods. The priesthoods of Augustus may have been found in thirty-four cities, but those of Tiberius, who comes closest to rivaling this figure, were only found in eleven cities of Asia Minor. Priests and temples of the later periods were more often dedicated to the Sebastoi, that is, the collective of emperors past and present, or the *autokrator*, the "generic," unspecified emperor.[20]

These trends indicate not the decline of the imperial cult (which continued to flourish until at least the late second century AD) but a "routinization," according to Price, in Anatolian constructions of the Roman emperor and his authority. Augustus' charismatic leadership marked a climactic moment not only in the life of the Empire as a whole, but also in the communities of Asia Minor that more than felt its repercussions. The ensuing process of routinization reflected, among other things, the stabilization of the system (i.e. what was shared knowledge no longer needed to be asserted as forcefully), but it also served as a means of transferring Augustus' personal charisma to the *institution* of the emperor itself, thereby rendering his authority into terms more transferable to his successors, even if they were indeed less capable or accomplished. Whereas charismatic authority might die with an individual emperor, authority based on office could more easily be passed on.[21] In support of this, we find the remark of Dio that the title "Augustus" ("Sebastos" in the east) taken by Octavian's successors made known

---

18. Mitchell, *Anatolia, Vol. I*, 103.
19. *IEph* 211 (= *OGIS* 493I).
20. Price, *Rituals and Power*, 57–8.
21. Price, *Rituals and Power*, 59.

"the splendor of their position" (τὴν τοῦ ἀξιώματος λαμπρότητα).[22] That the emperors came to be more frequently honored as a collective, the Sebastoi, may be seen as evidence of Price's theory: increasingly, cultic veneration in Anatolia shifted its focus from the charismatic figure of Augustus to the power of office held by his successors.

The developmental trajectory of Roman imperial cults in Anatolia from Augustus to the end of the first century AD can therefore be summed up as follows. Beginning with Augustus, the longstanding institution of the ruler cult in Anatolia acquired a definitively Roman orientation. Augustus and his successors were ritually commemorated as benefactors of the polis whose authority transcended the walls of the polis—in fact, emanating from Rome and encompassing the entire known world, as various inscriptions suggest. In the Julio-Claudian period (up to the first half of the first century AD), cultic rituals were more focused on individual emperors, including individual members of the imperial family. By the end of the first century, however, the emperors were more likely to be venerated as a collective, the divine Sebastoi, pointing to a shift in focus from the personal charisma of the individual emperor (most especially Augustus) to the institution of the emperor itself. This last development is, in large part, what enables us to speak of a relatively coherent ideological orientation amid the diversity we find in the imperial cults—that is, a construction of the world that is configured around the person of the Roman emperor and his empire.

2.1.2 Ritual and Infrastructure

As will be clarified in the next section, there was not one "normative form" of cultic veneration of the emperor and his family. We can, however, observe several recurrent features in the evidence. Further discussion of imperial festivals and temples, as well as how these shaped the perception and experience of temporal rhythms and spaces, will be elaborated in subsequent chapters (especially Chapters 3 and 5). For now, however, I confine myself to a rough sketch of the basic elements of the imperial cults.

In speaking of imperial *cults*, we immediately evoke a core aspect of religion in antiquity: the sacrifice.[23] Imperial sacrifices were offered on a variety of occasions and by a variety of people (individuals or groups), and constituted a key aspect of the various festivals honoring the emperor and the imperial family. The chief aspects of these sacrifices were the burning of incense and the slaughter of animals, typically a bull. Offerings could also take the form of libations or

---

22. 53.18.2 (Cary trans.). "The evolution of Augustus's name into the title for the office that he created advertised both the source and the existence of the charismatic power attaching to that position" (Ando, *Imperial Ideology*, 31).

23. The following summary of imperial sacrifices is primarily drawn from the discussion in Price, *Rituals and Power*, 207–33.

ritual cakes, though these were less common. The singing of hymns was often an integral part of more public celebrations.[24] It is important to note that these sacrifices could take place in conjunction with sacrifices to traditional divinities or independently of them, honoring specific emperors and members of the imperial family.[25] The records bear witness to both sacrifices *for* the emperor—that is, for his health, safety, and preservation of his reign by the gods—as well as sacrifices *to* him. Instances of the former are, by far, more frequently attested.[26] The officiants of these sacrifices were designated priests, both male and female, who were frequently elite members of the community and held civic office.[27]

These sacrifices could, in turn, be accompanied by festivals that lasted anywhere from one to several days and included processions, public banquets, athletic contests, and other forms of social entertainment in their agenda. These celebrations could often be elaborate, and drew people from far and near into the towns and

---

24. The singing of hymns by specially designated choirs was a prominent feature of festivals in the Classical, Hellenistic, and Roman periods. Song accompanied animal sacrifices and constituted an integral part of the gift to the gods (S. R. F. Price, *Religions of the Ancient Greeks* [Cambridge: Cambridge University Press, 1999], 37). See the discussion of the imperial hymnodes of Pergamum in Section 3.2 below.

25. On which, see below.

26. The co-existence of both types of sacrifices raises the question of the precise relationship of the emperor (and the imperial family) to the gods. There is no uniform "theology" extractable from the evidence, and the question as to whether or not the emperor (clearly referred to as θεός in inscriptions) was regarded as "divine" depends, in turn, on intricate questions as to what constitutes "divine" and "human" for both ancients and moderns. On this, see Price, "Gods and Emperors"; idem, *Rituals and Power*, 210–20; and Friesen, *Twice Neokoros*, 146–52. Friesen argues (rightly, I think) that the sacrifices have little to do with the emperor's ontology:

> My proposal is that ancient imperial sacrifices should not be understood as a way of indicating who was divine and who was human. Particular kinds of sacrifice were appropriate in the context of particular relationships. It was appropriate for the inhabitants to sacrifice to the emperors because the emperors functioned like gods in relationship to them. It was also correct for inhabitants of the empire to sacrifice to the gods on behalf of the emperors because the emperors were not independent of the gods. Put succinctly, sacrifice was not so much a means for expressing divinity as a way of demonstrating and maintaining a variety of relationships. Sacrificing to the emperors and sacrificing to the gods on behalf of the emperors were not contradictory actions. They were two complementary aspects of the larger sacrificial system (*idem*, 150).

27. Mitchell, *Anatolia, Vol. I*, 107.

cities in which they took place.²⁸ The imperial cults were not simply "religious events" in any isolated sense—they also decisively transformed social life by shaping how people experienced rest, entertainment and leisure, associating these domains in new ways with the emperor. This point can be illustrated by a list of imperial priests inscribed in the temple to Roma and Augustus in Ankara, Galatia, which tells us also of the benefactions provided by each.²⁹ According to this list, the imperial priests who served during the reign of Tiberius sometimes gave to the city new buildings, but more often they sponsored one or more of the following: (1) oil for use at the gymnasium; (2) multiple animal sacrifices; (3) public banquets; (4) gladiatorial shows and other forms of public entertainment (e.g., fights involving bulls and wild animals); and (5) distribution of grain, perhaps for free or at a low cost. Vital social institutions became recast in imperial terms. The list also points to an important form of social realignment: in Ankara and elsewhere, local elites (in this case, those who served as priests) were given new opportunities to foster ties with Rome and increase their prominence in the community via sponsorship of sacrifices, celebrations, and buildings associated with the imperial cults.

Rituals commemorating the emperor and his family necessitated new infrastructures—altars, sacred precincts (*temenoi*), and temples dedicated to the cause. Sometimes, buildings were consecrated exclusively for imperial veneration. In these instances, they most often occupied a prominent place that ensured their visibility to local inhabitants—as we see in Ankara, Pessinus, and Pisidian Antioch. At other times, imperial cultic structures were integrated into existing ones already consecrated to traditional deities, as with a room which appears dedicated to Hadrian in the sanctuary of Asclepius in Pergamum.³⁰ The ease with which a new

---

28. For a description of these features of imperial festivals, using Ankara as an example, see Mitchell, *Anatolia, Vol. I*, 107–13 (but see also the synoptic analysis in Price, *Rituals and Power*, 101–32).

One of the richest documentations of a civic festival, though not of an imperial feast as such, comes to us from a detailed and well-preserved inscription, dating to the reign of Hadrian, from Oenanda in Lycia. The text, originally published by Michael Wörrle in *Stadt und Fest im kaiserzeitlichen Kleinasien: Studien zu einer agonistichen Stiftung aus Oinanda* (Vestigia 39; Munich: Beck, 1988), has been translated into English and furnished with commentary by Stephen Mitchell in "Festivals, Games, and Civic Life in Roman Asia Minor," *Journal of Roman Studies* 80 (2012): 183–93. It stands as testimony to an elaborate theater festival, detailing the responsibilities of various participants—from the duties of the presider (*agonothete*) right down to the involvement of surrounding farms and villages. It also lists a complete program of events. Though the sacrifices on this occasion were offered to Apollo, the document nevertheless specifies that (1) images (in the form of relief portraits) of the emperors were to be carried in the festal procession by ten appointed officials (*sebastophoroi*) appointed for the task; and (2) imperial priests and priestesses were to participate by sacrificing one bull.

29. Mitchell, *Anatolia, Vol. I*, 107–13 (list translated in Table 8.1, 108).

30. Price, *Rituals and Power*, 148.

altar or image could be introduced into various spaces meant that the imperial cults could, quite literally, be inserted into just about any domain of public life. The placement of imperial altars in the bouleuterion of Miletus and the bath-gymnasium complex in Ephesus, as well as statues of Augustus and Livia in the gymnasium of Pergamon, exemplified a new imperial moment in the life of these cities.[31]

It is important to bear in mind in the course of this study that the inherently public and formal nature of much of the evidence affords us no direct access to the psyche of its practitioners or the depth of its reception among the people. Any attempts to reconstruct the meaning of these cults and their rituals for the practitioners—which even then can only be discussed in terms of an "archetypal practitioner"—thus remain precarious. Partly in response to older tendencies in scholarship, Price (drawing from the work of Clifford Geertz) has argued for a focus on the public, symbolic significance of the imperial cultic rituals rather than on the internal response or mental states of individual participants. Not only does the latter pursuit presume a disjuncture between religious action and religious feeling that may have well been foreign to ancient practitioners, but it also reads the data through a modern preoccupation with the individual as subject.[32]

Focus on the symbolic nature of these imperial rituals also means that we can avoid generalizations about what they "must have meant" to entire populations. What is produced or enacted by a system of symbols—in the case of our interest, an ideology or worldview—cannot so casually be equated with how all of its participants received it. Hence, Steven Friesen makes the appropriate distinction between the *production* of the imperial cults and their *consumption*.[33] That consumption or reception can be every bit as complex and diverse as the process of production itself: "Just as there was no single imperial cult, there was also no single audience, and no single response."[34]

---

31. Friesen, *Imperial Cults*, 71–4.

32. Price, *Rituals and Power*, 7–15, esp. 9–11. Price regards the emphasis on personal faith and religious feeling as "covertly Christianizing" (10). Jonathan Z. Smith has defended the intriguing thesis that the modern study of religions of Late Antiquity has for a long time been haunted by Protestant critiques of Catholicism that emerged during the Reformation—that is, that these "pagan" traditions, like Catholicism, are ritualistic and empty of sincere, personal faith; see his *Drudgery Divine: On the Comparison of Early Christianities and the Religions of Late Antiquity*, Jordan Lectures in Comparative Religion 14 (London: School of Oriental and African Studies, University of London, 1990), 1–35.

33. Steven J. Friesen, "Normal Religion, Or, Words Fail Us: A Response to Karl Galinsky's 'The Cult of the Roman Emperor: Uniter or Divider?'" in *Rome and Religion: A Cross-Disciplinary Dialogue on the Imperial Cult*, ed. Jeffrey Brodd and Jonathan L. Reed (Atlanta, GA: Society of Biblical Literature, 2011), 24.

34. Friesen, "Normal Religion," 25. Likewise Mitchell (*Anatolia*, 1:117): "[the imperial cults] meant different things to different participants and observers." I apply this also to my reading of 1 Peter: what the text endeavors to communicate to its readers cannot simply be equated to how every one of its readers must have heard it.

There surely were, as there always have been, individuals in the Roman world whose religious practices and experiences differed from those of the community in which they lived.[35] In the present study, we are thus only able to speak of the imperial cults as a complex of symbols that was to some extent shared by its collaborators (the emperor, the Senate, Roman and local government officials, local elites, non-elite participants, etc.) and regarded by them as efficacious responses to Roman presence in Anatolian territory.[36] All interpretations as to what these symbols meant, both to them and to others implicated by these imperial rituals, can only be adduced with a limited measure of confidence and must remain tenuous.

We will return to these features above as they become relevant later. This brief outline serves only to highlight some concrete aspects of the imperial cults and pave the way for the following discussion of their ideological component.

2.1.3 Their Remarkable Diversity

Any study of the imperial cults must respect their heterogeneous character.[37] In a very real sense, there was no monolithic "imperial cult" but rather a federation of "imperial *cults*."[38] While this often seems to be forgotten in New Testament

---

35. Cf. Mary Beard, John A. North, and Simon R. F. Price, *Religions of Rome, Volume I: A History* (Cambridge: Cambridge, 1998), 316.

36. Here, the following description of the nature of Roman religion in general encapsulates also the imperial cults: "... in communities throughout the empire, distinctively Roman and distinctively local traditions were integrated as a response to (and articulation of) the power of Rome" (Beard, North, and Price, *Religions of Rome, Vol. I*, 363).

37. The following point is, in part, related to the heterogeneity of the evidence itself. It is noteworthy that there exists no extensive contemporaneous treatment of the imperial cults in the provinces. For one, practitioners in Anatolia, whether Roman or indigenous, generally felt no need to record or describe their practices for outsiders. The data that remain come to us primarily through non-literary forms and bear attendant difficulties. The past must be made to speak via archeology, sculpture, numismatics, and, above all, the wealth of inscriptions that bear witness to this ancient and widespread institution. These sources are not only diverse in kind but also spread out temporally and geographically, spanning the imperial period of some 300 years and reaching around 180 communities scattered throughout Asia Minor. The communities ranged from small villages to large cities, and were by no means demographically or culturally uniform. On these and other cautions regarding the evidence, see Price, *Rituals and Power*, 2–19.

38. Karl Galinsky, "The Cult of the Roman Emperor: Uniter or Divider?" in *Rome and Religion: A Cross-Disciplinary Dialogue on the Imperial Cult*, ed. Jeffrey Brodd and Jonathan L. Reed (Atlanta, GA: Society of Biblical Literature, 2011), 3. This view is heartily affirmed in Steven Friesen's response to Galinsky's paper in the same volume: "Normal Religion, Or, Words Fail Us: A Response to Karl Galinsky's 'The Cult of the Roman Emperor: Uniter or Divider?'" 23–6.

scholarship—exegetes still tend to speak of "the imperial cult" in Philippi or Thessalonica as if it were more or less identical to what happened in Rome—this caveat is of paramount importance with reference to our investigation of imperial ritual in Anatolia. Not only was its terrain geographically vast, but it was also imbued with rich and diverse religious legacies, both indigenous and shaped by preceding conquests. It was generally speaking not a matter of Roman policy to impose Rome's own religious traditions on conquered populations or to annihilate local cultic practices. This was even more so in mainland Greece and Asia Minor, where the respect of the Romans for Greek language and culture meant that extant practices were less likely to be modified.[39] Cults to the emperor and his family developed under different circumstances in different places, taking on a variety of forms. The contours of this complexity can be traced quite easily.

An important distinction can be made, in the first place, in terms of how a particular imperial cult was organized. The procedures for the establishment of a new cult of the emperor at the provincial level were more formalized and complex than one at the municipal level. The former generally required approval from the Roman Senate and the emperor and were thus more regulated, whereas the latter tended to be set up by local initiatives and were more free in form.[40] One consequence of this difference is that in the municipal cults we tend to see a wider engagement of members of the imperial family, with more cults dedicated to the wives and progeny of the emperors, and a more generous application of the term θεός to the emperors.[41]

The emperor and his family were also integrated into religious life in a variety of ways. In some cases, cultic veneration was offered directly to the emperor (as in the instances recorded by Dio above),[42] and in others his cult was incorporated into those of traditional deities of the various locales.[43] At times, emperors and

---

39. Beard, North, and Price, *Religions of Rome, Vol. I*, 314, 342. Nevertheless, despite Rome's non-interventionist approach, indigenous cults acquired a new hue under Roman rule even when they were not directly affected by the imperial cults, transformed as they were by new relations of power to the imperial center. This could happen, for example, on the basic level of funding, as when a Roman party (whether the governor or a military official) contributed toward a temple for local divinities or took part in its ceremonies (*idem*, 343).

40. For detailed studies of how mechanisms differed at the provincial and municipal levels, see Friesen, *Imperial Cults*, 25–103.

41. On these and other differences between provincial and municipal imperial cults, see Friesen, *Imperial Cults*, 75–6.

42. See also, e.g., *SEG* 1.282; *AGRW* 81; *TAM* V 914; *IGR* 4.713.

43. See, e.g., *SEG* 21.703 (with Athena Polias); *IGladiateurs* 257 (with Apollo Chresterios ["of the Oracle"]); *IAssos* 26 (with Zeus Sotēr and Athena); *IGR* IV.144 (with Athena Polias); *IGR* IV.318 (with Hermes and Hercules). A list of additional examples is given in Galinsky, "The Cult of the Roman Emperor," 4–5. See the detailed discussion in Price, *Rituals and Power*, 146–62.

members of his family were even openly identified with divinities of the traditional pantheon: Augustus was honored as the son of Zeus Eleutherios,[44] Livia as the new Hera,[45] Nero as the new Apollo,[46] and so forth. This deep embedding of imperial cults into existing forms of religious life warns us against treating them as though they were a class of unique phenomena that can be easily "extracted" from the broader context of Anatolian religious practice. They were, in fact, rooted in older traditions of ruler cults, even if they were transformed, no doubt, by a new Roman hue.[47]

A third determinant of variegation was the composition and status of the local community—especially with regard to its ties to Rome (e.g., whether or not it was a designated colony). In Pisidian Antioch, the imperial temple reflected a robust sense of *Romanitas*, boasting of the city's status as a colony with its triple dedication to Jupiter Optimus Maximus, Augustus, and the Genius of the Colony, whereas in predominantly-Hellenic Aphrodisias, the divine Sebastoi shared a temple with its patron Aphrodite and the (local) *Demos,* and were artistically rendered in forms reminiscent of the Greek pantheon.[48] It is also noteworthy that, in the excerpt from Dio Cassius discussed above, the Romans living in Ephesus and Nicaea were said to have been "commanded" by Augustus to set up cults to Roma and the lately-divinized Julius. In these cases, the cults functioned as markers and expressions of Roman citizenship in the provinces.[49] Communities that lacked official Roman status of any sort, on the other hand, were quite free to determine the forms of the cults independent of official Roman channels.[50]

These differences in context of establishment, form, and practice have led various scholars to stress plurality in their study of the imperial cults. Prompted by his examination of the evidence, Elias Bickerman wrote:

> A universal cult of the ruler did not exist in the Roman Empire. Each city, each province, each group worshipped this or that sovereign according to its own discretion and ritual.[51]

---

44. *AGRW* 280.

45. *IAssos* 19.

46. *IG* II/III² 3278 (Athens), in E. M. Smallwood, *Documents Illustrating the Principates of Gaius, Claudius and Nero* (Cambridge: Cambridge, 1967), para. 145.

47. Beard, North, and Price, *Religions of Rome, Vol. I,* 360: "Cults of the emperor, which were modelled on the traditional forms of civic cults of the gods, did not displace traditional cults; they fitted alongside them."

48. A key study of both these cultic sites is Rubin, "(Re)presenting Empire." I have relied on this work for the detailed discussion presented in Chapter 6 below.

49. On cultic allegiance to Rome as an expression of citizenship, see Beard, North, and Price, *Religions of Rome, Vol. I,* 317.

50. Beard, North, and Price, *Religions of Rome, Vol. I,* 355.

51. Elias Bickerman, "Consecratio," in *Le culte des souverains dans l'Empire romain,* ed. Willem den Boer, Entretiens sur l'Antiquité classique (Geneva: Fondation Hardt, 1973), 9.

This finding is reiterated in the more recent work of Beard, North, and Price:

> There was no such thing as "*the* imperial cult"; rather there was a series of different cults sharing a common focus in the worship of the emperor, his family or predecessors, but ... operating quite differently according to a variety of different local circumstances—the Roman status of the communities in which they were found, the pre-existing religious traditions of the area, and the degree of central Roman involvement in establishing the cult.[52]

In proceeding, then, we must bear in mind that the terms "imperial cult" and "imperial cults" are operational definitions that designate particular (Roman) instantiations within a wider set of diverse religious practices. What holds them together is the modifier "imperial," marking out their common focus on the Roman emperor and his family.

2.1.4 Indigenous Initiatives or Imperial Impositions?: Hybridity

As noted above, the imperial cults must be studied together and not in isolation. As a collection of phenomena, they were rooted in Asia Minor's long tradition of ruler cults and emerged within the religious complexity of its various communities. Nevertheless, it cannot be denied that they also were, in a very real way, products of a "new moment"—the Roman occupation of Anatolia. As such, they must also be counted among the innovations triggered by this historical process, not solely as "religious phenomena," but as part of a much broader program of political, social, and economic change inaugurated by imperial presence in the land.

In considering the imperial cults as agents of ideological change—that is, the means by which imperial ideology was constructed—we can begin by asking, "Who were the makers and/or participants in this process?" How this question is answered will help us understand better their function as means by which that imperial ideology was constructed and disseminated.

There has long been a question among historians of the subject as to whether these cults were impositions "from the center"—that is, initiatives by imperial authorities to consolidate Roman power—or spontaneous, indigenous responses on the part of Rome's subjects to imperial presence. This is often answered by appealing to a dichotomous model that appeals to allegedly differing policies in the western and eastern parts of the Empire. The approach is concisely exemplified in the statement of Duncan Fishwick: "In origin the impetus to establish the ruler cult came from the east; but in the west provincial cult, at least, was for the most part installed by Augustus and his successors."[53] In his more recent work, the idea

---

52. Beard, North, and Price, *Religions of Rome, Vol. I*, 318. I have adhered to this strong caution by consistently using the plural form, "imperial cults," throughout.

53. Duncan Fishwick, *The Imperial Cult in the Latin West: Studies in the Ruler Cult of the Western Provinces of the Roman Empire*, vol. 1.1 (Leiden: Brill, 1987), 92.

persists: imperial cults in the West were subject to "central orchestration and control" from Augustus down to the third century, whereas "[i]nitiative from below was ... the norm in the Greek world."[54]

As with so many binaries, this perspective has been criticized for oversimplifying the data, not the least because it is built on longstanding Eurocentric stereotypes about the Greek-speaking East.[55] At the core of this bias is the persistent notion that the Latin West was more rational (and, by this fact, implicitly superior), whereas the Greek East was more superstitious and prone to religious impulses. While the former had to be compelled to worship the Roman emperor and did so quite reluctantly, the Greek-speaking East more enthusiastically prostrated in adulation before his footstool, either out of piety, or flattery, or both.[56] From this angle, the imperial cults in the western empire must be seen as political devices,[57] whereas in the eastern reaches of the Empire like Asia Minor, they were primarily out-workings of Hellenistic religiosity—Greek productions, as it were.[58]

---

54. Duncan Fishwick, *The Imperial Cult in the Latin West: Studies in the Ruler Cult of the Western Provinces of the Roman Empire*, vol. 3.1 (Leiden, Boston, and Köln: Brill, 2002), 219. Although he acknowledges that there are exceptions highlighted by scholars such as Price and Friesen (*idem*, n. 23), these do not seem to destabilize his position in any significant way.

55. The most influential critique has been that of Simon Price (see esp. *Rituals and Power*, 7–19), who confronts head-on this framework, which he regards as the product of Christianizing tendencies. Other critics of this model include Mitchell, *Anatolia, Vol. I*, 100–17; Rubin, "(Re)presenting Empire."

56. A position traceable back to at least Edward Gibbon, who described the practice of deifying the emperor as a departure from "[the Romans'] accustomed prudence and modesty." "The Asiatic Greeks," he continues, "were the first inventors ... of this servile and impious mode of adulation." The cult of the emperor in the West, on the other hand, was received as "an institution, not of religion, but of policy" (*The History of the Decline and Fall of the Roman Empire. With Notes by H.H. Milman*, vol. 1 [Philadelphia, PA: Porter & Coates, 1845], 84–5).

57. Fishwick, *The Imperial Cult*, 1.1:273: "One must always remember that in the west the imperial cult at the provincial level was basically a political device designed to weld the empire together." This idea is reiterated in a later volume in the series: "By and large provincial cult in the West appears as an instrument of imperial policy, a device that could be manipulated in whichever direction the purposes of the central authority might require" (Fishwick, *The Imperial Cult in the Latin West*, 3.1:219).

58. Rubin ("[Re]presenting Empire," 21–2) accuses Price of perpetuating the view of eastern imperial cults as essentially Greek initiatives and denying Roman responsibility for their formation. This charge, however, seems misguided, as Price clearly acknowledges the role of Roman authorities both in initiating and in regulating the cults (*Rituals and Power*, 65–77). In one place, Price explicitly cautions that "an excessive emphasis on Greek initiatives in the establishment of the [imperial] cults fails to take into account the actual intervention of Romans, whether in the provinces or in Rome itself, and also fails to allow for the constant and covert pressure exercised by Rome" (*Rituals and Power*, 173).

In a recent study, Fernando Lozano argues that this model distorts the available evidence and ignores a whole range of forces at play in the emergence of the imperial cults both in the western and eastern parts of the Empire.[59] Using a series of examples, he shows how the dynamics involved in the establishment and development of imperial cults, both in the west as well as in the east, were products of complex political, social, and economic variables. They cannot simply be reduced to either impositions from the imperial center or spontaneous responses from provincial communities, since they were shaped not only by a central imperial authority (e.g., the emperor) but also by a whole network of collaborators: senators, provincial governors, local elites, and the like.[60]

With regard to the eastern provinces that are our concern here, Lozano points out that the imperial cults were something more than spontaneous, indigenous initiatives. Roman governors in the provinces, acting as representatives of Caesar, often played a decisive role in the imperial cults. In addition to Paulus Fabius Maximus' role in promoting the Augustan cult in Asia (discussed in detail in the following chapter), Lozano draws from the case of a governor of Achaia, P. Memmius Regulus. Regulus took an active role in establishing and promoting the cult of Gaius throughout his tenure, including elevating the careers of its priests, at least one of whom obtained Roman citizenship.[61] Furthermore, the sudden proliferation, beginning in the mid first century AD, of the cult to the collective Sebastoi and its attendant priesthoods[62] can be more adequately explained by recourse to some form of initiative from imperial authorities. It seems highly unlikely that such cults would have emerged merely as localized initiatives.[63] In a similar way, the consistency of images of the emperor in coinage and statuary throughout the eastern provinces, though Greek in idiom, also suggests that their production was systematized and regulated by provincial authorities in some fashion.[64] All across the Empire, portraits

---

59. Fernando Lozano, "The Creation of Imperial Gods: Not Only Imposition versus Spontaneity," in *More Than Men, Less Than Gods: Studies on Royal Cult and Imperial Worship. Proceedings of the International Colloquium Organized by the Belgian School at Athens (November 1-2, 2007)*, ed. Panagiotis P. Iossif, Andrzej Stanisław Chankowski, and Catharine C. Lorber (Leuven: Peeters, 2011), 475–519.

60. Lozano, "The Creation of Imperial Gods," 479–80.

61. Lozano, "The Creation of Imperial Gods," 488–90.

62. Cf. the Price's explanation of "routinization," discussed above.

63. Lozano, "The Creation of Imperial Gods," 490–1.

64. Lozano, "The Creation of Imperial Gods," 491–2. Lozano is not alone here. Price (*Rituals and Power*, 172–4) argues that the consistent and thus recognizable depictions of the emperor must have stemmed from prototypes chosen and approved by high Roman officials, or even the emperor himself. Similarly, the remarkable stability in imperial representations has led Clifford Ando to state: "without imperial supervision of the processes of distribution it would be difficult to account for the speed and extent of the spread of official portrait types, or indeed, for their longevity: the *Haupttypus* of Antoninus Pius remained unchanged for the twenty-three years of his reign" (Ando, *Imperial Ideology*, 229–30).

of Augustus from the last thirty-five years of his reign, do not show him in old age, and are almost identical down to details in his hairstyle.[65] Lastly, Lozano emphasizes that when we treat the imperial cults simply as spontaneous Hellenistic institutions, we do not take into sufficient account the role of class and status in each case: elites in these communities in all likelihood held more sway in shaping the cults than did less privileged groups.[66] Lozano's work affirms the diversity of the imperial cults, not only in terms of their character but specifically in terms of their genesis. Their origin and development cannot simply be reduced to imposition from the imperial center or spontaneous response on the part of Rome's subjects. Rather, they constitute "a multiplex phenomenon, which cannot be explained in terms of a single and somewhat narrow theoretical line."[67]

When we speak of the imperial cults as a whole, therefore, we cannot regard them merely as Roman productions—or Greek ones, for that matter. On one level, this ought not to surprise us. Benjamin Rubin refers to the Roman occupation in Anatolia as "a dialogic process" that resulted in the fusion of Roman and provincial cultures, with the imperial cults being manifestations of this exchange. They are simultaneously, he says, both outcomes and catalysts of this process:

> Anatolian elites worked together with Roman administration to develop a shared set of cultural codes (i.e. art, architecture and rituals), which they could use to articulate and negotiate the new, social realities of Roman imperial rule. As a result, the ideological program of the Roman imperial cult in Asia Minor was neither truly Greek nor Roman, but rather a hybrid synthesis of multiple cultural systems.[68]

The concept of cultural hybridity, here applied to the imperial cults, is adopted from postcolonial and cultural studies, especially the work of Homi Bhabha.[69] Though there is no single view of hybridity, and Bhabha's theory on the matter has been both influential and disputed,[70] the outline of the idea itself can be helpful for our purposes.

---

65. Price, *Rituals and Power*, 172.

66. Lozano, "The Creation of Imperial Gods," 493.

67. Lozano, "The Creation of Imperial Gods," 494.

68. Rubin, "(Re)presenting Empire," 22–3. Rubin (*idem*, chs 4 and 5) conclusively shows, moreover, that Anatolian imperial cults were also influenced by Egyptian and Persian traditions, the threads of which have been obscured by scholars' preoccupation with their Roman and Greek origins.

69. Rubin, "(Re)presenting Empire," 23 n. 41. See Homi K. Bhabha, "Signs Taken for Wonders: Questions of Ambivalence and Authority under a Tree Outside Delhi, May 1817," *Critical Inquiry* 12, no. 1 (1985): 144–65. Also helpful is the summary of Bhabha's thought, with examples of application to a reading of Revelation, in Moore, *Empire and Apocalypse*, 86–96, 109–21.

70. For other ways of thinking about hybridity and criticisms of Bhabha, see Loomba, *Colonialism/Postcolonialism*, 173–83.

In its most general and neutral sense, hybridity characterizes the transactions and interactions between colonizer and colonized. It is premised on the idea that neither colonizer nor colonized are stable cultural entities, i.e. they are in themselves always growing and changing. For this reason, they do not exist in binary opposition to one another (though either side might construe it this way). In the colonial encounter, both parties—each of which is already an evolving culture—engage one another in complex ways that are inflected by their asymmetrical relations of power. For the purposes of our study, it is important to note that hybridity can work in the favor of either the colonizer or the colonized. Hybrid cultural forms, such as the mastery of English by a subjugated people, can cut both ways: fluent "non-native" speakers of English can be co-opted as imperial officials or cultural attachés, for example, but they can equally use that same language to critique and undermine the colonizers.

As hybrid productions, the imperial cults not only provided the colonizer, i.e. Rome, with entry points into Hellenistic political and religious life. These "contact zones" between Roman and Hellenistic cultures also afforded the colonized new ways of relating to Roman power and harnessing it to their advantage—as in the case of city elites who assumed the prestigious offices of imperial priesthood, or the Aphrodisians, who forged special ties with the Augustan family through a common, if mythical, ancestor (see Section 5.2.2). Nonetheless, the hybrid nature of the imperial cults must not be allowed to obscure a recurrent, unifying theme: the imperial cults wove the Roman emperor into the fabric of life—into daily rhythms and everyday spaces (argued in Chapters 3 and 5 to follow), into pantheons, into the cosmos—indeed, into reality itself, for those who lived in the shadow of Roman rule. This did not necessarily mean that the emperor always held preeminence or the supreme position in the worlds constructed by the imperial cults,[71] though it did mean that, wherever they were established, they infused these worlds with a distinctly Roman tenor and conditioned the particular ways in which people thought about and responded to imperial presence.

2.1.5 Representing Roman Power

What sort of picture did the imperial cults give of imperial power and its place in the world? Richard Gordon draws attention to ways in which the imperial cults played a part in advancing the agenda of Rome.[72] The cults and their attendant rituals and images, he argues, naturalized the socioeconomic order of Roman rule, "tacitly proposing and imposing a scheme of perception in terms of which the distribution of power and social advantage is as it must and can only

---

71. Though in some cases, as with the decree of the province of Asia discussed below, the emperor did seem to take center-stage.

72. Homi K. Bhabha, *The Location of Culture* (London and New York, NY: Routledge, 1994), esp. 145–74.

be."[73] Ultimately, they served as instruments for the Empire's self-preservation and perpetuation, but they fulfilled this function not necessarily by directly legitimating imperial authority in the minds of the Empire's subjects, but by "re-describing" the order of things—that is, re-framing the status quo (i.e. of Roman occupation) within a broader cosmic order in which the emperor occupied a pivotal role.[74] On this point, Gordon's argument dovetails nicely with Catherine Bell's description of royal cults: "The king's cult creates the king, defines kingliness, and orchestrates a cosmic framework within which the social hierarchy headed by the king is perceived as natural and right."[75]

In this reconfiguration of the socio-cosmic order, two groups of people played crucial roles by propagating the imperial cults. The first of these were Roman citizens living in Asia Minor. By instituting the cults in various localities, they set themselves up as privileged mediators between the local populations and the center of power in Rome. Likewise, members of the local elite, such as former kings and tribal leaders of indigenous communities, by contributing to the celebration and benefactions of the imperial cult, acquired status by virtue of their special position with respect to the emperor. Together, these two groups overlaid the realities of the Roman takeover and re-conceived it as a privileged relationship to the occupying superpower. By means of the benefactions of the cult (sacrifices, festivals, games, banquets, etc.), they enacted the emperor's solicitude, provision, and care for his subjects, yet these benefactions were precisely premised on power differentials and socioeconomic inequalities in these Anatolian communities. In this way, these celebrations insidiously naturalized the disparities of the status quo.[76]

The legitimation of imperial power can also be seen, Gordon argues, from the way images of the emperor were employed to create and disseminate fictive notions of Caesar's power. For one, the placement of his images into various domains—not only in temples but also in public spaces such as fora, baths, amphitheaters, and even rooms of private residences—imbued the emperor with a god-like aura, an apparent ability to transcend the limitations of space and time.[77] Even outside designated cultic spaces, these images were not merely ornamental or didactic, but objects that manifested the emperor's presence. Under the Julio-Claudian emperors, for instance, images of a new emperor were distributed to

---

73. Richard Gordon, "The Roman Imperial Cult and the Question of Power," in *The Religious History of the Roman Empire: Pagans, Jews, and Christians*, ed. John A. North and S. R. F. Price. Oxford Readings in Classical Studies (Oxford: Oxford University Press, 2011), 45. Catherine Bell (*Ritual: Perspectives and Dimensions* [New York, NY: Oxford University Press, 1997], 135) argues that this is the function of political rituals in general.

74. Gordon, "The Question of Power," 46. For a similar point, see Philip A. Harland, "Imperial Cults within Local Cultural Life: Associations in Roman Asia," *Ancient History Bulletin/Zeitschrift für alte Geschichte*, no. 17 (2003): 105–6.

75. Bell, *Ritual*, 129.

76. Gordon, "The Question of Power," 48.

77. Gordon, "The Question of Power," 54.

legionary camps throughout the Empire so that soldiers could swear allegiance to him.[78] "As a stand-in for the emperor's person, a portrait could witness an oath, receive cult acts, put the seal on diplomatic arrangements, or offer refuge to the oppressed."[79] Like the gods, the emperor was, in effect, omnipresent.

Perhaps most importantly, the imperial cults emphasized the emperor's role as mediator between the Empire and the divine realm, and thus as guarantor of the stability of the cosmic order. Imagistically, this was achieved by portraying him as the principal sacrificant of the Empire. A coin from Caesarea Maritima dating to the Trajanic period depicts the emperor offering grains of incense on a portable altar while holding in his left hand the cornucopia, a symbol of domestic peace and agricultural fecundity. The specimen thus conveys not only the emperor's role in preserving the *pax deorum*, but also his actual ability to do so. The order of the world rests, as it were, on him.[80] He occupies an essential place in the cosmos, and in his hands lies the potential to sustain (or thwart) the well-being of entire societies. His power was derived neither from consent nor veneration, but rather justified them. If, as Price says, the imperial rituals functioned as a "way of conceptualizing the world"—"a system whose structure defines the position of the emperor"[81]—then this coin captures *in nuce* the core idea undergirding the imperial cults in their various manifestations. In his person, the emperor of Rome is the one who, as the *koinon* of Asia said of Augustus, exists for "the common good fortune of all."

For Stephen Mitchell, "emperor worship was arguably the most significant way in which provincial subjects were made aware of and came to terms with imperial power within the framework of their communities."[82] Likewise, in Keith Hopkins' estimation, the imperial cults "provided the context in which inhabitants of towns spread for hundreds of miles throughout the Empire could celebrate their membership of a single political order and their own place within it."[83] This reality was due not only to the distribution of the imperial cults across the vast terrain of Roman Anatolia, but also to the specific ways in which the emperor was

---

78. Ando, *Imperial Ideology*, 230. In his book, Ando devotes an entire chapter (ch. 7) to images of the emperor. For an even more extensive treatment of the role of imperial images, see Paul Zanker, *The Power of Images in the Age of Augustus*, trans. Alan Shapiro (Ann Arbor, MI: University of Michigan Press, 1988).

79. Ando, *Imperial Ideology*, 232.

80. Gordon, "The Question of Power," 60–2. The role was intensified by the title *Pontifex Maximus*, taken up by Augustus and never abandoned by his successors. In becoming the supreme guardians of cult, the Caesars also became the supreme mediators between their realm and the gods. Hence it was important for Augustus to present himself as the restorer of the temples of Rome in the *Res Gestae* (20.4).

81. Price, *Rituals and Power*, 7–11.

82. Mitchell, *Anatolia, Vol. I*, 113.

83. Keith Hopkins, *Conquerors and Slaves*, Sociological Studies in Roman History (Cambridge/New York, NY: Cambridge University Press, 1978), 242.

symbolically constructed in ritual, image, and infrastructure. Gordon's analysis stresses the notions of power enacted in the ritual life of these cults. Their evolution from earlier forms of ruler cults embodies the assimilation of a foreign, Roman self-understanding into the cultural frameworks of the Empire's Anatolian subjects. This process was complex, a synthesis in which Roman and indigenous traditions engaged one another (though not necessarily symmetrically) and developed symbols of shared meaning. On one level, the cults can be seen as local attempts to make sense of Roman incursions into their world. This, however, should not obscure the fact that the cults were also genuinely Roman in character in that they imagined a universe in which the emperor occupied pride of place. In this way, they served as carriers of imperial ideology.

2.2 First Peter: Establishing Parameters for Ideological Analysis

We turn now to some prefatory matters that frame my reading of 1 Peter as an ideological document. The aim, as will soon become obvious, is not to reach any definite conclusions regarding the letter's authorship, dating, provenance, or readership. Rather, these discussions serve to develop a working hypothesis regarding the letter's historico-geographical context in order to facilitate the discernment of its ideological stance.

2.2.1 Authorship and Date of Composition

While scholars' views regarding 1 Peter's authorship tend to be linked to the position taken on its date of composition and provenance as well, for ease of discussion, each of these topics will be dealt with in sequence.

The present scholarly consensus leans in favor of 1 Peter as a pseudonymous text, against the letter's own explicit claim to have been written by Peter the apostle (1.1). The primary reasons in favor of this conclusion can be summed up as follows:[84]

1. The rather polished Greek of the letter makes it unlikely that it would have been written by Peter, a fisherman (Mk 1:16) who was, as early traditions admit, "uneducated" (ἀγράμματος, Acts 4:13). In conjunction with this, the letter's reliance on and complex handling of the Septuagint[85] points to an author whose command of Greek likely surpassed his knowledge of Semitic languages, making the Galilean's authorship improbable.

---

84. For a more comprehensive coverage of the debate over 1 Peter's authorship, see Elliott, *1 Peter*, 118–30.

85. On which see Steve Moyise, "The Old Testament in 1 and 2 Peter, Jude," in *The Old Testament in the New: An Introduction* (London: T&T Clark, 2001); Steve Moyise, "Isaiah in 1 Peter," in *Isaiah in the New Testament*, ed. Steve Moyise and M. J. J. Menken (New York, NY: T&T Clark, 2005), 175–88.

2. The letter cannot be so easily linked to the historical Peter. Though it exhibits familiarity with early traditions about Jesus,[86] its reflection on his passion, death, and resurrection is characteristic of the early church's kerygma and scriptural interpretation, and does not necessitate composition by the apostle, even if the author claims to have been "witness of the sufferings of Christ" (5:1).[87]
3. Since internal evidence of the letter points to a date of composition in the early 70s at the earliest (see below), the apostle Peter, martyred under the reign of Nero according to early Christian tradition,[88] cannot have been its author.

In turn, defenders of the traditional view that the letter was in fact written by the apostle Peter have offered corresponding rejoinders:

1. The employment of an amanuensis for the letter (the candidate for which is most likely, though not necessarily, Silvanus; cf. 5:12) renders moot any argument based on the quality of the Greek of 1 Peter, since it was common for the secretary to exercise his own linguistic prowess over the text's final form by revising earlier versions, or even drafting it afresh. If Peter did employ an amanuensis, "then stylistic considerations, of little value in any instance, are worthless."[89]
2. As for the lack of traces of the apostle himself, it can equally be said that the letter was driven by a specifically pastoral strategy and not a personal one (compare, for example, Paul's self-defense in 2 Corinthians), thus making personal details of the author's life unnecessary and even irrelevant for his purposes. The absence of references to Peter's own life does not in itself constitute a legitimate point against the traditional view of Petrine authorship.[90]

---

86. On this, see David G. Horrell, "Jesus Remembered in 1 Peter? Early Jesus Traditions, Isaiah 53, and 1 Pet 2.21–25," in *Early Jesus Traditions in James and 1–2 Peter*, ed. Alicia J. Batten and John S. Kloppenborg, LNTS 478 (London and New York, NY: Bloomsbury T&T Clark, 2014), 123–50.

87. The word μάρτυς here need not necessarily mean "eye-witness," but can have a more general sense of "one who observes and testifies to the actuality and veracity of something" (Elliott, *1 Peter*, 818). See also Achtemeier, *1 Peter*, 323–4; David G. Horrell, *The Epistles of Peter and Jude* (Peterborough: Epworth, 1998), 92.

88. Cf. Tertullian, *Scorp.* 15; Eusebius, *Hist. eccl.* 2.25, 3.1; Lactantius, *Mort.* 2.

89. Michaels, *1 Peter*, lxii.

90. Williams, *Persecution in 1 Peter*, 26. As Williams insightfully points out, scholars also frequently argue for the *pseudonymous* authorship of 2 Peter precisely on the grounds that it contains too many references to the historical Peter!

The key problem here, it seems to me, is the lack of solid criteria for what counts as "Petrine" since, as Michaels (*1 Peter*, lxii) admits plainly, "there is no acknowledged Petrine corpus with which 1 Peter can be compared." Difficulties in attributing traditions to the historical Peter also apply to arguments that 1 Peter was composed by a "Petrine circle" (in

3. While arguments for the dating of the letter are in themselves disputable, a later date would not invalidate authorship by the apostle if one remains open to the possibility, as suggested by other early sources, that Peter outlived the Neronian persecution.[91]

While it may be impossible, despite the consensus, to establish definitive answers in this debate, the patterns of coalescence in arguments from both sides can be illuminating for the present inquiry.

Disagreements about the quality of Greek in 1 Peter, even if they be somewhat subjective, serve to point out that 1 Peter is, unambiguously, a cultural amalgam. Whether 1 Peter exhibits a "polished Attic style"[92] or Semitic interferences indicative of an author "for whom Greek is a second language,"[93] of greater interest here is the indisputable fact that 1 Peter articulates Jewish and Christian traditions in a language indicative of cultural accommodation. The debate over the quality of its Greek is, largely, one about how smoothly this was executed. It is hardly controversial that the author of 1 Peter was reliant on the Septuagint, itself a hybrid product of Hebrew and Aramaic texts rendered into Greek and thus adapted to the Hellenistic modes of thought,[94] though the letter's use of Jewish traditions goes

---

Rome)—a theory first proposed by Ernest Best (*1 Peter* [London: Oliphants, 1971], 62–3) and defended by John Elliott, most recently in his commentary (*1 Peter*, 127–30). This theory has been cogently refuted in David G. Horrell, "The Product of a Petrine Circle?: Challenging an Emerging Consensus," in *Becoming Christian: Essays on 1 Peter and the Making of Christian Identity*, LNTS 394 (London and New York, NY: Bloomsbury T&T Clark, 2013), 7–44 (on the lack of criteria for "Petrine traditions," see esp. 31–2).

91. For a discussion of this body of evidence, see Michaels, *1 Peter*, lx–lxi.

92. Elliott, *1 Peter*, 120.

93. Karen H. Jobes, *1 Peter* (Grand Rapids, MI: Baker, 2005), 7. (This position is elaborated in the excursus of 325–38.)

94. The hybrid nature of the Septuagint is made concrete in studies of the translation techniques used by its translators. The gap between the *Vorlage* and the final product was more than a semantic one, and at times necessitated strategies that negotiated habitual, culturally-embedded patterns of thought and expression as well as meanings of words, phrases, and idioms. For examples of this, see Hans Ausloos and Bénédicte Lemmelijn, "Content-Related Criteria in Characterising the LXX Translation Technique," in *Die Septuaginta—Texte, Theologien und Einflüsse: 2. Internationale Fachtagung veranstaltet von Septuaginta Deutsch (LXX.D), Wuppertal 23.-27. Juli 2008*, ed. Wolfgang Kraus, Martin Karrer, and Martin Meiser, WUNT 252 (Tübingen: Mohr Siebeck, 2010), 357–76; Hans Ausloos, Bénédicte Lemmelijn, and Valerie Kabergs, "The Study of Aetiological Wordplay as a Content-Related Criterion in the Characterisation of LXX Translation Technique," in *Die Septuaginta—Entstehung, Sprache, Geschichte: 3. Internationale Fachtagung veranstaltet von Septuaginta Deutsch (LXX.D), Wuppertal 22.-25. Juli 2010*, ed. Siegfried Kreuzer, Martin Meiser, and Marcus Sigismund, WUNT 286 (Tübingen: Mohr Siebeck, 2012), 273–94.

well beyond this and has been amply demonstrated.[95] Disputes as to whether or not Peter the apostle, being himself a Galilean, would have been sufficiently fluent in Greek emerge precisely because of the cultural pluralism that characterized the Roman-dominated Mediterranean. Greek was, quite certainly, not the only language used by the earliest Christians who both wrote and read the texts of the New Testament, but more importantly, early Christian traditions cannot simply be reduced to the labels "Jewish" or "Hellenistic," despite earlier attempts to do so. Insofar as language, thought, and culture are enmeshed with one another, 1 Peter, like the imperial cults of Anatolia, comes to us as a hybrid product. It is a text at the intersection of Jewish, Hellenistic, and Roman worlds.

The ongoing discussion regarding the link between 1 Peter and the apostle, despite differing findings, highlights rather than obscures the fact that the letter is attributed to Peter the apostle.[96] What is disputed is the veracity of this self-claim. Even if one assumes the view that the letter is pseudonymous, the attribution in 1:1 still speaks to the importance of Peter's apostolic authority for its Anatolian readers and the early church as a whole.[97] First Peter is an unambiguously *Christian* text and thus, as is significant for our purposes here, representative of at least one stream of thought in early Christianity. On the basis of its positive reception in other early Christian texts, we can infer that it was regarded as an authoritative (as opposed to marginal) voice by the churches in Asia Minor and elsewhere.[98]

---

95. A primer on the use of Jewish traditions and other streams of influence in 1 Peter can be found, with accompanying bibliography, in David G. Horrell, *1 Peter*, T&T Clark New Testament Guides (Edinburgh: T&T Clark, 2008), 31–44. More detailed treatments include William L. Schutter, *Hermeneutic and Composition in 1 Peter* (Tübingen: Mohr Siebeck, 1989); Richard Bauckham, "James, 1 and 2 Peter, Jude," in *It Is Written—Scripture Citing Scripture: Essays in Honour of Barnabas Lindars, SSF*, ed. D. A. Carson and H. G. M. Williamson (Cambridge: Cambridge, 1988), 303–17; and, most recently, Alan Chapple, "The Appropriation of Scripture in 1 Peter," in *All That the Prophets Have Declared: The Appropriation of Scripture in the Emergence of Christianity*, ed. Matthew R. Malcolm (Milton Keynes: Paternoster, 2015), 155–71. On the possibility of Platonic influence, see Reinhard Feldmeier, "Salvation and Anthropology in First Peter," in *The Catholic Epistles and Apostolic Tradition*, ed. Karl-Wilhelm Niebuhr and Robert W. Wall (Waco, TX: Baylor, 2009), 203–13, 437–41.

96. Compared to the far more nebulous identity of John the Seer in Revelation, this is indeed some comfort.

97. Horrell, "A Petrine Circle?" 39–40.

98. Depending on the position one takes on its dating, the earliest indicator is perhaps 2 Pet. 3:1. Significantly, Polycarp, bishop of Smyrna in Asia, writing to Christians in Philippi in the first half of the second century, already showed familiarity with 1 Peter (*Phil.* 1.3; 2.1, 2; 5.3; 6.3; 7.2; 8.1, 2). Though Polycarp does not explicitly state that he is quoting 1 Peter, this was obvious to Eusebius (*Hist. eccl.* 4.14.9). In his study of the reception of 1 Peter in Polycarp, Michael W. Holmes ("Polycarp's Letter to the Philippians and Writings That Later Formed the New Testament," in *The Reception of the New Testament in the Apostolic Fathers*,

We can now turn to discussions of the dating of 1 Peter. As with the question of authorship, and with the dating of New Testament texts in general, there has been no conclusive answer. Most scholars would, nonetheless, date 1 Peter to some point between the 60s and the 90s AD.[99] The outcomes of these discussions are, in part, dependent on one's views regarding authorship. If one were to accept the early witnesses that Peter the apostle wrote the letter *and* was later martyred under Nero, 1 Peter would have to have been written prior to 68 AD, the year of Nero's death.[100] If, on the other hand, Peter outlived Nero, or if one adheres to the majority view that 1 Peter was not written by the apostle, then its date of composition can extend to the end of the first century, bounded by its possible familiarity to the author of 1 Clement (*c.* 60s to 90s AD), Ignatius of Antioch (98–138 AD), and Polycarp (first half of first century AD).[101]

Other considerations are based on internal evidence.[102] The lack of evidence for a mono-episcopal ecclesial structure suggests that 1 Peter was written before the letters of Ignatius of Antioch, in which this form of leadership had apparently become quite widespread in Asia. Proposals for a date after 70 AD, however, are supported by (1) the use of "Babylon" (5:13) for Rome, as was common in Jewish

ed. Andrew Gregory and Christopher Tuckett [Oxford and New York: Oxford University Press, 2005], 223) concludes: "it appears virtually certain that Polycarp made relatively extensive use of 1 Peter." Bruce Metzger (*The Canon of the New Testament: Its Origin, Development, and Significance* [Oxford and New York: Clarendon Press, 1987], 62) states, more conjecturally, that the bishop must have known 1 Peter "by heart."

Beyond the Anatolian communities to whom it was addressed, the use of 1 Peter by Irenaeus of Lyons (*Adv. Haer.* 4.9.2; 4.16.5) suggests that it was already known among the communities of Gaul, especially given his care with regard to what Christians ought to accept as authoritative. Eusebius (*Hist. eccl.* 3.3.1) states that the canonical status of 1 Peter was unquestioned in the earliest centuries. On the acceptance of 1 Peter in the early centuries, see Elliott, *1 Peter*, 148–9.

99. The arguments over more precise dating cannot be ignored, though they are not decisive for my work here. They are taken up with more detail in, e.g., Williams, *Persecution in 1 Peter*, 22–34; Elliott, *1 Peter*, 134–8; Michaels, *1 Peter*, lv–lxvii.

100. Since most scholars accept that 1 Peter was familiar with Pauline traditions (see, e.g., Horrell, "A Petrine Circle?" 12–20), a date before the 60s is highly unlikely.

101. For the dating ranges of these texts, see Michael W Holmes, *The Apostolic Fathers: Greek Texts and English Translations* (Grand Rapids, MI: Baker Academic, 2007), 35–6 (1 Clement), 170 (letters of Ignatius), 275–6 (Polycarp's letter to the Philippians), and discussions noted there.

102. On the following, see Horrell, *Epistles*, 8–10.

and Christian literature after the destruction of the Jerusalem Temple;[103] as well as (2) references in the letter to markers of later Christian developments: the office of the presbyter (5:1–5), the household code (2:18–3:7), and the label "Christian" (4:16) as a term of hostility. Attempts to tie 1 Peter's references to persecution to the reigns of specific emperors (Nero, Domitian, Trajan) have also yielded differing timeframes.[104]

For the purposes of this study, the timeframe ranging from the 60s to the end of the first century constitutes a sufficient framework. A more precise date would not, as far as I can tell, make any significant differences to the readings of 1 Peter set forth in later chapters. In fact, in terms of a comparative study in ideology, this range of dating in the second half of the century is quite helpful. As discussed earlier, the Roman imperial cults had by then become fixtures in the Anatolian landscape, signaling what Price considered a cultic "routinization" of the emperor's power of office.

2.2.2 Provenance and Destination

First Peter presents itself as a letter written in Babylon (5:13). This may be taken to refer to the actual name of the city, or it may have served as a cipher. If the first option is taken, then the primary candidates for the letter's origin are Babylon on the banks of the Nile Delta in Egypt, or Babylon on the Euphrates, capital and heart of the ancient Babylonian empire (cf. Mt. 1:11–12, 17; Acts 7:43). Attributing 1 Peter's composition to either site, however, can only be done with great difficulty. Babylon on the Nile was a Roman military outpost,[105] and its only possible—and remote—link to 1 Peter is by way of Mark (mentioned in 5:13b), who is said by Eusebius to have preached the gospel in Egypt.[106] As for Babylon in Mesopotamia,

---

103. See *2 Bar.* 10:1–2; 11:1; 67:7; *4 Ezra* 3:1–2, 28, 31; *Sib. Or.* 5.143, 158–9; and, of course, Rev. 14:8; 16:19; 17:5; 18:2, 10, 21. With regard to the book of Revelation most, though not all, scholars accept "Babylon" as a designation for Rome. For the minority report, see, e.g., David Chilton, *The Days of Vengeance: An Exposition of the Book of Revelation* (Fort Worth, TX: Dominion Press, 1987); and Kenneth L. Gentry, *Before Jerusalem Fell: Dating the Book of Revelation* (Fountain Inn, SC: Victorious Hope Publishing, 2010). Not coincidentally, both of these also date Revelation prior to 70 AD, and thus Revelation's indictment against Babylon as a condemnation of the fallen Jerusalem—a position idiosyncratic in current scholarship.

104. Elliott, *1 Peter*, 136. To date, the most exhaustive study of the causes and nature of persecution in 1 Peter has undoubtedly been Williams, *Persecution in 1 Peter*. In a scholarly *tour de force*, Williams shows that the legal standing of Christians became endangered with the reign of Nero, whose policies set precedents that rendered Christianity effectively illegal in the Empire (see esp. ch. 6).

105. Strabo (17.1.30) identifies this Babylon as a fortress city and home to one of three Roman legions stationed in Egypt.

106. *Hist. eccl.* 2.16.1.

it is at least possible that Peter's mission to the Jews (cf. Acts 15:7; Gal. 2:8) may have taken him there, since there was a Jewish population that remained from the time of the Exile.[107] (Nevertheless, Josephus records that this remnant by the second half of the first century AD had been largely driven out of the city and taken refuge in surrounding cities.[108]) What is crucially missing in this case, as in the first, is any explicit links of a Petrine tradition to this location that would make it a plausible, not merely possible, option.[109]

We are left, then, with "Babylon" as a figurative designation. There are several reasons to commend the position that Babylon in 5:13 refers to Rome: (1) after the destruction of Jerusalem in 70 AD, "Babylon" had become a common term for Rome in both Jewish and Christian literature, such that its use in 5:13 is in fact quite typical;[110] (2) early Christian traditions attest to Peter's presence and ministry in Rome,[111] with Eusebius (*Hist. eccl.* 2.15.2) specifying the tradition, based on the authorities of Papias and Clement of Alexandria, that Peter wrote the letter while there; and (3) affinities between 1 Peter and two other texts traced back to Rome, Paul's epistle to the Romans and 1 Clement,[112] further suggest that common traditions may have been developed there.[113] The collective weight of these reasons has persuaded most scholars to conclude that "Babylon" in 5:13 refers to the imperial metropolis, and 1 Peter was therefore written there—or at least depicted as such.[114] This conclusion, of course, is far from certain. What is more relevant for

---

107. Josephus, *Ant.* 15.14.

108. *Ant.* 18.371–372.

109. Elliott, *1 Peter*, 882–3.

110. See n. 103 above.

111. Ignatius, *Rom.* 4.3; Eusebius, *Hist. eccl.* 2.15.2; 3.39.15 (cf. Mark's role in 3.39.15); Irenaeus, *Adv. Haer.* 3.1.5.

112. For parallels with Romans, see Horrell, "A Petrine Circle?" 12–19. For 1 Clement, see Elliott, *1 Peter*, 138–40, though see also the critique of these parallels in Andrew Gregory, "1 Clement and Writings That Later Formed the New Testament," in *The Reception of the New Testament in the Apostolic Fathers*, ed. Andrew Gregory and Christopher Tuckett (Oxford and New York: Oxford University Press, 2005), 154 n. 101.

113. David G. Horrell, "Re-Placing 1 Peter: From Place of Origin to Constructions of Space," in *The Urban World and the First Christians*, ed. Steve Walton, Paul Trebilco, and David W. J. Gill (Grand Rapids, MI: Eerdmans, 2017).

114. So Elliott, *1 Peter*, 131–4, 882–7; Michaels, *1 Peter*, 310–11; Horrell, *Epistles*, 7–8; Jobes, *1 Peter*, 322–3; Achtemeier, *1 Peter*, 63–4, 354; Goppelt, *1 Peter*, 373–5; Ceslaus Spicq, *Les Epîtres de Saint Pierre* (Paris: Gabalda, 1966), 181; J. N. D. Kelly, *A Commentary on the Epistles of Peter and of Jude*, Black's New Testament Commentaries (London: Adam & Charles Black, 1969), 218–20; Charles Bigg, *A Critical and Exegetical Commentary on the Epistles of St. Peter and St. Jude* (Edinburgh: T&T Clark, 1956), 75–7; Peter H. Davids, *The First Epistle of Peter*, 2nd ed. (Grand Rapids, MI: Eerdmans, 1990), 202–3.

our understanding of ideological construction, as Chapter 6 will show, is the author's use of the evocative name, "Babylon," for the letter's place of origin.

The intended destination of 1 Peter is significantly clearer. The prescript states that the letter was addressed to readers in "Pontus, Galatia, Cappadocia, Asia, and Bithynia" (1:1). These place-names appear to be those of the provinces into which the Romans had parceled out Asia Minor.[115] The order of their mention, beginning with Pontus and ending with Bithynia, is most plausibly explained as the route of a letter carrier—whether actual or hypothetical—who would have entered the region via one of the ports of Pontus (Amastris or Sinope) and proceeded southwards through Galatia and Cappadocia before journeying westwards into Asia, completing the circuit in Bithynia.[116] Since 1 Peter was an encyclical intended for distribution across a large area, we lack the contextual specificity afforded by other letters in the New Testament addressed to particular communities (as with Paul's Corinthian or Roman correspondences). Nevertheless, since the letter had to have been disseminated by way of known Roman roads connecting these provinces, it would have been first read in urban centers, including those in generally less developed regions (e.g., Ankara in Galatia and Caesarea in Cappadocia).[117] Most importantly for our study, this also means that its recipients

---

115. Some difficulty is presented by the fact that 1:1 mentions Pontus and Bithynia separately. Beginning in 63 BC, Pompey had assigned the newly-created province of Pontus (formerly the Mithridatic kingdom) and placed it under the governor of Bithynia, so that the two provinces were administered as one (David Magie, *Roman Rule in Asia Minor, to the End of the Third Century after Christ* [Princeton, NJ: Princeton University Press, 1975], 369; Mitchell, *Anatolia, Vol. I*, 31). Following this, it has been suggested that the designations in 1.1 are those of districts rather than provinces as such (e.g., Spicq, *Saint Pierre*, 12, 41), though, as Williams (*Persecution in 1 Peter*, 63 n. 1) points out, a list of districts should have yielded more specific district-names included in this vast area, e.g., Paphlagonia, Pontus Galaticus, Phrygia, Pisidia, and Lycaonia. Writers after Pompey likewise found it useful to speak of Pontus as a province in recounting the region's history (Livy, *Per.* 102; Strabo, 7.3). The most parsimonious reading is, therefore, to regard the list in 1.1 as names of provinces.

116. This explanation is traceable to F. J. A. Hort, *The First Epistle of St. Peter, I.1–II.17: The Greek Text with Introductory Lecture, Commentary, and Additional Notes* (Eugene, OR: Wipf & Stock, 2005), 17, 183–4. Kelly (*Commentary*, 42) notes that, according to Josephus (*Ant.* 16.21–23), Herod the Great, accompanied by Augustus' son-in-law Marcus Agrippa, had made a similar journey in 14 BC from Sinope in Pontus to Ephesus in Asia.

117. For arguments for a predominantly urban setting for 1 Peter, see David G. Horrell, "Aliens and Strangers? The Socio-Economic Location of the Addressees of 1 Peter," in *Becoming Christian: Essays on 1 Peter and the Making of Christian Identity*, LNTS 394 (London and New York, NY: Bloomsbury T&T Clark, 2013), 100–32 (esp. 118–20); Williams, *Persecution in 1 Peter*, 69–74.

were likely to have been Christian communities in sites where the imperial cults loomed large.[118]

2.2.3 Formulating a Working Hypothesis for 1 Peter

From the preceding sections we can construct the following picture of 1 Peter. Though the letter may well have been a pseudonymous composition, it comes to us as a text attributed to Peter the apostle and invokes his authority. While a precise date and place of composition is impossible, it was likely to have been composed in Rome, spoken of as "Babylon," between the 60s and the 90s AD—in a time when the imperial cults were already established throughout Anatolia. The opening of the letter indicates that it was written for circulation in the Roman provinces of Anatolia north of the Taurus mountains. The sequence in which these provinces are named corresponds to the route a letter carrier might have taken if using the network of known roads in the second half of the century. Since these roads linked cities across the provinces, the first recipients of 1 Peter were, in all likelihood, Christian communities that met in these urban centers. Because of this, there is good reason to believe that, in the locations where they met and/or lived, cults to the Roman emperor and his family occupied a prominent part of the civic landscape.

As can be seen from the preceding survey of early Christian traditions that surround the origin of 1 Peter as well as its familiarity to key figures in early Christianity, the letter no doubt served as an authoritative voice for the first generations of believers. This warrants our approach to the letter as a text that both reflects and constructs an influential form of early Christian ideology. Its smooth

---

118. Contra Elliott (*A Home for the Homeless: A Social-Scientific Criticism of 1 Peter, Its Situation and Strategy* [Minneapolis, MN: Fortress, 1981], 62–3; *1 Peter*, 90) who argues for a predominantly rural setting for 1 Peter and thus conjectures that readers in "the hinterlands of Bithynia, Pontus, Galatia and Cappadocia" would not have been confronted with the imperial cults to the same degree as its readers in Asia (*A Home for the Homeless*, 62). Both Horrell and Williams (see n. 117 above) have rightly rejected Elliott's proposal for such a demographic. While Elliott is right that populations in the central provinces were largely rural in the time of 1 Peter, the letter's route of distribution via the network of roads would have meant that it first reached populations concentrated at urban centers along the route. An important distinction must be made between the *overall* demographic of the provinces and the *specific* populations that would have come into contact with 1 Peter.

With respect to the imperial cults, Mitchell (*Anatolia, Vol. I*, 102) shows that, within three years of annexation to Rome, cults to the emperor had already spread to the largely rural regions of Paphlagonia and Cappadocia, rivaling the rate of growth we see in Asia. In 43 AD, the same year Lycia was made a province, it already had a Caesareum. Even granting Elliott's unlikely reconstruction of the readership demographic, contact with the imperial cults would have been near inevitable.

journey of acceptance into the collection of authoritative texts now known to us as the New Testament reveals, furthermore, that the power of its ideas traversed well beyond its points of origin and destination, to Christian communities scattered elsewhere in the Empire. First Peter was more than just another voice in the plurality of voices that characterized early Christianity. It was a formative document for the churches in Anatolia, first of all, but also for the movement as a whole.

In what ways did this text of ideology compete with imperial ideology for the minds and hearts of its readers? The following chapters will look at the constructions of time and space in 1 Peter, evaluating these in light of the imperial cults of Asia Minor. In each case, the imperial cults will be examined first so as to provide the dominant ideological context against which we can "read" time and space in 1 Peter. We begin by looking at time in the imperial cults.

Chapter 3

TIME IN THE IMPERIAL CULTS[1]

Toward the end of the second century AD, in the course of what came to be known as the Quartodeciman Controversy, Pope Victor I of Rome attempted to excommunicate all the churches of Asia for keeping Pascha according to an (allegedly) aberrant date. In accord with their local tradition, the Asian communities kept the feast on the fourteenth of Nisan, the same day as the Jewish Passover, while churches elsewhere observed it on the Sunday following. Victor was dissuaded from doing so by his fellow bishops, among which was the influential Irenaeus, bishop of Lyons in Gaul, who defended the Asian practice on the basis of its antiquity and apostolicity.[2]

This earlier Anatolian controversy, a matter of fierce in-house debate among the early Christians but today little more than a blip in the history of Christianity, stands as a reminder that the manner in which time is reckoned carries a significance that is often lost to the modern imagination. Indeed, one of the premises underpinning this study is that in both the imperial cults and 1 Peter, the construal of time is tied to particular ways of seeing and moving in the world—a basic sense of the cosmic order and one's relationship to that order. This notion is not simply an artifact of the past: the revolutionaries of late eighteenth-century France attempted to inaugurate a new sociopolitical order by instituting a calendar which began on the date of the revolution, September 22, 1792, and broke with the Judeo-Christian roots of the seven-day week by imposing instead a ten-day cycle. The new world they imagined needed to be expressed in a new way of counting and moving in time.

Contesting time, whether in ancient times or modern, in Roman Anatolia or revolutionary France, was—and perhaps has always been—far more than disputing astronomical calculations. The process carried within itself questions about meaning and the authority to create meaning. In this chapter, I will examine the view of time

---

1. Some of the material in Chapters 3 and 4 appeared earlier in Wei Hsien Wan, "Whose Time? Which Rationality? Reflections on Empire, 1 Peter, and the 'Common Era'," in *Postscripts* 7, no. 3 (2011): 279–94; as well as David Horrell and Wei-Hsien Wan, "Christology, Eschatology and the Politics of Time in 1 Peter," in *Journal for the Study of the New Testament* 38, no. 3 (2016): 263–76.

2. Eusebius, *Hist. eccl.* 5.23–25.

in the Roman imperial cults as suggested by the evidence in the Anatolian provinces. This will provide the axes for comparison with the view of time presented in 1 Peter. While the diversity of practices subsumed under the umbrella term "the imperial cults" does not permit us to securely construct any single, official and programmatic view of time as such, the following observations attempt to sketch some broad themes in the cultic notions of time, with particular attention to its meaning and trajectory. I take these modes of representation to be dialogical, meaning that they are not merely Roman "impositions" on provincial subjects, but rather forms of discourse shaped by participants on both sides of Rome's colonial project. In this section, I will examine three particular time-related aspects of the imperial cults: (1) the new calendar of Asia proclaimed around 9 BC; (2) the celebration of imperial festivals known throughout Asia Minor; as well as (3) belief in the perpetuity of Roman rule as attested in documentary evidence, imperial images, and architecture.

3.1 A New Calendar for Asia and the Reinterpretation of Time

Around 29 BC, the council of the Province of Asia instituted a competition, awarding a crown to the one who succeeded in proposing the highest honors for Augustus. A worthy recipient of this reward was only found some twenty years later, in 9 BC. It was none other than the Roman proconsul of the province himself, one Paullus Fabius Maximus, who proposed that all of Asia honor Caesar by adopting a single calendar with the birthday of Augustus as its starting point. In a letter to the council, Maximus recommended that the emperor's birthday, September 23, be henceforth designated the beginning of the new year.[3] This date was also to be the one on which new municipal officials began their term of service.

Until Maximus' proposal, each city-state in the province, as was customary in Hellenistic kingdoms and the eastern Mediterranean in general, had its own way of counting time, yielding calendars that varied from place to place.[4] Starting the

---

3. The proconsul's letter to the council and the council's response have come down to us as a composite document preserved in the important inscription found in several Asian cities. The fullest of these is *OGIS* 458 (= *IvP* 105) found in Priene, thus earning the document a shorthand title, "the Priene inscription." On its textual history and other known fragments, see Sherk, *Roman Documents from the Greek East*, 328–9.

4. Bradley Hudson McLean, *An Introduction to Greek Epigraphy of the Hellenistic and Roman Periods from Alexander the Great Down to the Reign of Constantine (323 B.C.– A.D. 337)* (Ann Arbor, MI: University of Michigan Press, 2002), 169. As John Scheid (*An Introduction to Roman Religion* [Edinburgh: Edinburgh University Press, 2003], 41–2) points out, there was no universal religious calendar for the whole Empire: "Each city, even a Roman colony, established its own, which did not necessarily mirror that of Rome" (41). He provides as an example the Western colony of Urso in Spain, whose chief magistrates (*duouiri*) bore the tasks of defining the local religious calendar and organizing the celebration of the festivals therein.

calendar year on a date that marked some momentous event in the life of a local community was not unprecedented in the Roman world,[5] but the scale of this reform, i.e. at the provincial level, made it novel. Maximus' innovative recommendation would consolidate the divergent calendars in various cities and set forth a uniform, synchronized calendar for the entire province. The rationale behind Maximus' new calendar lay in the accomplishments of Augustus himself, of which the proconsul wrote:

> [It is difficult to know whether] the birthday of the most divine Caesar is a matter of great pleasure or great benefit. We could justly consider that day to be equal to the beginning of all things. He restored the form of all things to usefulness, if not to their natural state, since it had deteriorated and suffered misfortune. He gave a new appearance to the whole world, which would gladly have accepted its own destruction had Caesar not been born for the common good fortune of all. Thus a person could justly consider this to be the beginning of life and existence, and the end of regrets about having been born.
>
> Since on no (other) day could each one receive a starting point more beneficial for corporate and personal improvement than the day that has been beneficial to all;
>
> And since it happens that all the cities of Asia Minor have the same date for entrance into local office, which is an arrangement that has clearly been formed according to some divine counsel in order that it might be the starting point of honors to Augustus;
>
> And since it is difficult to give thanks equal to such benefactions as his unless we devise some new manner of reciprocation for each of them;
>
> And since people could celebrate more gladly the birthday common to all because some personal pleasure has been brought to them through (his) rule;
>
> Therefore, it seems proper to me that the birthday of the most divine Caesar be the one, uniform New Year's day for all the polities. On that day all will take up their local offices, that is, on the ninth day before the Kalends of October, in order that he might be honored far beyond all ceremonies performed for him and that he might rather be distinguished by all, which I consider to be the greatest service rendered by the province. A decree of the koinon of Asia should be written encompassing all his virtues, so that the action devised by us for the honor of Augustus should endure forever. I will command that the decree, engraved on a stele, be set up in the temple, having arranged for the edict to be written in both languages.[6]

---

5. Dio, for example, records a similar calendric change in Alexandria: "The day on which Alexandria had been captured [by Octavian] they [the Romans] declared a lucky day, and directed that in future years it should be taken by the inhabitants of that city as the starting-point in their reckoning of time" (51.19.6; Cary trans.).

6. *OGIS* 458.3–30 (Friesen trans.).

Because this text was inscribed and displayed alongside the decree of the *koinon* of Asia which he requested, its representation of time merits detailed consideration.

Foremost, it must be observed that this new calendar did not merely alter the counting of time, but its very *meaning*. More precisely, it tied the "form" of time to its "substance." The justification for a new starting point for the calendar was the fresh cosmic beginning marked by Augustus' birth. Maximus describes the emperor's birthday as a day "equal to the beginning of all things" (τῆι τῶν πάντων ἀρχῆι ἴσην). In his grand interpretation of the significance of Augustus' life, the proconsul also presented a particular evaluation of the past: the entire cosmos had, up to the point of his birth, been descending into chaos and self-destruction, and would have gladly seen its own decimation had Augustus not averted its path and raised it up from dilapidation. With a single sweep, entire legacies of Asian society—past conquests, kingdoms, and accomplishments—are cast as histories plagued by destruction (φθορά) and misfortune (ἀτυχής), transformed only by the good fortune (εὐτύχημα) of Caesar's birth. As such, the feats of Augustus can be said to parallel those of the gods who fashioned and ordered the universe, for "he restored the form of all things to usefulness, if not to their natural state (τῆι φύσει)," and in doing so truly "gave a new appearance to the whole world."[7] The Augustan era was, according to Maximus, one of renewal—a happy rupture from Asia's past of decay and effacement, and the very inauguration of a new order. The new creation, as it were, launched by his birth constituted "the beginning of life and of existence" (ἀρχὴν τοῦ βίου καὶ τῆς ζωῆς) for everyone, extinguishing any regret anyone could have had about being born, for it made every life itself worth living. What the world had never experienced, Augustus gave to one and all.[8]

All time, then, found its renewal and culmination in the life of Augustus and the embrace of his empire. What did this mean, however, for the daily grind of city life? Maximus' proposal ensured a worthy two-pronged response. First, beginning the new year on Augustus' birthday would be a most fitting way to celebrate the cosmic

---

7. On the theme of (visual) appearances in the decree, see Holly Haynes, *The History of Make-Believe: Tacitus on Imperial Rome* (Berkeley and Los Angeles, CA: University of California Press, 2003), 75–7.

8. Admittedly, Augustus was not the only emperor whose birth was said to mark a new epoch. On the occasion of Gaius' visit to their city, the people of Assos declared: "Since the announcement of the rule of Gaius Caesar Germanicus Augustus, which all men had hoped and prayed for, the cosmos has found no way of measuring its joy, and every city and each people has been eager regarding the appearance of the god, as if the happiest age of men had now begun" (*IAssos* 26, Philip Harland, trans., "Oath of Assos and the Roman Businessmen on the Accession of Gaius Caligula [37 AD]," in *Associations in the Greco-Roman World: A Companion to the Sourcebook*, accessed June 25, 2013, http://www.philipharland.com/greco-roman-associations/?p=6555/). Perhaps tellingly, however, in their oath of allegiance to Gaius himself, the Assians invoked as divine witnesses Zeus Sotēr, "the god Caesar Augustus," and Parthenon (Athena). Still, no emperor after Augustus was accorded higher honors at the provincial level.

rejuvenation inaugurated by Caesar's appearance in the world. No longer was the starting point of the year based on the solar and lunar cycles of the natural world, as in existing Asian calendars of the time.[9] In place of these celestial rhythms (which were still used in the calculation of the lengths of months and the year itself), we have the non-recurring event of the emperor's birth which is nevertheless used to mark the beginning of a recurring—and, indeed, still solar—cycle of 365 days. It is not the case, however, that we have abandoned cosmic or natural rhythms in favor of a "human" event in the new calendar. Maximus' letter gives no intimation of such a shift. It is, rather, that we have set aside one set of cosmic events (lunar and solar cycles) in favor of a more crucial (but equally) cosmic event—that of Augustus' birth. This is precisely why Maximus opens his proposal by highlighting the rejuvenating effect of that birth on the natural, cosmic order. It is this day that ought to henceforth govern the rhythms of human life, for it genuinely constituted a new beginning for the entire world.

That governance would be made most tangible in the political cycle of the *polis*. Since all municipal officials already took office on the same day in the province— already a providential sign, as he saw it—the proconsul suggested that they transfer this date to the newly instituted new year's day.[10] Given the long tradition of political autonomy in Greek cities, this marks a sharp departure from extant practice and illustrates clearly the emergence of a new phase of political hybridity in Asia—one in which Rome exercised decisive and palpable influence. This change in political practice surpassed, Maximus opined, even the honors bestowed by the ceremonies of the imperial cults. No matter how grand and magnificent these celebrations throughout the province—sacrifices, games, festivals, and all— they would reach only those who were present and were able to participate in some way. In requiring that all municipal officials honor Augustus by taking up office on that day, the cities could ensure that the emperor would "be distinguished by all," since its repercussions would be felt not only by inhabitants of all the cities, but also by those whose lives were in any way dependent on the sociopolitical rhythms of the *poleis*.

The import of this revolutionary shift can hardly be overstated. Calendric reforms, far from being innocent alterations on the administrative level, mark pivotal ideological shifts and bear pervasive implications for social and political life. Calendars are not merely utilitarian devices for coordinating communal life. Rather, they are means by which a community shares, not simply on the level of abstract ideas but in embodied practices, a common perception of time and its flow, measured and segmented according to particular patterns of recurrence (e.g.,

---

9. Price, *Rituals and Power*, 106.

10. Though the text of the decree proper does not explicitly state that this was to be carried out, we may infer from the promulgation of Maximus' rescript alongside the decree that this was in fact instituted. Otherwise, it would have seemed odd for the *koinon* of Asia to publicly commemorate a suggestion from its proconsul which it failed to carry out.

hours, months, weeks, seasons, etc.). As social instruments that structure and shape human experience of reality, calendars embody ideology, serving as repositories and tradents of a community's worldview.[11] In this sense, they are inherently political, and the ability to regulate or implement them is the subject of political contest. Nancy Munn observes:

> Authority over the annual calendar (the chronological definition, timing, and sequence of daily and seasonal activities) ... not only controls aspects of the everyday lives of persons but also connects this level of control to a more comprehensive universe that entails critical values and potencies in which governance is grounded. Controlling these temporal media variously implies control over this more comprehensive order and its definition, as well as over the capacity to mediate this wider order into the fundamental social being and bodies of persons.[12]

In short, power over the calendar translates into power over bodies.

Seen in this light, Maximus' suggestion that municipal officials begin their terms of office on Augustus' birthday cannot simply be thought of as a matter of administrative convenience. By being sworn into office on Augustus' birthday, municipal officials throughout Asia thus demonstrated to their constituencies that their authority was exercised only by derivation—a distributed share in the power emanating from the emperor himself, legitimated by his empire's ascendancy according to the dictates of Providence.[13] In doing so they acknowledged the legitimacy of Roman rule for themselves and their fellow citizens—and with it, the entire cargo of values and potencies borne by the imperial freight of Rome. Not least among these was Maximus' manifestly Romanocentric interpretation of time past, present, and future, as well as his explication of a divine cosmo-logic for Augustus' power over them. These were the terms by which the people of Asia were to structure the rhythms of their everyday life and, according to Maximus, discover existential purpose—"the beginning of life and of existence, and the end of regrets about having been born."

The significance of the proconsul's initiative emerges even more clearly as we turn to the response of the *koinon*, which responded favorably to Maximus' idea. Its decision, promulgated in a decree which included the proposal of the proconsul, records the turn of events in this manner:

> Whereas the providence that ordains our whole life has established with zeal and distinction that which is most perfect in our life by bringing Augustus, whom

---

11. Sacha Stern, *Calendars in Antiquity: Empires, States, and Societies* (Oxford: Oxford University Press, 2012), 1–2.
12. Munn, "The Cultural Anthropology of Time," 109.
13. Cf. Friesen, *Imperial Cults*, 33–4.

she filled with virtue as a benefaction to all humanity; sending to us and to those after us a savior who put an end to war and brought order to all things; and Caesar, when he appeared, the hopes of those who preceded [...] placed, not only surpassing those benefactors who had come before but also leaving to those who shall come no hope of surpassing (him); and the birth of the god was the beginning of good tidings to the world through him; and [when the high priest] was Lucius Valcacius Tullus and when the secretary was Pap[ias ...] Asia passed a decree at Smyrna [that a crown should be given] to the one who could devise the greatest honors to the god; and Paullus Fabius Maximus the proconsul—sent for the well-being of the province by his right hand and decision—has made myriad benefactions to the province, the extent of which benefactions no one could adequately express; and now that which was unknown until this time by the Hellenes he devised regarding the honor of Augustus: calculating time to have begun at his birth.

The *koinon* continued, announcing its resolution:

For this reason, with good fortune and for salvation this was decided by the Hellenes of Asia. The new year will begin in all the cities on the ninth day before the Kalends of October, which is the birthday of Augustus. In order that the day be always aligned in every city, the Roman date will be used along with the Greek date. The first month will be observed as Kaisar(eios), as decreed earlier, beginning from the ninth day before the Kalends of October. The crown that was decreed for the one proposing the greatest honors on behalf of Caesar will be given to Maximus the proconsul, who also will always be proclaimed publicly in the athletic contests at Pergamon, the Romaia Sebasteia, with, "Asia crowns Paullus Fabius Maximus, who most reverently proposed the honors for Caesar." Likewise he will be proclaimed in the Kaisareia, the games celebrated in the city. The rescript of the proconsul and the decree of Asia will be inscribed on a marble stele, which will be set up in the temenos of Rome and Augustus. The public advocates for the year will see to it that the rescript of Maximus and the decree of Asia will be engraved on marble steles in the leading cities of the districts. These steles will be placed in the Kaisareia.

The months shall be observed as follows: Kaisar(eios), 31 days; Apellaios, 30 days; Audnaios, 31 days; Peritios, 31 days; Dystros, 28 days; Xandikos, 31 days; Artemisios, 31 days; Daisios, 31 days; Panemos, 30 days; Loos, 31 days; Gorpiaios, 31 days; Hyperberetaios, 30 days.[14]

It is immediately obvious that the council, in its response, concurred with Maximus' letter in several ways. It affirmed, above all, the epochal nature of Augustus' arrival

---

14. *OGIS* 458.31–71 (Friesen trans; cf. Sherk, *Roman Documents from the Greek East*, 331–2). Mitchell (*Anatolia, Vol. I*, 113) conjectures that this Asian calendar was probably adopted by some of the other Anatolian provinces as well.

on the stage of history. If, according to Maximus, the world would have collapsed on itself had it not been for Augustus, the council proclaimed the genius of Providence in providing a savior (σωτήρ) who rescued humanity from destroying itself through war, bringing order to all things (κοσμήσοντα ... πάντα). Like Maximus, the *koinon* described Augustus as the zenith of history: not only did his predecessors pale in comparison, but the emperor's achievements left "to those who shall come no hope of surpassing (him)." The present moment had been transformed by his birth, the event which marked the beginning of glad tidings (εὐαγγελία) to the entire cosmos.

In their resonance with Maximus' position, the words of the provincial council reflect what amounts to a comprehensive interpretation of history. The present age, seen precisely as a radical break with all that had come before it, was characterized by cosmic order and the glad tidings of Caesar's benefaction. It could only be properly understood, in fact, in terms of Augustus' reign. In light of his glory, ages past can only be summed up by their most salient, totalizing feature—war (πόλεμος). The council's positive narration of the present thus implicated the entirety of Asia's past, in agreement with Maximus' characterization of it as a long blur of "destruction" and "misfortune." Not only that, but all possible futures were circumscribed by the Augustan "now"; no successor to the Roman throne could ever hope to outdo the reigning *imperator*, whose birth had inaugurated an era of peace and stability that would continue for generations to come ("to us and to those after us"). The present was the apex of time, the unrivaled summit between the valleys of past and future.

This arc of history did not merely exist as an abstraction or belief. It was mediated by—one could even say "incarnated in"—a specific hierarchy of imperial relationships.[15] According to the decree, Providence had ordained and filled Augustus with virtue, but it was the emperor himself who manifested this destiny and carried out on earth the divine benefactions to all humanity. He did not do so directly or unaided, however. Rather, it was the proconsul, sent by the savior's right hand and will (ἀπό τῆς ἐκείνου δεξιᾶς καί γνώμης ἀπεσταλμένος), who administered "well-being" (σωτηρία) to the province. In this particular instance, it was also the proconsul who directed the proper response of the province to the emperor, since the honors given by the *koinon* began with Maximus himself. The provincial nature of the calendar also meant that it reinforced the Roman administrative system, which took the province rather than the *polis* as its basic administrative unit and signaled a departure from longstanding Hellenistic tradition.[16] This new way of reckoning time translated itself into the concrete,

---

15. Mitchell, *Anatolia, Vol. I*, 113.

16. We can therefore say that the new Asian calendar reworked not only time but also spatial conceptions—in this case, of Anatolia. At this point, however, it is best to reserve further consideration of imperial geography as engendered in the imperial cults to the next major chapter of this work.

embodied imperial relations necessary for its outworking, embedding in the rhythm of life in Asia the very "critical values and potencies" in which Roman governance was grounded.

Nevertheless, it must be emphasized that this imperial reconfiguration of time cannot simply be caricatured as a totalizing act. The implementations called for by the provincial council reflect a more complex, hybrid sensibility. To begin with, one ought to note that one of the months, Artemisios, was named after a chief deity in Asia, the goddess Artemis, who held pride of place especially in the provincial capital of Ephesus. As a whole, the calendar seems to have incorporated existing Syro-Macedonian names for months into the Roman (Julian) calendar year.[17] We would simply be mistaken to regard the calendar as a thoroughly Roman product, since it reflected such a prominent element of Hellenistic religious and political heritage. There are further clues, moreover, pointing to its dialogical character.

Significantly, the final version of the calendar indicates that the *koinon* made a decision to alter some details in Maximus' proposal. A fragment of the Latin version of Maximus' rescript called for the last four months of the year to have 30, 31, 30, and 31 days respectively, but the conciliar version has a sequence of 30–31–31–30 days—evidently an adjustment that was necessary so that all months could begin on the same day of the Julian calendar (i.e. the ninth before the Kalends). The conciliar version was thus actually better aligned to the Roman (Julian) calendar than what Maximus had set forth. The proconsul, it appeared, had not paid sufficient attention to the finer astronomic points, and the provincial council did not hesitate to correct him. This emendation simultaneously reflects, on the one hand, the council's (perhaps obliged) receptivity to Maximus' initiative, but also its exercise of provincial autonomy on the other.[18]

Several scholars have also drawn attention to the delicate balance preserved in the language of the promulgating document. Price states that Maximus' letter "shifted significantly between suggestion and instruction,"[19] and Sherk notes that the "[the governor's] suggestion is worded in such a way as to constitute virtually a directive."[20] Stern's opinion further testifies to this tension in the document: he argues that, although Maximus refers to his own words as a διάταγμα (the Greek equivalent of *edictum*) and thus "implies something therefore quite authoritarian," the tone of the letter is noticeably gentle and "makes it read more like a recommendation."[21] Collectively, these observations point to the nature of Maximus' letter as an attempt to navigate the boundaries of Roman power in Asia.

The calendar introduced a uniform date for the new year, but it did not, judging from its "history of effects," entirely obliterate preexisting calendars. While it superimposed an imperial grid of months onto existing local calendars, evidence

---

17. McLean, *Greek Epigraphy*, 169.
18. Stern, *Calendars in Antiquity*, 276–7.
19. Price, *Rituals and Power*, 70.
20. Sherk, *Roman Documents from the Greek East*, 334.
21. Stern, *Calendars in Antiquity*, 274 n. 106.

suggests that the older, local calendars continued to be used, perhaps even remaining the primary calendar in many places. It appears that Ephesus and Smyrna, two influential cities with provincial imperial temples, along with Miletus and Cyzicus, retained their older calendars at least through the first century AD. The older, Greek names of months continued to be used into the second century AD in Magnesia-on-the-Maeander and Chios.[22] Similar versions of the Asian calendar adopted in other parts of the Empire also began the new year on a different date—some on September 22 and others on September 24—variations that may have emerged as celebrations of Augustus' birthday diminished in importance after his death.[23] Maximus envisioned a world in which all time had already been reconfigured around the cosmic event of Augustus' birth, but older and alternative traditions—and ways of conceiving time—persisted.

Both the new calendar and the dynamics of its reception were thus marked by complex Roman and local interactions. While the calendar was a Roman initiative (originating from an imperial official), its genesis, we must remember, took place within the context of a competition independently organized by Rome's subjects. The proconsul's calendric reform depended substantially on the provincial council as well as other cities which received it, each (it would seem) in its own way. The final Asian calendar and its recensions were therefore products of dialogue, even though the partners in that conversation stood in a starkly asymmetrical relationship with one another. The Roman voice was dominant in this instance, yet it was akin to the lead voice in a choir, not a solo, and worked precisely because it acknowledged, rather than drowned out, the others.

Nevertheless, in anchoring a luni-solar year on an artificial event (Augustus' birth) that was, ironically, independent of both lunar and solar calculations, the calendar's *raison d'être* was undeniably imperial. The justifications provided for its promulgation, both on the part of Maximus and the *koinon*, were likewise rooted in Rome's rise to global domination under its hallowed *princeps*. Its adoption by Asia was, after all, motivated not by social necessity strictly speaking, but rather by political necessity—as an act of loyalty and homage to the emperor.[24] One cannot escape the fact that the calendar, regardless of variations in its concrete implementation, brought all the cities of Asia under a single ideology of time simply by establishing a new date for the beginning of the year. In lieu of these complex forces at work, Friesen rightly regards the calendar as evidence of Rome's "flexible hegemony" in Anatolia.[25]

---

22. For the epigraphic evidence and discussion, see Magie, *Roman Rule in Asia Minor*, 481, 1343 n. 40. For a comparative list of the older names for months retained by various Asian cities, see McLean, *Greek Epigraphy*, 169–70.

23. On this point and the broader argument that many of these variances were based on different calculation methods and not on scribal errors, see Stern, *Calendars in Antiquity*, 280–3.

24. Stern, *Calendars in Antiquity*, 277.

25. Friesen, *Imperial Cults*, 125–6.

3.2 Imperial Festivals: Shaping the Rhythm of Time

We have already seen that Paullus Fabius Maximus, the proconsul of Asia who proposed the calendric reform of Asia, held that transferring the new year to Augustus' birthday would ensure that the emperor was "honored far beyond all ceremonies (θρησκεία) performed for him." Despite the seeming juxtaposition of calendar and ceremony in Maximus' logic, however, there was historically speaking no inherent antithesis between the two—at least as far as the imperial cults were concerned. The former, after all, served as an *ordo* for the latter: it was precisely the city's calendar that provided a shared temporal framework for the bulk of cultic ceremonies that honored the emperor.

Imperial festivals, Price writes, "formed the essential framework of the imperial cult," for in and through them "the vague and elusive ideas concerning the emperor...were focussed in action and made powerful."[26] In celebration and ritual performance, they enacted the "critical values and potencies" (to use again Munn's expression) on which Roman imperialism was grounded. At the heart of these lay the centrality of the emperor to the well-being of society, both in Rome and in its provinces. Even without taking into consideration the Asian calendric realignment of 9 BC, the imperial festivals which punctuated the year would have been sufficient to reshape the rhythms of life for Rome's Anatolian subjects—arguably in even more direct ways than any calendar itself could. In fact, there is a sense in which the dissemination of the ideology that underpinned Asia's new calendar was dependent on the festivals that emerged from and embodied its rationale. The orchestration of feasts throughout the year ensured that devotion to the emperor could extend through time, punctuating its very cadences and infusing people's lives with an inescapably imperial tenor.

Imperial festivals were organized both on special occasions and at regular intervals. We will first look at some examples of the former. Often, the accession of the emperor or some other good news about him warranted the celebration.[27] The city of Assos offered sacrifices at the beginning of Gaius' rule, and Aphrodisias likewise commemorated the accessions of Decius and Herennius.[28] In Ephesus, the commencement of Antoninus Pius' reign was honored by a festival on his birthday.[29] News of the emperor's military victory and safe return could also prompt a festival, as when the people of Lesbos offered sacrifices to all gods and goddesses in thanksgiving for Augustus' triumph.[30] On the occasion of the coming

---

26. Price, *Rituals and Power*, 102. On imperial festivals as a whole, see *idem*, 101–32; Peter Herz, "Herrscherverehrung und lokale Festkultur im Osten des römischen Reiches (Kaiser/Agone)," in *Römische Reichsreligion und Provinzialreligion*, ed. Hubert Cancik and Jörg Rüpke (Tübingen: Mohr Siebeck, 1997), 239–64.
27. Price, *Rituals and Power*, 103, 212–14.
28. Assos: *IAssos* 26; Aphrodisias: *MAMA* VIII.424.
29. *OGIS* 493 = *IEph* 21.
30. *IG* XII, Suppl. 124.

of age of Augustus' son and heir, Gaius, the people of Sardis offered sacrifices and prayers for his safety.[31] Later, in 2 AD, when Publius Cornelius Scipio, the proconsul of the province of Achaia, learned of the future emperor Gaius' successful defeat of the enemies of Rome, he instituted thanksgiving sacrifices and lavish festivities.[32]

Generally speaking, imperial celebrations that took place according to regular festal cycles were of two kinds: joint celebrations honoring the emperor with other gods, and festivals honoring the emperor alone. As mentioned earlier (see Section 2.1.3), emperors and members of the imperial family were often incorporated into the local pantheon by means of the joint dedication of shrines, assimilation, or identification. As a corollary, celebrations of the emperor were at times taken up in the festal cycles of the traditional gods themselves. Sometimes, this meant that two distinct festivals were celebrated in conjunction with each other, as were the Caesarea and Isthmia at Corinth. At other times, a single unified festival honored both the emperor and other gods, like the Dionysia Caesarea of Teos. Another example comes from Samos, where the festival honoring the goddess Hera was fused with an imperial one, yielding the Sebasta Heraea.[33]

The majority of regular festivals solely dedicated to the emperor bear the names of their imperial honoree—the Sebasteia, Caesarea, Hadrianea, Antoninea, Severeia and so forth—and were most often associated with imperial birthdays. These festivals were held according to a four-year, two-year and/or annual cycle, depending on the organizing city or province. For instance, Mytilene celebrated imperial games every four years as well as annual sacrifices in the temples of Zeus and Augustus, usually on the emperor's birthday. In addition, its inhabitants also offered sacrifices on the commemoration of Augustus' birthday at the beginning of each month.[34] In Gortyn on the island of Crete, the birthday of Rome, the accession of Marcus Aurelius as well as the birthdays of three members of the imperial family were jointly celebrated with feasting and distribution of goods by wealthy benefactors. Such combined festivals, known as "imperial days," were recorded also in Gytheum, Rhodiapolis, Thyatira, and Lagina in Panamara.[35]

A second-century AD altar found in Pergamum in 1885 offers further insight into the cultic calendar of a city with a provincial imperial temple. The altar, inscribed on all four sides, was dedicated to the emperor Trajan by a group of hymnodes, a men's religious choir, of the cults of Augustus and Roma.[36] Inscriptions

---

31. *IGR* IV.1756.
32. *SEG* 23.206. Cf. Price, *Rituals and Power*, 70.
33. Price, *Rituals and Power*, 103–4.
34. *OGIS* 456 = *IGR* IV.39; Price, *Rituals and Power*, 105, 217–18.
35. Price, *Rituals and Power*, 104–5, with epigraphic evidence.
36. *AvP* 8, 2:260, 264. Here I have relied on the translation and discussion in Friesen, *Imperial Cults*, 109–13.

pertaining to regulations for the convening of the hymnodes indicate that they performed at four large, annual festivals.³⁷ These were:

1. a three-day festival beginning with the celebration of the birthday of Livia and culminating in the Augustan (Asian) New Year (September 21 to 23);
2. the Kalends of January in the month of Peritios, i.e. the New Year according to the Julian calendar (January 1);
3. a three-day celebration of Rosalia, a festival commemorating the dead, beginning on the Augustan day of the month of Panemos (May 24 to 26); and
4. the entire month of Loos for the imperial mysteries (June 23 to July 23).

In addition, the hymnodes were also to perform during "the monthly celebration of the birthday of Augustus and on the other birthdays of the emperors," during which they were to be bestowed crowns by an official bearing the title *eukosmos* (probably similar to a master of ceremonies). Working from this information, Friesen estimates that the hymnodes would have gathered approximately 19 times each year, averaging about once every three weeks.³⁸

Although we cannot generalize the ritual calendar of this Pergamene group to the imperial cults in other cities, the altar nonetheless gives us one example of how local time was restructured by imperial celebrations. The public nature of these commemorations leads one to imagine a year pervaded by festivals into which the Roman emperor was incorporated, as in the case of the Kalends of January and Rosalia. At times, the emperor and his family took center-stage, as in the case of celebrations of the Augustan new year or imperial birthdays. Yet even when imperial presence took a more auxiliary form, as it may have when the hymnodes gathered to sing on Rosalia, it nonetheless wove Roman rule firmly into the fabric of everyday life. In very concrete ways, imperial festivals filled time with empire.

On the most basic level, imperial festivals introduced an ordinal change to Anatolian time. Local calendars were overlaid with a series of imperial celebrations that were sometimes integrated into other celebrations—as, for example, when the emperor was honored alongside other divinities in a traditional festival. At other times, stand-alone imperial celebrations took on a rhythm and life of their own, e.g., the birthday of an emperor and/or members of the imperial family. In some cities, years even ceased to be reckoned by the tenures of their magistrates; rather, these were designated according to the terms of their imperial priests. If the province of Asia took the initiative to rename the first month of its new calendar

---

37. The term "hymnodes" does not mean that the responsibilities of these men were restricted to choral singing. A provincial decree from Asia dating to 41 AD suggests that hymnodes may also have participated directly in the offering of sacrifices as well as the hosting of feasts during imperial festivals (*IEph* 3801 = *SEG* 4.641).

38. Friesen, *Imperial Cults*, 111.

after Caesar (Kaisareios), other cities followed suit, most likely to mark the imperial festival commemorated in the respective months.[39]

As in the case of the Asian calendar, to regard such changes as merely pertaining to calendric reconfigurations would, of course, be misleading. To appreciate their significance more thoroughly, we must consider how these ordinal changes reconfigured the lived experience of time for all who were subject to them. In a fundamental way, the patterns of Anatolian life, marked as they were by cycles of work, rest, and festivity, acquired a new set of associations with the birth, reign, and achievements of the emperor, as well as those of the imperial family as a whole. This would have been clearly the case with festivals dedicated to the emperor and his family, but even the festivals of the gods which "absorbed" the emperor and the imperial family were altered to some extent by this modification. Through it, local and traditional worship acquired an imperial valence.[40] The cadences of life in the city and the countryside became interwoven in both overt and subtle ways with imperial threads.

The festivals did not simply give form to imperial ideology, as a container might give form to water or a light bulb to electricity. Rather, they played an essential role in *constructing* the emperor's power over his subjects, not simply displaying his authority but creating it.[41] Imperial festivals, whether they were one-off celebrations or recurrent ones, entailed the *temporal expansion* of the emperor: the emperor quite literally took up the people's time. Celebrations transformed events in the emperor's life, such as the birth of offspring or a military victory, into events that concerned entire populations living even in the remotest reaches of the Empire. In this way, they made tangible the power of the emperor over the people's lives as well as delineating the borders of his territorial domain, that is, the expanse of the Empire itself. They comprised, to borrow an expression from Clifford Geertz's analysis of state cult in Bali, "an argument, made over and over again in the insistent vocabulary of ritual,"[42] for the centrality of the emperor in the order of things.

Other relations of power in Anatolian life underwent a corresponding transformation. Since they were major events in public life, the organization of imperial festivals engaged important offices both on the municipal and provincial level. Priests and high priests were necessary to offer sacrifices and lead prayers; in this they would have required the cooperation of the *neokoroi*, officials appointed as keepers of the sacred precincts. Athletic and musical contests, which were essential components of the festivals, required a presider, an *agonothete*. In addition

---

39. Price, *Rituals and Power*, 106.

40. For an example of this transformation within the city of Rome itself, see Mary Beard, "A Complex of Times: No More Sheep on Romulus' Birthday," *The Cambridge Classical Journal (New Series)* 33 (1987): 1–15.

41. Bell, *Ritual*, 86, 128–9.

42. Clifford Geertz, *Negara: The Theatre State in Nineteenth-Century Bali* (Princeton, NJ: Princeton University Press, 1980), 102.

to these, generous benefactors were needed to sponsor oil used in the gymnasium, animals for the sacrifices, food and drink of festal banquets (*demothoiniai*), gladiatorial shows and wild beast fights, and distribution of grain and oil, which sometimes accompanied the celebrations, to those in the city and countryside.[43] These responsibilities, as one might expect, were taken up by wealthy local elites, who frequently played multiple roles at once. The list of imperial priests found in Ancyra and dating to the reign of Tiberius, for instance, indicates that the priests were themselves the chief (if not sole) providers in the city's imperial celebrations.[44] What was novel was not so much that political power lay in the hands of such a group of people, since governance of the Hellenistic *polis* had always been led by a class of elites. Rather, what was new was the shape of that power, which, thanks to the imperial festivals, was now concretely expressed in terms of proximity to Caesar and his family. The festivals gave new opportunities for wealthy and able citizens to show benefaction towards the city and its vicinity, whether by assuming key offices, such as priest or *neokoros*, or by providing financially for feasts, competitions, or distributions of gifts. Civic and personal advancement, previously based on an elite's benefactions to the city itself, were now rendered into an imperial grammar.

This was true not only for individuals but also for cities at the provincial level. Positively, imperial festivals provided new occasions for cities to relate diplomatically to one another. In keeping with Hellenic tradition, cities continued the practice of inviting each other to their festivals, and delegations sometimes traveled great distances to participate in sacrifices and games.[45] These festivals, however, also became occasions for cities to vie with one another for honor. Under Roman occupation, the status of a city was no longer defined in terms of the honor it received when other cities recognized its festivals, but rather in terms of its diplomatic standing before Rome. The competition for status had now been transposed to an imperial key. Lesser cities expressed grievance about having to pay for the maintenance of priesthoods in more important cities, and did not take lightly the subordination implied by participation in imperial sacrifices organized by the latter.[46] Another common point of contention was the order which a city's delegation occupied in the festal procession, taken as a marker of its importance in the province. Bitter disputes in processional rank are recorded between Nikomedeia and Nikaia in Bithynia, and among Ephesus, Pergamon, Miletus, and Smyrna in Asia. To grasp just how important this was for municipal pride, one need only to look to Magnesia-on-the-Maeander, which announced proudly in its coinage that

---

43. For a detailed discussion of the organization of festivals in general and their impact on city life, see Mitchell, "Festivals, Games, and Civic Life in Roman Asia Minor." On the various forms of benefaction during festivals, see Mitchell, *Anatolia, Vol. I*, 109–11.

44. Mitchell, *Anatolia, Vol. I*, 107–9.

45. Price, *Rituals and Power*, 128.

46. Price, *Rituals and Power*, 130.

it was seventh among the cities of Asia, most probably indicating that it also occupied seventh place in the provincial procession.[47] A related development was the new trend in which cities took pride in assuming the honorary title of *neokoros* (loosely, "temple steward") with relation to cults of the Sebastoi. This practice originated in Ephesus as a means of asserting its status over other cities in Asia, and later spread as far as Macedonia and Samaria.[48]

Whether they were individuals or cities, then, key players of the cults drew people (themselves included) into new relationships with the imperial center.[49] The public nature of imperial celebrations—processions, prayers, sacrifices, games, and banquets—meant that many in the cities and those in surrounding areas participated in, or at least witnessed, them.[50] These festivals assured that time itself unfolded into a theater of power, a spectacle of the state to be witnessed by all. While socio-religious institutions such as sacrifices, games, and civic benefactions predated the advent of the imperial cults in an already-Hellenized Anatolia of the first century AD, they nevertheless gradually came to be articulated within the structures of Roman occupation, and formed an essential component of the framework by which the emperor's provincial subjects felt tangibly the reach of his influence.

There is, of course, no need to imagine that every inch of Anatolia was impacted in exactly the same way. It is more helpful—and more reasonable—to think of the reconfiguration as occurring along a spectrum, more concentrated in some places (say, in more urbanized areas) and less so in others. Nevertheless, given what we know about the spread of imperial cultic activity, these effects must have been quite ubiquitous, since no group of honorees enjoyed a more widespread cultic veneration than the Roman emperors and members of the imperial family. Price, therefore, cannot be charged with exaggeration for concluding that "time itself was changed by the imperial cult."[51] By means of their festivals, the imperial cults exercised decisive, albeit differentiated, influence on the life of Anatolian cities and their dependants.

---

47. Herz, "Herrscherverehrung und lokale Festkultur," 247–8.

48. Friesen, *Twice Neokoros*, 50–9. The title *neokoros* was initially the title of an official appointed as the steward of a particular deity's cult, generally charged with the maintenance of the cultic space, its equipment, and funds. The office may have also entailed assisting the priests of the cult in offering sacrifices.

49. Gordon, "The Question of Power," 47–8.

50. Price, *Rituals and Power*, 107. There is no reason, as Herz does ("Herrscherverehrung und lokale Festkultur," 255–6), to restrict participation in imperial festivals to a city's citizens or a Greek-speaking minority. In its typical form, the efficacy of an imperial festival lies precisely, it seems to me, in the visual display of power (e.g., in processions) and the multiple points of entry through which one can participate in its rituals.

51. Price, *Rituals and Power*, 106.

3.3 "Imperium Sine Fine": The Future of an Empire without End

We have already seen that, in its decree promulgating the new calendar, the *koinon* of Asia stated that it could not envision a future ruler who would supersede the accomplishments of Augustus, "[who left] those who shall come no hope of surpassing [him]." This sentiment simultaneously affirmed the Augustan era as the zenith of history and delineated all possible futures—there could be no moment more glorious for the world than the present. In addition to this, there is another conviction about the future that surfaces in the evidence: that of the perpetual rule of Rome, to which the institutions of the Empire were committed.

The notion of an eternal Roman Empire, not surprisingly, seems to have originated during the imperial period.[52] The earliest intimation of this in the documentary evidence is to be found in Tibullus' application of *aeternae* to the city of Rome (*Elegiae* 2.5.23–24; *c*. 9 BC),[53] and Ovid's use of the same in *Fasti* 3.71–73.[54] F. G. Moore surmises that this emergence corresponds to the new age of optimism and hope following the end of civil wars and Augustus' rise to power.[55] In Virgil's *Aeneid* we find Jupiter promising to the descendants of Romulus an empire that will survive the ravages of time: "For these I set neither bounds nor periods of empire; dominion without end (*imperium sine fine*) have I bestowed."[56] Even when one adjusts for poetic flourish in these instances, the idea of an eternal empire survives in more sober historical writings. Suetonius mentions among the entertainments organized by Nero games called *Ludi Maximi* ("Greatest Games"), staged "for the eternity of the Empire" (*pro aeternitate imperii*).[57] Along similar lines, Livy described the Roman state as something "immortal,"[58] and Tacitus, in recounting various hardships endured by the Roman people, nevertheless declared, "Statesmen were mortal, the state eternal (*principes mortalis, rem publicam*

---

52. The foundational study of the concept of the eternity of Rome in the imperial period is that of F. G. Moore, "On Urbs Aeterna and Urbs Sacra," *Transactions of the American Philological Association (1869–1896)* 25 (1894): 34. See also, Martin Percival Charlesworth, "Providentia and Aeternitas," *The Harvard Theological Review* 29, no. 2 (1936): 107–32. On the persistence of this idea of an eternal empire into the twentieth century, see Kenneth J. Pratt, "Rome as Eternal," *Journal of the History of Ideas* 26, no. 1 (January 1965): 25.

53. "Romulus aeternae nondum formauerat urbis moenia, consorti non habitanda Remo" ("Not yet had Romulus traced the walls of the Eternal City wherein was no abiding for his brother Remus"; Postgate trans.).

54. "Iam, modo quae fuerant silvae pecorumque recessus, urbs erat, aeternae cum pater urbis ait . . ." ("And now what of late had been woods and pastoral solitudes was a city, when thus the father of the eternal city spake . . ."; Frazer trans., LCL).

55. Moore, "Urbs Aeterna," 46.

56. *Aeneid* 1.278–279 (Fairclough trans.).

57. *Nero* 11. I owe this and the following references to Livy, Tacitus, and Silius Italicus to the discussion in Whitlark, *Resisting Empire*, 105–6.

58. *Ab urbe condita* 6.23.7 (Foster trans.).

aeternam esse)."[59] Thus, the consul and poet Silius Italicus, writing in the second half of the first century AD, had no difficulty envisioning the perpetuity of the Empire: "So long as sea-monsters shall swim the deep and stars shine in the sky and the sun rise on the Indian shore, Rome shall rule, and there shall be no end to her rule throughout the ages (*hic regna et nullae regnis per saecula metae*)."[60] The concept finds cultic crystallization in the era of Hadrian, who built in the imperial city his magnificent temple to *Roma aeterna* and *Venus felix*. The eternity of the city and its empire thus "became an official formula, with distinctly religious associations."[61]

Corresponding belief in the longevity of the Roman Empire surfaces quite clearly in the Anatolian epigraphic evidence. A marble slab dating to 41 AD, recording the Ephesian hymnodes' honors for the imperial family, begins, "... on behalf of the eternal continuation of Tiberius Claudius Caesar Augustus Germanicus and his entire household..." (...[ὑπὲρ τῆς αἰωνί]ας διαμονῆς Τιβε[ρίου Κλαυδίου Καίσαρο]ς Σεβαστοῦ Γερμανικ[οῦ καὶ τοῦ σύμπαν]τος οἴκου αὐτοῦ...).[62] Another Ephesian text reads: "On behalf of the health of our Lord Emperor Titus Caesar and the permanence of the rule of the Romans (διαμονῆς τῆς Ῥωμαίων ἡγεμονίας), the damaged wall surrounding the Augusteion was repaired."[63] In Phrygia, a small marble altar memorializes the dedication of a certain "Euphrastos, slave of Caesar" who prayed "for the eternal continuation and victory (αἰωνίου διαμονῆς τε καὶ νείκης) of emperor Nerva Trajan Caesar Sebastos Germanicus Dacicus."[64] Dedications to the perpetual rule of the emperors and the Romans have also been found, among other places, in Smyrna, Hyllarima, Aphrodisias, Ankara, and Amastris (Bithynia).[65] While these "eternity" dedications may refer to the Caesars' eternal rule as deified emperors, they may also refer to the perpetuity of the Roman state established by them.[66]

The notion of perpetual rule found in imperial inscriptions is, of course, premised on the continuation of the imperial household. Thus it was that Velleius Paterculus spoke of Augustus' adoption of Tiberius as his successor as an event that fueled "the hopes which they [i.e. the Romans] entertained for the perpetual security and the eternal existence of the Roman Empire."[67] The importance of a continuing imperial house leads us to two aspects of the imperial cults that are

---

59. *Ann.* 3.6 (Jackson trans.).
60. *Pun.* 175–179 (Duff trans.).
61. Moore, "Urbs Aeterna," 45; see also Pratt, "Rome as Eternal," 28.
62. *IEph* 3801.
63. *IEph* 412.
64. *SEG* 31.1124 (AD 104).
65. Smyrna: *SEG* 28.884; Hyllarima: *BCH* 1887, 306–8, 1; Aphrodisias: *REG* 19, 1906, 100–2, 14; Ankara: Bosch, *Quellen Ankara* 245, 184; Amastris (Bithynia): *SEG* 35.1317.
66. Charlesworth, "Providentia and Aeternitas," 124.
67. *Hist.* 2.103.4 (Shipley trans.).

often overlooked: (1) the cultic attention given to members of the imperial family other than the emperor himself, and (2) the related emphasis on dynastic continuity by means of succession. As Price observes: "The stability of imperial rule was perceived to lie in the transmission of power within the imperial family and, in consequence, considerable importance was attached to the whole imperial house."[68] In face of the ever-present dangers of civil war and dynastic struggle, both the Roman public and Rome's provincial subjects in Anatolia and elsewhere possessed keen awareness that the stability and security of the Empire were essentially dependent on the smooth succession of the ruling dynasty.[69]

Wives and mothers of emperors, along with the emperor's progeny, numbered among the recipients of cult, for they too played a crucial role in ensuring the Empire's continuation. Thus, for example, not only Augustus but also his wife Livia and their sons were accorded temples in Eresos on Lesbos.[70] The birth of Drusus' twin sons was celebrated in Rome with a coin which depicted the boys emerging from two crossed cornucopiae, signifying the secure prosperity of the Empire's future.[71] Fittingly, the twins also received cult and an imperial priest in Ephesus.[72] In the Artemision of the same city, Marcus Aurelius is depicted alongside his wife, his son Commodus, and his five daughters.[73] After Domitian was subjected to *damnatio memoriae* by the Senate and his name excised from the title of the imperial priest of the provincial temple in Ephesus, the priest continued in service of his wife Domitia and the Flavian household.[74] These cases suggest that, in honoring the eternal continuance of Roman power, the cults were quite capable of adapting to disruptive shifts in the imperial center and imagining that longevity in terms broader than the reign of any single emperor. In the grand scheme of things, not only the emperor but other royalty crucial to that process also deserved veneration. "The empire was in the hands of a family."[75]

The ethos of the imperial cults also entailed commitment to the smoothness of the process of dynastic succession. A coin issued by Titus on his accession to the throne in AD 79 depicts his father Vespasian handing him a globe, symbolizing the legitimate succession of power as well as the handing on of the entire *oikoumenē*. Commenting on the significance of this imagery, Richard Gordon states eloquently:

---

68. Price, *Rituals and Power*, 162. He continues: "Modern historians tend to lay too much emphasis on the emperor alone, ignoring the role of the imperial family."
69. Peter Herz, "Emperors: Caring for the Empire and Their Successors," in *A Companion to Roman Religion*, ed. Jörg Rüpke (Malden, MA: Blackwell, 2007), 313.
70. *IG* XII Suppl. 124; Friesen, *Imperial Cults*, 75.
71. Herz, "Emperors," 314.
72. *IEph* 7.2.4337.
73. Price, *Rituals and Power*, 162.
74. Friesen, *Imperial Cults*, 56–60.
75. Price, *Rituals and Power*, 162.

[The emperors] are vast enough to pass the world from hand to hand as though it were indeed a ball. Moreover, insofar as the globe denotes power, power is represented as a quantum, as a concrete totality, reified as a sphere, almost as a possession. This power cannot leak away, is dependent neither upon negotiation nor political calculation, fears not the mood of the military nor the assassin's dagger.[76]

In Roman practice, the mechanics of succession were such that they could be adapted to a variety of situations. Several arrangements were possible if the emperor had no biological male heir: (1) his daughter could marry a possible successor; (2) another female member of the imperial family could marry the potential successor; or (3) the first two options failing, the emperor could adopt any suitable male as son and successor.[77] Regardless of the pathway, ceremonies of the imperial cults provided a medium by which provincials could express their confidence in the continuance of dynastic succession and simultaneously demonstrate allegiance to the imperial household.

The practice of taking and inscribing oaths, integrated into cultic veneration of the emperor, was one means of accomplishing this.[78] Whereas in the Hellenistic era we have no evidence that communities swore oaths of allegiance to the ruler's family, this appears to have become quite important in the Roman period. In Samos, a priest of the cult of Augustus, Gaius, and Marcus Agrippa led a delegation to Rome to express, on behalf of the people, an oath of loyalty to Augustus and "to his children" (τοῖς τέκνοις αὐτοῦ). A Paphlagonian oath from 3 BC was directed to Augustus, his children, and his descendants, and was sworn by Zeus, Gē, Helios, all the gods and goddesses, and Augustus himself. In Gangra, this oath was sworn at imperial temples, imperial games, and on altars of Augustus, and in Neapolis, at the altar of the Sebasteion. Loyalty and worship were promised to Tiberius, son of Augustus, "and all his house (οἶκος)" in Palaipaphos. In the same breath, divine status was accorded to Tiberius, "the sons of his blood, and no one else." (Notably, this oath also clearly situated the emperor within the traditional pantheon: it was sworn "by our Akraia Aphrodite, our Kore, our Apollo Hylates, our Apollo Kerynetes, our savior Dioscuri, the common Council Hearth [*Boulaia Hestia*] of the island, Augustus the god Caesar, descendant of Aphrodite, Eternal Rome, and the rest of the gods and goddesses.") These oaths were oriented to the well-being of the Empire not only in the present but also in the future. By conceiving succession in ideological terms, they emphasized imperial permanence, and were

---

76. Gordon, "The Question of Power," 70.
77. For a discussion and examples of these various pathways, see Herz, "Emperors," 313.
78. The following material has been drawn from the discussion of oaths in Rowe, *Princes and Political Cultures*, 135–9. Rowe's analysis, in turn, uses the epigraphic material as given in Appendix 1 of Peter Herrmann, *Der römische Kaisereid: Untersuchungen zu seiner Herkunft und Entwicklung* (Göttingen: Vanderhoeck & Ruprecht, 1968).

little concerned with the "messiness" of its actual, formal mechanisms. In this way, they enabled the imagination of an order that would extend itself for generations to come.[79]

Emphasis on the continuity of the dynastic line is also illustrated in some of the archeological remains.[80] Among the ruins of imperial buildings, we find evidence of sets of images that were most likely grouped for this purpose. In the imperial room of the portico in Thera, for example, an ancient inhabitant may once have beheld a family sculpture of the Antonine line. From the remnant of a single large base, we know that the original sculpture depicted Faustina, Marcus Aurelius, Lucius Verus, and perhaps Antoninus Pius himself. Another room in the imperial shrine in Xanthos contains a group of marble statues, though the only recognizable one at present is that of Marciana, Trajan's sister. Sculptural groupings like these stressed the role of the imperial cults in foregrounding the integrity of the dynastic monarchy.

In this regard, two sites boast of particularly interesting cases: Bubon in Lycia and Cestrus in Cilicia. In Bubon, we find the remains of an imperial building of approximately 5m x 6m and containing more than twenty bronze statues with their bases intact. These statues of emperors and their family members line the walls of the room and are arranged in chronological order. The time span of the group stretches over some 200 years: from Nero and his wife, Poppaea Sabina, of the middle of the first century AD to Gallienus and his wife, Cornelius Salonina, of the middle of the third century AD. At the second site, the imperial temple in Cestrus, the statue of Vespasian occupies the center of a group of sculptures. He is flanked by the heirs to his power: Titus, Nerva, Trajan, and Hadrian together with his wife Sabina. Given that the building is evidently full, the adjacent temple containing another group of imperial statues (the only recognizable one being that of Antoninus Pius) may have been built to house statues of imperial successors further down the line.

The chronological sequences of statues in Bubon and Cestrus share one remarkable feature: they both ignore the conventional dynastic partitions among the Julio-Claudian, Flavian, Antonine and later dynasties.[81] Also noteworthy is the fact that Domitian, subject to *damnatio memoriae* by the Roman Senate, seems to have been removed from both temples. It would seem from these points that creases in the saga of the Roman emperors were, at least in practice, ironed out. Within the cultic ethos, the emperors followed one another in an uninterrupted line without any known terminus. Thus, the fact that Hadrian was succeeded by an adopted son and not his biological heir is ignored in the Ephesian inscription

---

79. Rowe, *Princes and Political Cultures*, 139.

80. Here I will focus only on depictions of the imperial family for the purposes of emphasizing dynastic succession. I have relied, unless otherwise noted, on the excellent discussion in Price, *Rituals and Power*, 159–62. A fuller treatment of the deployment of imperial images and their impact on space will be given in Chapter 5.

81. Price, *Rituals and Power*, 161.

which speaks of Antoninus Pius' taking over "the kingdom given to him by his divine father" (τὴν παρὰ τοῦ θεοῦ πατρὸς πα[ραδοθεῖσαν] αὐτῷ βασιλείαν),[82] and Septimius Severus' usurpation of the Antonine dynasty is passed over in the sequence of statues of his "ancestors" in Bubon. Strikingly, the presence of a statue of Alexander the Great at the latter site indicates that the founding figure of the Hellenistic Empire was probably invoked as a "founder" in order to lend archetypal legitimacy to Roman rule, presenting it as an heir to Alexander's legacy.[83] This seamlessness of rule constituted an integral part of Rome's myth of its perpetual empire. Whether power was gained by just or unjust means, whether by legitimate succession or by intrigue, imperial cultic representation and ritual obliterated the disruptions of history. Like the much-later royal rituals of the Merina of Madagascar, the imperial cults "outflank[ed] mere human time" and over-wrote it with "the continuity of smooth replacement, of generation after generation, of king after king, who transfer to each other their power which therefore endures unchanging."[84]

Nonetheless, succession by itself, however smooth, would not have guaranteed the eternal continuation of Rome or any other empire. Its importance had to be complemented by another thread essential to the Roman narrative of a perpetuity: firm conviction regarding her guaranteed success—what Price has termed "the ideology of imperial victory."[85] This doctrine of victory encompassed Rome's predestined rise to power, her advancement into the future, and the futility of all attempts to resist this divinely ordained trajectory. The outlines of this creed, as it were, can be traced in at least two Anatolian imperial sanctuaries.[86]

The first of these is the Augusteum in Pisidian Antioch, built by cooperation of Roman colonists and the local Greco-Phrygian elites and completed in Augustus' own lifetime. The main entrance into the sanctuary is a triple-arched propylon adorned, as might be expected, with reliefs that celebrated Augustus' victories both on land and at sea—winged genii and nude captives, along with the apropos goddess, Victoria.[87] (These depictions may have chiefly been drawn from Augustus' victory at the Battle of Actium, a pivotal moment which dominated imperial representations during and after the Augustan era.)[88] Of special note, moreover, is

---

82. *OGIS* 493.19. See also Price, *Rituals and Power*, 57, 161.

83. Price, *Rituals and Power*, 162.

84. Maurice Bloch, "The Ritual of the Royal Bath in Madagascar: The Dissolution of Death, Birth, and Fertility into Authority," in *Ritual, History and Power: Selected Papers in Anthropology* (London: Athlone, 1989), 202.

85. Price, *Rituals and Power*, 157.

86. The following analysis of these two buildings is taken from Rubin, "(Re)presenting Empire," 72–116. For further analysis from a different angle, see Chapter 5.

87. Rubin, "(Re)presenting Empire," 149–50 (Figures 13–15).

88. On the evocation of Actium in imperial images, see Zanker, *The Power of Images*, 82–5.

the depiction here of Augustus' conception sign, Capricorn, most likely intended to reflect the belief that the emperor's rise to power had been preordained by the gods and signaled in the stars.[89] On the top of the propylon, the goddess Victoria accompanies Augustus and members of the imperial family. Near the statue of Augustus, a captive barbarian kneels before another draped male figure (which may have been Augustus himself, or another emperor), sending the clear message to all who beheld it: all attempts to challenge the rule of Rome can only end in defeat and humiliation.[90]

Our second sanctuary in Aphrodisias is a complex dedicated to "Aphrodite, the *Theoi Sebastoi*, and the *Demos*," though largely regarded as the site of a Sebasteion.[91] The structure likewise evokes Rome's triumphal past, but it does so by means of distinctive portrayals of the Roman emperors interacting with subjugated peoples carved onto the façades of its three-tiered porticoes. In one such depiction, Claudius, in warrior garb, is shown grabbing Britannia by the hair, his right hand raised to strike. Before him, the humiliated Britannia, right breast exposed by her torn tunic, makes a vain attempt to shield the blow with her right arm.[92] On the other hand, the Pirousthae, a people who offered little resistance to Rome, are depicted as a figure upright and fully clothed, donning a Corinthian-style helmet and bearing a small shield in her left hand.[93] These images demonstrate the "two ways" held out by the formidable armies of Rome: resist and be defeated, or submit and escape with dignity intact. The message is resonant with the Romans' vocation encapsulated in the words of Virgil: "to impose the ways of peace, to show mercy to the conquered and to subdue the proud" (*pacisque imponere morem, parcere subiectis et debellare superbos*).[94]

The temples in Pisidian Antioch and Aphrodisias communicated Rome's ideology of victory in stone. While the representations on their walls and pillars could only tell of the accomplishments of emperors past, their full value did not lie there. They stood not only as memorials of the past or explanations of the present—of how the Empire became what it was—but also as architectural keys to extrapolating Rome's future. Like known points on a graph, they compelled all who entered the sanctuaries to project for themselves the rest of that line of history—the inevitable, inexorable growth of the Caesars' empire. That empire was anchored not only in an unbreakable process of succession, but also in a predestined glory engineered by providence and inscribed in the heavenly constellations.

---

89. Rubin, "(Re)presenting Empire," 149 (Figure 12).

90. Rubin, "(Re)presenting Empire," 152 (Figure 20).

91. On findings at this site, see R. R. R. Smith, "The Imperial Reliefs from the Sebasteion at Aphrodisias," *Journal of Roman Studies* 77 (November 1987): 88–138; R. R. R. Smith, "Simulacra Gentium: The Ethne from the Sebasteion at Aphrodisias," *Journal of Roman Studies* 78 (November 1988): 50–77; Friesen, *Imperial Cults*, 77–95.

92. Rubin, "(Re)presenting Empire," 157 (Figure 30).

93. Rubin, "(Re)presenting Empire," 158 (Figure 32).

94. *Aeneid* 6.853.

3.4 Conclusion

Though the plurality of the imperial cults must ultimately dissuade us from any attempt to assign to them a systematic or unified "theology," the evidence suggests that they were premised in some way upon particular views of the meaning and directionality of time. For the *koinon* of Asia, the reign of Augustus in history held significance for the present age which simultaneously implicated the past and the future. Imperial festivals celebrated throughout the region of Anatolia in the Roman period reflected the basic conviction that undergirded the new calendar promulgated in Asia: time itself had in some sense become "Roman." Events in the life of the emperor and the imperial family became temporal markers which punctuated the rhythms of everyday civic life so that the passing of days and months—of work, rest, and celebration—were themselves permeated by the emperor's presence. In inscription, coinage and architecture, the narrative of Roman triumph projected into the realm of possible futures a stable conviction in "the permanence of the rule of the Romans." "The discourse of imperial cults," as Friesen puts it, "was committed to preventing the imagination from imagining the end of the world."[95] The empire without end necessitated a world without end. In this sense, one could say that the cults to the Sebastoi engendered an eschatology of their own, even if only in the form of an outline.

---

95. Friesen, *Imperial Cults*, 130.

Chapter 4

TIME IN 1 PETER

Having examined some of the ways in which the imperial cults of Roman Anatolia constructed time in their representation of the emperor and the Empire, I turn now to the construction of time in 1 Peter. As with the case of the imperial cults as a whole, the author of 1 Peter did not attempt to consciously articulate a comprehensive "philosophy of time" as such. Nonetheless, the contours of the letter do allow us to reconstruct the basic framework of his temporal imagination—an interpretation of time which he held and sought to communicate to the letter's recipients.

This being the case, the purpose of the present chapter is not to read 1 Peter for an abstract philosophy of time, as it were, but rather to understand its view of time against its Roman imperial counterpart as manifested in the imperial cults. Doing so will illumine a specific way in which this letter posed an alternative reality to that which undergirded imperial ideology and rule—that is, by configuring time in a manner that decentered Roman power. The author's distinctly Christian figuration of time, in turn, undergirded his exhortation to faithful discipleship for the Anatolian communities living under Roman domination.

4.1 From "Before the Foundation" to "the Last of the Ages" (1:20): A Primopetrine Thesis of Time

As I showed in the preceding chapter, the Asian provincial decree of 9 BC reconfigured Anatolian time around the person of Augustus, presenting the era marked by his birth and rule as one destined by the gods to become the zenith of cosmic history. The past and the future were defined in relation to the Augustan moment: behind this emperor was a long march of political chaos and decline, and after his reign there could be no possible rival to his accomplishments. As such, Augustus became the canon by which history was measured.

The legacy of Augustan rule in Anatolia produced a crucial ripple effect: increasingly, Anatolian time became synchronized to the imperial center, not only as Asian cities aligned themselves to the new calendar, but also as festivals in honor of the Caesars and their families proliferated across the landscape. Increasingly, time in various Anatolian communities acquired an imperial valence as cities and villages alike celebrated events such as birthdays and military accomplishments of the emperors and the imperial family. Not only was the present time subject to this imperial revisionism; even the future became recast in terms of the Empire's perpetual endurance. In the Christian imagination of 1 Peter, however, it is not these imperial time markers but the revelation of God in Jesus of Nazareth that takes center-stage as *the* key event in cosmic time.

To examine this perspective, I take as my point of departure 1 Pet. 1:19–20. In this text, the author likens Jesus to a sacrificial lamb "without defect or blemish" (v. 19) who was "foreknown before the foundation of the world, but was revealed at the last of the ages for your sake" (v. 20). Concise yet comprehensive in its evaluation of history, these words are foundational for the conception of time that undergirds the letter. The use of μὲν . . . δέ indicates a contrasting couplet:

> A προεγνωσμένου
>   μὲν
>   B πρὸ καταβολῆς κόσμου
> A' φανερωθέντος
>   δὲ
>   B' ἐπ' ἐσχάτου τῶν χρόνων

As the diagram above shows, in this verse Christ's being foreknown is counterbalanced by his being revealed, the inception of the world with its consummation.[1] The phrases πρὸ καταβολῆς κόσμου and ἐπ' ἐσχάτου τῶν χρόνων serve as temporal demarcations to highlight a pair of actions originating in the divine will: God's election of Christ and his appearance in the world. According to the author's schema, time can be divided into a succession of ages (χρόνοι) culminating in Christ's manifestation, since his role as God's agent of redemption was written into the story of creation from the start.[2] In the hands of the sovereign deity, the cosmos unfolds along a course of preparation that culminates in the revelation of the Messiah, when he is finally revealed for the readers' salvation (δι' ὑμᾶς). Time is thus understood as the gradual disclosure of God's cosmic plan, the

---

1. Given the symmetrical elegance of this verse, some commentators have posited its independent origin in early Christian creedal formulae, liturgical hymnody, or catechetical material, e.g., Spicq, *Saint Pierre*, 69; Kelly, *Commentary*, 75; Francis Wright Beare, *The First Epistle of Peter: The Greek Text with Introduction and Notes*, 3rd ed. (Oxford: Blackwell, 1970), 106. The suggestion made by Martin ("1 Peter," 108) that εἰδότες ὅτι in 1:18 signifies that traditional material was used in vv. 18–20 seems far-fetched, as this would also require the content of v. 18 (an appeal to the readers' experience) to have a similarly independent existence. Other commentators, like Achtemeier (*1 Peter*, 131), are more inclined to attribute it to the author (also Elliott, *1 Peter*, 377–8).

2. Early Jewish and Christian texts often speak of the Messiah as already existing in the heavenly realm, waiting to be revealed at the appointed time (e.g., *1 En.* 48:6; 62:7; *4 Ezra* 12:32; 13:26, 52; Ign. *Magn.* 6.1, 2; 2 Clem 14.2; *Herm. Sim.* 12.2–3).

goal of which is the manifestation of Christ and the salvation of those who receive him. Hence the author can confidently declare in another place that "the aim of all things has come near" (πάντων δὲ τὸ τέλος ἤγγικεν, 4:7), for he sees history as having arrived at its destination in the eschatological present.

The Primopetrine thesis of time is Christological because it is the entrance of Christ into the world that marks off the present as "the last of the ages." Time itself is reimagined around this single point of reference. In Jewish and Christian apocalyptic texts more or less contemporaneous with 1 Peter, the last age is typically regarded as the finale in a succession of periods of human history and characterized by tribulation of the elect, the coming of the Messiah, and God's decisive intervention in history (e.g., 4 Ezra 3:14; 12:9; 2 Bar. 13:3; 21:8; 27:15; 29:8; 30:3; 59:4; 76:2; Heb. 1:2; 2 Pet. 3:3; Jude 18).[3] While many communities that embraced apocalyptic convictions held that they too were already living in that long-awaited eschaton, the Petrine author, in keeping with a distinctively Christian conviction, regards that eschaton as having been inaugurated by the appearance of Christ in the world.[4]

The last age is, above all, one of redemption. This can be seen in the author's evocation of the ransom motif with ἐλυτρώθητε (1:18). Not only is it the age in which Christ is revealed, but it is the age in which he is revealed precisely as a sacrificial lamb (1:19; cf. 1:2) who, though once slain, is now raised and glorified (1:21). The redemptive-sacrificial aspect of this Christophany is augmented by the emphasis on its origin in divine foreknowledge (προεγνωσμένου, v. 20), thus "removing [Christ's passion and death] from the realm of the accidental."[5] His appearance cleaves all time in two—the ages preceding his appearance and the "now" of his manifestation, precisely because it cleaves darkness from light, the ages of slavery from the final age of liberation. Time is transformed into the measure of God's saving activity (2:9; cf. Isa. 42:16).

---

3. Elliott, *1 Peter*, 377. For a detailed study of Jewish and early Christian perspectives on this subject, see Mark Dubis, *Messianic Woes in First Peter: Suffering and Eschatology in 1 Peter 4:12–19* (New York, NY: P. Lang, 2002); Brant Pitre, *Jesus, the Tribulation, and the End of the Exile: Restoration Eschatology and the Origin of the Atonement* (Tübingen: Mohr Siebeck, 2005); Portier-Young, *Apocalypse Against Empire*. On thematic features generally classified as typical of apocalyptic literature, see John J. Collins, *The Apocalyptic Imagination: An Introduction to Jewish Apocalyptic Literature* (Grand Rapids, MI: Eerdmans, 1998), 1–42, esp. 2–11.

4. The Dead Sea Scrolls, for example, reveal a community that likewise saw itself as living in the eschatological age. As such, this "inaugurated eschatology" was by no means unique to 1 Peter or the early Christians as a whole. Rather, it is the centrality of Jesus of Nazareth to the scheme of things that sets Christian apocalypticism apart from its Jewish equivalents (Collins, *The Apocalyptic Imagination*, 256–79)—a theme that emerges with indefatigable conviction in 1 Peter.

5. Achtemeier, *1 Peter*, 131.

Taken as an encapsulation of the author's outlook on history and eschatology, 1 Pet. 1:20 reveals a perspective of time that is at once theocentric, Christological, and soteriological. It is theocentric because time's ultimate mover is the one true and sovereign God; Christological because Jesus the Messiah is the one through whom that God acts; and soteriological because time is articulated in terms of the divine plan to save. The world 1 Peter constructs is one ruled by divine agency, in which the sovereign God directs all events toward the flawless execution of a salvific blueprint.

Placed beside the imperial ideology we find in the cults, the potential of this temporal imagination to generate friction in its Anatolian context comes to the fore. The Asian decree couched the sweep of history in sociopolitical terms, evaluating past, present, and future in terms of the instability or stability of localized politics (from chaos to peace) and military and imperial accomplishments. Similarly, festivals of the imperial cult throughout the Anatolian provinces bound the rhythms of the city and its rural dependants to the life and actions of the Caesars and the imperial family, effectively becoming a metronome that kept rhythms of life coordinated to the practices and events of Roman statecraft. By contrast, in 1 Peter, time is reconfigured or "tied" around an entirely different pole. It is defined not in terms of the peace and stability of the state or the city, but rather in terms of God's decisive intervention in the world. The Christ-event, not events in the lives of the imperial family, becomes the chief indicator of time's meaning and forms the rationale for right living in the world. We might say that, whereas time is politicized and militarized in the imperial cults (that is, tied to the stability of the state), it is soteriologized in 1 Peter—that is, its passage must be understood as the unfolding of the salvation of souls (cf. 1:9). This soteriological aspect of time is in turn rooted in its theocentric and Christological properties: the action of a sovereign God through his appointed agent, Jesus Christ.

4.2 The Power of Now: The Present as a State of Eschatological Urgency

These "qualities" of time, inscribed into the cosmic foundations and belonging to the metaphysical substructure of reality itself, form the basis of the author's exhortations to discipleship in the present. Again and again, in 1 Peter we find an understanding of faithful praxis that is conditioned by the eschatological urgency of "the last of the ages."

That Jesus has appeared means that the readers are now living at the climax of history, in a time of unprecedented blessing—the eschatological age. This reality is fundamental to the Petrine author's call to obedient praxis issued to the Christian communities spread throughout Anatolia (1:2). Through faith, they are already receiving by way of foretaste the salvation of their souls (κομιζόμενοι τὸ τέλος τῆς πίστεως [ὑμῶν] σωτηρίαν ψυχῶν, 1:9), being protected by God's power as they await its fullness in "the final appointed time" (ἐν καιρῷ ἐσχάτῳ, 1:5). That salvation already-begun is the rationale for Christian joy amid present trials that test the genuineness of their faith (1:6–8). σωτηρία here is premised not on the stability of the Empire and its mechanisms, but rather on God's protection in the face of hardship (1:7).⁶ The power to protect and secure is thus relocated from the hands of Caesar to the hands of God, and it is the latter's servant, the Messiah, who becomes worthy of love and faith (1:8; 2:6-7).

4.2.1 The Ethical Imperative of the Present

The regeneration of all things at this climactic juncture of history lies neither in the birth of one Octavian nor the unsurpassable accomplishments of his reign. Rather, it is Jesus' resurrection from the dead that confers "new birth" (ἀναγεννήσας, 1:3) to the world and inducts it into "a living hope" (1:3), testifying to God's power to sweep aside even the penalty of crucifixion that is the Empire's ultimate weapon of terror. The God who is the source of life for Jesus is now also their "Father" (1:3), since they have been reborn from the imperishable seed of his living and abiding word (ἀναγεγεννημένοι ἐκ σπορᾶς ... ἀφθάρτου διὰ λόγου ζῶντος θεοῦ καὶ μένοντος, 1:23).⁷ This new existence orients believers toward an inheritance that is "imperishable, undefiled, and unfading" (ἄφθαρτον καὶ ἀμίαντον καὶ ἀμάραντον, 1:4; NRSV) even as the Messiah was shown to be imperishable in the face of

---

6. On the Greco-Roman use of σωτηρία to designate deliverance or protection offered by both human and divine agents, see Martin Williams, *The Doctrine of Salvation in the First Letter of Peter* (Cambridge: Cambridge University Press, 2011), 157-60, with literary and papyric evidence. As Williams points out, in its biblical use, σωτηρία is overwhelmingly the prerogative of the one true God of Israel.

7. The description here of the divine word as σπορά, which in the LXX has an exclusively agricultural sense (2 Kgs 19:29; 1 Macc. 10:30), sets up the comparison with floral metaphors (grass, flower) in 1:24. σπορά can also be used in relation to human procreation, however (e.g., Aeschylus, *Prom.* 871; Sophocles, *Aj.* 1290; Plato, *Laws* 729c; 783a). Its double sense may well serve to bind the floral imagery in 1.24 to that of human progeny in 2.2. Moreover, the transition from the agricultural to the human in 1:24 to 2:2 is not as sudden as it first appears once we keep in mind that the referent of χόρτος and ἄνθος χόρτου in 1:24 is, in fact, corporeal human life (σάρξ; cf. LXX Isa. 40:6). Since the σπορά in 1:23 is the agent of re-begetting, it is possible to understand it as God's sperm, a development of the theme of divine paternity announced in 1:3 (cf. Feldmeier, "Salvation and Anthropology in First Peter," 210-11). The image of God as a nursing mother implied in 2:2 (on which see n. 9 below), then, provides the maternal counterpart to divine parenthood. The word of God (i.e. the gospel) proclaimed to the readers is both sperm and breast milk. What joins the two images, therefore, is God's life-giving parenthood, manifested as both paternity and maternity. Thus, between sperm and milk there need not be any of the "metaphorical incoherence" posited by Karen H. Jobes, "Got Milk? Septuagint Psalm 33 and the Interpretation of 1 Peter 2:1-3," *Westminster Theological Journal* 64, no. 1 (2002): 3. This even more so when one considers the fact that, in ancient Greece, semen and milk were thought to be different stages of blood (Helen King, *Hippocrates' Woman: Reading the Female Body in Ancient Greece* [London and New York: Routledge, 1998], 10, 32-5, 97).

death.⁸ Into this inheritance they are to grow, being newborn infants fed on "the pure milk of the word" (τὸ λογικὸν ἄδολον γάλα, 2:2).⁹ In the order of spiritual kinship, they have now been constituted into a "brotherhood" (ἀδελφότης) that exists in solidarity throughout the world (2:17, 5:9; cf. 5:13). The full force of this re-begetting brings Christians into an entirely new set of social relations and, with it, a new way of relating to wider society.¹⁰

---

8. Feldmeier ("Salvation and Anthropology in First Peter," 206–11) argues that the understanding of divine rebirth in 1 Peter can be shown to have been influenced by Hellenistic understandings of the same, which perhaps entered into the Christian imagination by way of the Diaspora synagogue (*idem*, 206–7, 439–40 n. 26, 27). In particular, Feldmeier notes that the adjectives ἄφθαρτος and ἀμίαντος, used to describe the divine inheritance in 1:4 (cf. 1:23; 3:4), are attributes associated with the divine realm in Greek thought, and were later appropriated by Hellenized strands of Judaism (e.g., Philo, *Spec*. 1.113; *Leg*. 1.50; *Migr*. 31). Most striking, however, is Philo, QE 2.46, in which Moses' ascent to Mount Sinai in Exod. 24:16 is described as a "second birth" (δευτέρα γένεσις). According to Philo, this second birth was better than the first (from corruptible, natural parents) because the reborn Moses became a bodiless, pure spirit, having no mother but only one Father, God himself. First Peter lacks this decisive shunning of corporeality, though its concept of rebirth in the one Father (1:3) and by his imperishable seed (1:23), along with its corresponding reorientation to an imperishable inheritance, certainly provides stimulating fodder for comparison.

9. My translation. The meaning of τὸ λογικὸν ἄδολον γάλα is difficult, and has been the subject of much debate, chiefly due to the disputed meaning of the adjective λογικός (which appears in the NT only here and at Rom. 12:1). If one accords weight to the morphological connection between λογικὸν γάλα here and the divine λόγος in 1:23, this would associate "milk" with God's word, yielding the reading "wordly milk" or, more conventionally, "milk of the word" (KJV). Some commentators dismiss this reading on the grounds that λογικός bears no relation to λόγος (Hort, *The First Epistle of St. Peter*, 100; followed by Michaels, *1 Peter*, 87; and Jobes, "Got Milk?") though this is more asserted than demonstrated. Beare (*The First Epistle of Peter*, 115) believes that λογικός indicates "that which is proper to the Logos, and to life which is mediated through the Logos" (citing 1:23), but nevertheless prefers the translation "spiritual"—an option taken by several translations (e.g., RV, RSV, NRSV, ESV) and commentators (Selwyn, *The First Epistle of St. Peter*, 155; Michaels, *1 Peter*, 86–8). There remains, I believe, good reason to keep together λογικὸν γάλα in 2:2 and λόγος θεοῦ in 1:23. The thought-unit of 2:1–2 flows directly from the author's preceding reflection on divine rebirth by means of God's word (1.23–25), as indicated both by the connecting οὖν in 2:1 and the resumption of the motif of divine birth (ἀρτιγέννητα, 2:2). Given this flow of thought, λογικός here is most likely a reiteration of the life-giving force of the divine λόγος in 1:23. So Horrell, *Epistles*, 37; Kelly, *Commentary*, 85; Elliott, *1 Peter*, 401; Achtemeier, *1 Peter*, 147; Bigg, *The Epistles of St. Peter and Jude*, 126.

10. On this point I part ways with Elliott, who argues that the readers' relationships to outsiders were first determined by their actual sociopolitical status as resident aliens and

From the author's perspective, Christ's appearance in the world has ruptured time, not in some broad, "objective" sense, but in an existential sense. In the words of Eugene Boring, the Christ-event "bifurcates not only world history but the readers' own story."[11] A non-people who were previously alienated from God, they have now been constituted as his people (2:10). (The "then and now" dimension of this transposition is clear in the Greek: οἵ ποτε οὐ λαὸς νῦν δὲ λαὸς θεοῦ.) Their pre-Christian past was shaped by desires fueled by their ignorance (1:14) that enshrouded not only them but also their ancestors, from whom they inherited a uniformly futile way of life (1:18). That life, governed by submission to human desires and dominated by moral disorder and dissipation (4:2–4), belongs to an age that has now passed (ὁ παρεληλυθὼς χρόνος, 4:3). In 1 Peter, immoral living is characteristic of Gentiles in their state of anachronistic stupor. Elliott is thus right that the contrast invoked here between Anatolian Christians and their non-believing neighbors is primarily *temporal* in nature.[12] In other words, the author engages in allochronistic critique, strategically other-ing Gentiles wholesale by relegating their way of life to the past.[13]

Christians, however, must no longer live in that outmoded way. Rather, they ought to spend their remaining days doing God's will rather than pursuing the dictates of human desires (4:2). Christ's coming and the new birth they have received initiate them into a new identity with its own ethic—one fitted for the last age. Since they have been re-begotten by reception of the divine word (1:23–25), they must rid themselves of all evil and the vices of guile, insincerity, envy and slander (2:1),[14] and "abstain from the desires of the flesh that wage war against the soul" (2:11). The "now" (νῦν) of their Christian existence stems from their status as

strangers (πάροικοι; παρεπίδημοι), which they already possessed prior to becoming Christians (see Chapter 6 below). With their conversion to Christ, they are invited by the author of 1 Peter to see their marginalization as "an opportunity and a challenge" to "manifest also the religious dimension of their social strangerhood" (*A Home for the Homeless*, 35; though this position is somewhat modified in *1 Peter*, 101–2). As I argue in Section 6.1.1, I do not find Elliott's reading of the evidence tenable, and so read 1 Peter as a Christian attempt to make sense of the changes in social relations effected by the readers' conversion, not by their socio-legal standing.

11. M. E. Boring, "Narrative Dynamics in 1 Peter: The Function of Narrative World," in *Reading First Peter with New Eyes: Methodological Reassessments of the Letter of First Peter*, ed. Robert L. Webb and Betsy Bauman-Martin, LNTS 364 (New York, NY: T&T Clark, 2007), 31.

12. Elliott, *A Home for the Homeless*, 43.

13. On allochronism, see Section 1.3.1 above.

14. The link between their new birth and the imperative to strip off these vices is indicated by the use of οὖν in 2:1: "Ἀποθέμενοι οὖν πᾶσαν κακίαν...." A similar connection is made in 1:12–13: their hearing (and receiving) the gospel proclaimed (v. 12) bears a moral imperative (v. 13).

God's people and recipients of divine mercy (2:10); their return to the true Shepherd and Guardian after a history of straying (2:25); and the good conscience before God conferred by baptism (3:21). In place of their "old" past of idolatry and ignorance there is a "new" past—the past of Israel, into which the readers have now been grafted. For the author, the readers' embrace of the gospel means that they have reappropriated Israel's biblical identity in the fullest sense—in Achtemeier's words, "without remainder."[15] As such, he does not hesitate to describe them with the biblical titles accorded to Israel: "a chosen race, a royal priesthood, a holy nation, God's own people" (2:9–10; cf. Exod. 19:5–6). This is the identity out of which the readers must now live. They must become who they already are.

Keeping in step with such a translation of identity requires that they "know the time," so to speak. As privileged recipients of a long-anticipated proclamation withheld from both prophets and angels (1:12), they are called to nothing short of a cognitive revolution. They must "gird up the loins" of their mind (1:13) and abandon the ignorance (ἄγνοια, 1:14) of their past, remaining sober and vigilant (cf. 4:7; 5:8a) lest they lapse into Gentile ways typical of the old order. The command to "gird up the loins" (ἀναζωσάμενοι τὰς ὀσφύας) draws from the Hebraic practice of gathering a long garment in preparation for movement or action, usually in moments of urgency or conflict (2 Kgs 4:29; 9:1; Job 38:3; 40:7; Jer. 1:17; Nah. 2:1; Jn 21:18; Acts 12:8). In Exod. 12:11, it is commanded as a ritual act during the observance of Passover, Israel's archetypal feast of redemption, and embodies preparedness for flight:

> This is how you shall eat [the Passover Lamb]: your loins girded [LXX: περιεζωσμέναι], your sandals on your feet, and your staff in your hand; and you shall eat it hurriedly. It is the passover of the LORD. (NRSV)[16]

In 1 Peter, the qualification τῆς διανοίας transforms this into an act of mental preparation—hence the NRSV's freer rendering, "prepare your minds for action."[17] That this command to gird up immediately follows (διό, 1:13) the author's declaration that the gospel has been announced to his readers in 1:12 indicates

---

15. Achtemeier (*1 Peter*, 69): "In 1 Peter, the language and hence the reality of Israel pass without remainder into the language and hence the reality of the new people of God."

16. Kelly (*Commentary*, 65) suggests that the Exodus narrative is at the front of the author's mind here. Achtemeier (*1 Peter*, 118) acknowledges the possibility but is more cautious.

17. Michaels (*1 Peter*, 54) posits that διάνοια here refers not to natural human intellect but to "a capacity that is [the readers'] by virtue of their redemption in Jesus Christ." He is virtually alone, however, in seeing a more supernatural aspect here. Other commentators are content with a more "natural" meaning, i.e. simply "mind" or "understanding" (Elliott, *1 Peter*, 356; Hort, *Epistle*, 65; Achtemeier, *1 Peter*, 118). For Kelly (*The Epistles of Peter and Jude*, 66–7) διάνοια refers not to the intellect but to one's "whole spiritual and mental attitude."

that it is the appropriate response to what has happened—the revelation of Christ. It is, so to speak, the mental stance demanded by the present age.

An examination of ἄγνοια, against which διανοία is juxtaposed,[18] offers further insights. In 1:14, ἄγνοια is coupled with ἐπιθυμία (desire; ταῖς πρότερον ἐν τῇ ἀγνοίᾳ ὑμῶν ἐπιθυμίαις), a term associated with base human nature elsewhere in the letter (2:11; 4:2–3). It is the ignorance of those who do not know God and live accordingly (likewise in Acts 17:30; Eph. 4:18; Wis. 14:22; cf. Wis. 13:1). More importantly for our discussion, ἄγνοια is also in this verse regarded as a feature of the readers' pre-Christian past (πρότερον).[19] It "belongs to the old order of existence that is passing away as a result of the coming of Christ."[20] In contrast, the call to readers to gird up the loins of their διανοίας in 1:13 entails mental vigilance (νήφοντες) against spiritual recidivism so that they do not "fall back" in time. Rather, they must build hope (ἐλπίσατε—the principal imperative in 1:13) on the grace being brought to them in the eschatological present (τὴν φερομένην ὑμῖν χάριν ἐν ἀποκαλύψει Ἰησοῦ Χριστοῦ).[21] Here and elsewhere in the letter, as we shall see, time is "ethicized"—times past, present, and future demand appropriate moral responses.

---

18. Elliott, *1 Peter*, 356; Michaels, *1 Peter*, 54.

19. Hort, *Epistle*, 69. "πρότερον ... means the former time before they received the Gospel." Cf. Achtemeier, *1 Peter*, 120 n. 45; Elliott, *1 Peter*, 359.

20. Michaels, *1 Peter*, 58.

21. The apparent contradiction between the future-oriented nature of hope (ἐλπίσατε; ἐλπίς) and the present form of φερομένην in this clause has caused some disagreement among commentators. This is, moreover, aggravated by the ambiguity of the expression ἐν ἀποκαλύψει Ἰησοῦ Χριστοῦ, which can refer to either Christ's first manifestation in history (ἀπεκαλύφθη, 1:12; 1:20) or his second coming (1:7; 5:4). Some commentators have resolved this tension by taking φερομένην as a present participle with a future meaning (Michaels, *1 Peter*, 56; Achtemeier, *1 Peter*, 119; Best, *1 Peter*, 85). Others prefer to retain the present force of the participle (Hort, *Epistle*, 66–7; Kelly, *Commentary*, 67; Spicq, *Saint Pierre*, 60–1; E. G. Selwyn, *The First Epistle of St. Peter: The Greek Text with Introduction, Notes and Essays* [London: Macmillan, 1946], 140; Elliott, *1 Peter*, 356–7; David C. Parker, "The Eschatology of 1 Peter," *Biblical Theology Bulletin: A Journal of Bible and Theology* 24, no. 1 [1994]: 29). The latter position seems more probable, since the author elsewhere speaks of grace as something already experienced in the present (4:10; 5:5, 10, 12). Hort (*Epistle*, 67) takes the "strictly present" force of φερομένην to mean that grace "is ever being brought, and brought in fresh forms, in virtue of the continuing and progressing unveiling of Jesus Christ," and thus sees ἀποκάλυψις here and elsewhere (1:7; 4:13) not as a discrete moment but as "a long and varying process, though ending in a climax" (*idem*, 45). The author invites his readers to let this grace (already being experienced) form the basis of their hope in God's future. (On grace as the foundation and not the object of hope in this verse, see Hort, *The Epistle*, 66 ["not the thing hoped for, but that which makes it possible"]; Norbert Brox, *Der erste Petrusbrief*, 4th ed., Evangelisch-Katholischer Kommentar zum Neuen Testament 21 [Zurich & Neukirchen-Vluyn: Benziger & Neukirchener, 1993], 75; Achtemeier, *1 Peter*, 119).

Each instance of the letter's summons to sobriety (νήφοντες, 1:13;[22] νήψατε, 4:7, 5:8a) is, in fact, related to awareness of time. Though νήφω can be used in the plain sense of being sober as opposed to being drunk with wine,[23] its six occurrences in the New Testament—half of these in 1 Peter—are tied specifically to alertness in an eschatological context (cf. 1 Thess. 5:6, 8; 2 Tim. 4:5) or, to use Elliott's expression, "eschatologically conditioned."[24] In 1 Peter, its deployment at key points in the letter body—at the beginning of the first section (1:13), the conclusion of the second (4:7), and the end of the body closing (5:8)—occurs in parenetic contexts, and signals the importance of knowing time in the letter's pastoral strategy.[25]

In 1:13, νήφοντες enjoins the stance required for perseverance to the end—a decisive clear-mindedness about what God has accomplished in Christ (1:10–12) and the grace being poured out upon them. For Norbert Brox, this is a call not merely to assume a mental state, but also to embrace the practice of ascetical self-discipline, without which such clear-mindedness would no doubt be impossible (cf. NRSV: "discipline yourselves").[26] After all, actual drunkenness was a clear and present danger in the company of non-believers (οἰνοφλυγίαι, κῶμοι, πότοι, 4:3).[27] In 4:7, as indicated by the use of the conjunction οὖν, sobriety is demanded by the eschatological intensity of the present: "the end of all things has come near; therefore..." (NRSV). Self-control is required not only for efficacious prayer (εἰς προσευχάς),[28] but also for the practice of fraternal concord and service in the communities (4:8–11).[29] Used here with σωφρονήσατε, νήψατε emphasizes "the

---

22. I am here attributing imperatival force to the participle νήφοντες in 1:13 (so NRSV, NAB, RSV, ASV, KJV). In this verse, it works in tandem with ἀναζωσάμενοι to build momentum leading to the first direct imperative of the letter, ἐλπίσατε. On the use of imperatival participles in the New Testament, with special attention to 1 Peter, see Travis B. Williams, "Reconsidering the Imperative Participle in 1 Peter," *Westminster Theological Journal* 73 (2011): 59–78.

23. See, e.g., Plato, *Sym.* 213e; Josephus, *Ant.* 11.3.3.

24. Elliott, *1 Peter*, 356.

25. For the sake of discussion, I am here following the outline of the letter in Achtemeier, *1 Peter*, 73–4. The structure of 1 Peter has been the subject of considerable and ongoing debate, yielding some broad patterns of consensus, though exegetes vary on how the subsections of the letter body are to be reckoned, as well as their relationship to each other. See, e.g., Mark Dubis, "Research on 1 Peter: A Survey of Scholarly Literature since 1985," *Currents in Biblical Research* 4, no. 2 (2006): 206–9; Achtemeier, *1 Peter*, 58–62; Williams, *Persecution in 1 Peter*, 339–49.

26. Brox, *Der erste Petrusbrief*, 75. He continues: "Das Gegenteil wäre *Trunkenheit* als bewußtlose, orientierungslose, hemmungslose Existenz" (emphasis in original). The NASB's "keep sober in spirit" is thus too narrow a rendering.

27. Selwyn, *Epistle*, 140. Contra Michaels, *1 Peter*, 246.

28. Cf. Col. 4:2; Eph. 6:18. Polycarp, *Phil.* 7.2b draws a similar link between sobriety and prayer (νήφοντες πρὸς τὰς εὐχὰς), to which is added the injunction to fast.

29. So also Achtemeier, *1 Peter*, 294; Beare, *Epistle*, 184.

need for a disciplined life focused on the urgencies of the moment."[30] Finally, in 5:8, coupled with the injunction to stay awake (γρηγορήσατε), the command νήψατε finds its most vivid—and perilous—context. Sobriety is now necessitated by the wiles of their enemy, the devil, who prowls about like a predatory "roaring lion," seeking their destruction so as to rob them of future exaltation (5:6, 10).[31] In the triple charge to be sober, we see the call to Christian conduct motivated by attentiveness to the significance of the present, the momentous "now" opened up by Jesus' suffering, resurrection, and glorification.[32]

4.2.2 Valorizing Estrangement and Suffering in the Present

Sobriety and vigilance are crucial stances because, contrary to the era of peace described in the Asian decree and Rome's widespread propaganda of a *Pax Romana*, the present in 1 Peter is fundamentally a period of destabilization. Though the cosmos has entered its last age, those outside the community of faith continue to live out of sync with this new reality and remain stuck in a state of dyschronia. Gentile ignorance and immorality, as I have shown above, are largely defined by attachment to the ways of the old order. Those who follow Christ, who are keeping in step with what God is doing in the world, will necessarily find themselves out of step with wider society.

It is telling that, in calling his readers to be ready to share Christ's suffering "in the flesh" (4:1), the author associates this suffering with the rupture between their lives and those of non-believers. It is no wonder, he states, that their non-believing family members, friends, and co-workers should feel alienated by the fact that Christians are no longer "running together" with them in dissolute living (μὴ συντρεχόντων, 4:4). Disciples ought not to be surprised at "the fiery testing" that has come upon them, as though it were something alien, but rather rejoice in this opportunity to commune in Christ's own passion (4:12). Their embrace of the gospel means that they have been transposed into the life of the new age while the rest of the world lags behind, drunk and half asleep. As such, they cannot be people of their time, for there can be no rest while the enemy is hot on their heels (5:8). Social estrangement must be accepted as the norm, since the last χρόνος is also the age of exile (τὸν τῆς παροικίας ὑμῶν χρόνον, 1:17).

---

30. Elliott, *1 Peter*, 748.

31. On the leonine image here as an allusion to *ad bestias* executions, see David G. Horrell, Bradley Arnold, and Travis B. Williams, "Visuality, Vivid Description, and the Message of 1 Peter: The Significance of the Roaring Lion (1 Peter 5:8)," *Journal of Biblical Literature* 132, no. 3 (2013): 697–716.

32. On the importance of eschatological alertness for followers of Jesus, see also Mt. 24:42; 25:13; Mk 13:32–37; Lk. 12:37; 21:36; Acts 20:31; 1 Cor. 16:13; 1 Thess. 5:1–10; and *Did.* 16.1.

We thus see that, as a constitutive feature of its view of the present, the eschatological intensity of 1 Peter serves to normalize the Anatolian Christians' experience of non-belonging within wider society. Authentic discipleship is life in sync with the rhythms of the final age—with what God has done in Christ—and moral deviance symptomatic of the non-believers' dyschronia. The letter provides, on the basis of this temporal imagination, an explanation as to how and why Christians are out of step with those outside the community. One of the outcomes of this social arrhythmia is the readers' suffering, the understanding of which the author seeks to transform by valorization. Patient endurance in the face of "many trials" (ποικίλοις πειρασμοῖς, 1:6), according to the letter, must not be seen simply as the passive tolerance of hardship, but actual sharing in the sufferings of Christ (3:21; 4:13).

This strategy of valorizing suffering explains what appears to be the author's recurrent focus on the effects of authentic Christian living upon non-believers. After his programmatic exhortation that the readers embrace their identity as "aliens and strangers" who must leave behind the desires of their past (2:11), he enjoins them in 2:12 to maintain honorable conduct so that, even if "the Gentiles" were to speak against them as evildoers (καταλαλοῦσιν ὑμῶν ὡς κακοποιῶν), their good works might yet be evident and lead their opponents to glorify (δοξάσωσιν) God in "the day of [his] visitation" (cf. Mt. 5:16).[33] These verses serve as a thesis statement for the ensuing injunctions (2:13–3:12) that are primarily concerned with living out Christian identity amid (potentially) hostile outsiders.[34]

---

33. Following Michaels (*1 Peter*, 119–20) and Achtemeier (*1 Peter*, 178), who see the ἐν ἡμέρᾳ ἐπισκοπῆς in 2:12 as a reference to the final judgment and vindication mentioned elsewhere in the letter (1:5, 7; 4:7, 13; 5:1, 4, 10; likewise Beare, *Epistle*, 138). Elliott (*1 Peter*, 471), on the other hand, moves away from this reading, understanding the phrase to refer to "an occasion of testing when they [non-believers] are confronted with the winsome behavior of the believers and are thereby motivated to join the Christians in their glorification of God." Selwyn (*The First Epistle of St. Peter*, 171) is in general agreement with this position. However, as Achtemeier (*1 Peter*, 178 n. 82; with extensive citations) points out, the expression as it is used elsewhere in biblical (e.g., LXX Isa. 10:3; LXX Jer. 6:15; Wis. 3:7–8; Lk. 1:68; 19:44) and Qumranic literature refers to a decisive moment of judgment.

34. Commentators are in agreement that 2:11 inaugurates a new section in the body of the letter, marked off by the use of ἀγαπητοί as well as παρακαλῶ: Hort, *Epistle*, 9–10; Selwyn, *Epistle*, 4–6; Beare, *Epistle*, 134; Kelly, *Commentary*, 102; Michaels, *1 Peter*, 115; Achtemeier, *1 Peter*, 169; Goppelt, *1 Peter*, 153; Horrell, *Epistles*, 47; Elliott, *1 Peter*, 81; Reinhard Feldmeier, *The First Letter of Peter: A Commentary on the Greek Text*, trans. Peter H. Davids (Waco, TX: Baylor, 2008), 144–5. Elliott (*1 Peter*, 81, 474–6) views 2:11–12 as constituting "a major transitional unit or hinge" that bridges the aspects of Christian identity expounded in 1:3–2:10 and the exhortations to live out this identity in 2:13–3:12 (but also through 5:11). Likewise, Selwyn (*Epistle*, 169), for whom vv. 11–12 are "at once resumptive and prefatory." Cf. also Michaels, *1 Peter*, 115.

Christians are told in 2:13–15 to accept the authority of the emperor and his governors "for the sake of the Lord" because this is God's will (ὅτι οὕτως ἐστὶν τὸ θέλημα τοῦ θεοῦ), that they might "silence the ignorance of the foolish"—that is, their false accusers (cf. 3:16). The tone of this counsel, which describes the imperial authorities as those vested with authority "to punish those who do wrong and to praise those who do right" (2:14), expresses basic confidence in the Roman mechanisms of justice. For the author, the imperial system is capable of meeting well-doing with praise (ἔπαινος), though this praise is perhaps *qualitatively* different from that in 1:7 on account of its "creaturely" origin (ἀνθρώπινη κτίσις, 2:13).[35] Nonetheless, he anticipates a forthcoming moment of divine judgment far more universal (4:5)—about which more will be said below.

In addressing slaves (2:18–25), the author exhorts them to be obedient to their masters, whether good or abusive ones, because their endurance of unjust suffering is "grace before God" (χάρις παρὰ θεῷ, 2:20).[36] What follows this statement, grating as it might be to modern ears, bears witness to the author's convictions regarding the transformative power of patient endurance. He appeals to Christ who has left them an "example" (ὑπογραμμός, 2:21) and underscores the redemptive effects of his suffering: it was by similarly enduring wrongful suffering that Christ healed their wounds, rescued them from straying, and brought them back to God (2:24–25). The implication here is quite clear: just as Christ's suffering of injustice was efficacious in transforming the world, so too would theirs be.

---

35. On κτίσις in 2:13 meaning "creature" rather than "institution" (NRSV), see Williams, "The Divinity and Humanity of Caesar"; Michaels, *1 Peter*, 54.

36. The difficult expression χάρις παρὰ θεῷ most likely reiterates τοῦτο γὰρ χάρις in 2:19 (Michaels, *1 Peter*, 142), since the two verses have in common the subject of unjust suffering that is patiently endured. Most exegetes interpret χάρις in vv. 19–20 as "favor," in which case endurance of innocent suffering wins God's approval or favorable judgment (so Kelly, *Commentary*, 116; Beare, *Epistle*, 146–7; Best, *1 Peter*, 118; Michaels, *1 Peter*, 142; Achtemeier, *1 Peter*, 198; Davids, *Epistle*, 108; Elliott, *1 Peter*, 522; reflected in the NRSV: "you have God's approval"). This makes good sense of the contrast between divine χάρις and human κλέος ("report," or NRSV: "credit"; *hapax* in NT) in 2:20a. Goppelt (*1 Peter*, 199–200), however, posits that χάρις here and elsewhere in 1 Peter is something more than a subjective disposition or attitude on God's part; rather, it is a form of divine presence. This fits better with the letter's treatment of χάρις as something that is imparted (cf. φερομένην, 1:13; δίδωσιν, 5:5) by "the God of all grace" (5:10). Its recipients must act as good stewards (οἰκονόμοι) by manifesting it in embodied practice—that is, as one's "gift" (χάρισμα) to the community (4:10; cf. Rom. 12:6; 1 Cor. 12:4–6). Thus, Goppelt takes 2:19–20 to mean that unjust suffering is a form of "God's bestowal of himself" (199) that configures the believing slave to Christ (cf. 2:21; 4:13). (For a similar interpretation, see Feldmeier, *Letter*, 171–2.) It seems to me that on this point, the divergent readings are rooted in different theological paradigms and approximate earlier Reformation-era debates over the meaning of χάρις (God's favor vs. metaphysical impartation of divine life) as well as the "modality" of Christ's suffering (vicarious vs. substitutionary).

The counsel to wives makes more explicit this doctrine of efficacious endurance.³⁷ The women are advised to accept the authority of their husbands so that the men "may be won over without a word" by their purity and reverence (3:1-2). Indeed, the Christian wife's quiet and gentle spirit is "very precious in God's sight" (3:4). Sarah is marshaled as the model obedient wife (3:6)—one who went so far as to call her husband "lord," and whom the women should imitate in doing good and standing fearlessly in the face of intimidation.³⁸ These elements raised by the author—the preciousness of the wife's submissive spirit, the radical demand of her submission, and threatening situations in which the response of fear must be resisted—suggest that the author is aware of household dynamics that must be navigated with great care. Nonetheless, he is convinced that a Christian wife's submission will effect transformation even in her non-believing husband (εἴ τινες ἀπειθοῦσιν τῷ λόγῳ, 3:1).³⁹

The author's faith in the transformative power of endurance goes beyond the *Haustafel* passages. He shows conviction, for example, that Christians falsely accused will be vindicated by their good conduct, even if enduring this involves unjust suffering (3:16b). Not coincidentally, it is at this point that he launches into what otherwise appears to be an aside on Christ's suffering and glorification (3:18-22)—in actuality, no aside at all, since he consciously draws from this narrative arc an invitation to patient suffering, as indicated by the transitional οὖν in 4:1. What cannot be missed in this arc is his emphasis on the salvific efficacy of Christ's suffering of injustice: "in order to bring you to God" (3:18). This efficacy is amplified to a cosmic level, since even "the spirits in prison" heard this proclamation of victory (3:19)—a victory that has exalted Christ at God's right hand, above even the celestial powers (3:22).⁴⁰ Just as Christ's suffering was not in vain, so their suffering is also not in vain; in and through it they become "blessed ones" (μακάριοι; 3:14; 4:14) who bear God's Spirit (4:14; cf. Isa. 11:2)—the very same Spirit who raised Jesus from the dead (3:18). In 1 Peter, as Achtemeier points out, "the events of Christ's passion become the pattern for the temporal structure of the Christians' life and fate."⁴¹

---

37. For a discussion of 3:1-6 in light of contemporaneous views of household management in Greco-Roman and Jewish sources, see Balch, *Let Wives Be Submissive*, 95-105.

38. The injunction μὴ φοβούμεναι μηδεμίαν πτόησιν (3:6; "fear no intimidation," NAB) is probably an allusion to LXX Prov. 3:25 (οὐ φοβηθήσῃ πτόησιν ἐπελθοῦσαν). The most proximate source of intimidation in context is probably the non-believing husband, though it may also apply to hostility from others (see Elliott, *1 Peter*, 574; Achtemeier, *1 Peter*, 216-17; Kelly, *Commentary*, 132).

39. On this last point, see Balch, *Let Wives Be Submissive*, 99-100.

40. For the argument that 3:18-20 refers to the announcement of Christ's victory rather than the proclamation of the gospel, and that it is a journey of ascent rather than descent, see William J. Dalton, *Christ's Proclamation to the Spirits: A Study of 1 Peter 3:18-4:6*, 2nd, fully rev. ed., Analecta Biblica 23 (Rome: Editrice Pontificio Istituto Biblico, 1989 [1965]), esp. 121-90.

41. Achtemeier, *1 Peter*, 68.

In this way, suffering becomes, in 1 Peter, the "Christian condition" in the eschaton—at least "for a little while" (ὀλίγον ἄρτι, 1:6) until their final vindication (1:7). Christ's own suffering establishes this as the norm for discipleship, just as his exaltation points to "the glory to be revealed" (5:1) for those who are faithful. The call to patient endurance and imitation of Christ issues, then, from within a particular temporal schema—one in which the present has acquired the status of the final, critical stage in the outworking of God's cosmic plan. By divine design, time is indeed "soteriologized," and by virtue of this fact bears in itself the imperative for moral action.

The robust eschatological outlook we find in 1 Peter is focused on the present with a palpable urgency—understandable, since from the author's perspective the present has become the hinge of history by virtue of the Christ-event. This construction of the present, as does any attempt to express the meaning of "now," implicates both the past and the future in particular ways. To these we now turn.

4.3 The Past in 1 Peter: Writing Empire Out of History

Within 1 Peter's temporal framework, the preceding ages emerge, above all, as periods of preparation for Jesus' manifestation, such that the past leans forward into the present eschatological moment. We see this view encapsulated in 1:20, with its assertion that Christ's manifestation was an event destined by God even before the foundation of the world. The meaning of the past is thus fully disclosed only in and through the arrival of Christ on the stage of history.

4.3.1 The Present in the Past: Reinterpreting Scripture, Reinterpreting History (1:10–12)

To elaborate more specifically the author's understanding of the past, we can turn to his handling of the biblical testimonies of Israel. While the author's interpretation of scriptural texts has been subject to much discussion,[42] both in terms of their reframing within the epistle as well as the author's view of his readers' relationship

---

42. For these, see Chapter 2, n. 95. Chapple's essay ("The Appropriation of Scripture in 1 Peter") is the most recent (2015), and helpfully engages earlier studies on the subject. I think Bauman-Martin's argument ("Speaking Jewish") that 1 Peter's appropriation of the Jewish scriptures constitutes a form of colonial violence is too reductionistic, and does not adequately take into consideration the dynamics of hybridity that have been much-discussed in postcolonial studies. Contesting interpretations or reinterpretations of texts are not inherently colonial (as Bauman-Martin contends), though they can of course be harnessed for such purposes—and often have been. We have to bear in mind, moreover, that we are here dealing with a case of two subaltern groups (Jews and early Christians), whose complex identities and agencies cannot simply be viewed as functions of the colonizer's (i.e. Rome's) strategies.

to Israel of old, here I wish to focus only on the *fact* that he has drawn from them and deployed them in the letter. I contend that such use of scripture is premised on a particular way of thinking about the past and its relationship to the present. The author's hermeneutic of scripture is derived from his hermeneutic of history: he is able to read scripture Christologically precisely because *time itself*—in this instance, past time—is inherently Christological.

This is most evident in 1:10–12, a passage which William Schutter regards as key to understanding the author's hermeneutic.[43] Here, the author states that the salvation accomplished in Christ, which the readers were already receiving by faith (κομιζόμενοι, 1:9), was long foretold by the prophets who anticipated its arrival.[44] These "made careful search and inquiry" (ἐξεζήτησαν καὶ ἐξηραύνησαν) regarding the details of the manifestation of the Messiah in history: his identity and the appointed time of his appearing (τίνα ἢ ποῖον καιρὸν),[45] as well as the suffering and glorification destined for him (τὰ εἰς Χριστὸν παθήματα καὶ τὰς μετὰ ταῦτα δόξας).[46]

---

43. See Schutter, *Hermeneutic and Composition in 1 Peter*, esp. 100–23.

44. Precisely which prophets did the author have in mind? Kelly (*The Epistles of Peter and Jude*, 59) suggests that the "obvious and natural sense" of προφῆται here is the prophetic writings of ancient Israel, and indeed, the Hebrew Bible as a whole, which the earliest Christians interpreted Christocentrically (e.g., Lk. 24). With this Achtemeier (*1 Peter*, 108 n. 42) and Bauckham ("James, 1 and 2 Peter, Jude," 310) concur. Selwyn's proposal (*Epistle*, 134) that προφῆται here includes Christian prophets is unlikely given that νῦν in 1:12 emphasizes the disclosure to the prophets as opposed to the proclamation of the gospel in the present (Chapple, "The Appropriation of Scripture in 1 Peter," 270 n. 24; similarly, Elliott, *1 Peter*, 346). For further critique of Selwyn's proposal, see Best, *1 Peter*, 83–4.

45. It is possible to take τίνα as an adjective coordinate with ποῖον so that they both modify καιρόν. In this case, the phrase τίνα ἢ ποῖον καιρόν means "what or [at] what sort of time"—that is, "when or under what circumstances" these prophecies would come to pass (so the majority of commentators: Feldmeier, *Letter*, 92; Horrell, *Epistles*, 28; Michaels, *1 Peter*, 41–2; Goppelt, *1 Peter*, 98; Kelly, *Commentary*, 60; Selwyn, *Epistle*, 135; Beare, *Epistle*, 91; Hort, *Epistle*, 51; ASV, NAB, NJB, NIV, and NLT). Spicq (*Saint Pierre*, 54) more freely renders: "quelles circonstances et quelle époque." On the other hand, if we take τίνα as a pronoun independent of ποῖον, it can mean "what person" or "what sort of person" (so Elliott, *1 Peter*, 345; Jacques Schlosser, *La Première épître de Pierre*, Commentaire biblique: Nouveau Testament 21 [Paris: Les Éditions du Cerf, 2011], 76; NRSV, RSV, NASB). This option reflects, in some way, the Petrine author's concern with the "who" of Christ—that is, his role in God's plan (e.g., 2:4–8, 21–25; 3:18–22). A balanced discussion is provided by Achtemeier (*1 Peter*, 109), who cautiously sides with the former interpretation, though he is most likely right to conclude that "certainty in this matter is unattainable."

46. There remains a question as to whether τὰ εἰς Χριστὸν παθήματα καὶ τὰς μετὰ ταῦτα δόξας ought to be understood as referring to Christ's sufferings and glorification (εἰς Χριστὸν as meaning "destined for Christ"), or that of the readers themselves (εἰς Χριστὸν as meaning "for the sake of Christ" or "the sufferings of the Christward road" [Selwyn]). See, e.g., the

It is noteworthy that the diverse historical contexts and circumstances in which these prophets lived and ministered, along with their concern for their contemporary world, are passed over entirely. What binds them together as a cluster of προφῆται is only the fact that they strained to look forward in time, into the eschatological salvation disclosed to the readers—"the grace meant for you" (1:10). Indeed, it was the very "Spirit of Christ" in these prophets (τὸ ἐν αὐτοῖς πνεῦμα Χριστοῦ, 1:11) who animated their feats of foretelling. Whether "πνεῦμα Χριστοῦ" is interpreted as an objective genitive construction or a subjective one,[47] the forcefully Christological nature of the author's view of time remains evident. The past, for him, is permeated by Christ's presence—whether understood as his pre-incarnate, Spirit-mediated presence at work in the seers of old, or by the prophetic anticipations of his arrival. Christ is established as protagonist in the historical drama of Israel—a story that now extends into the lives of the letter's recipients: "to [the prophets] it was revealed that they were serving not themselves but you" (1:12). This point is underscored by the emphatic recurrence of pronouns in the Greek: οἷς ἀπεκαλύφθη ὅτι οὐχ ἑαυτοῖς ὑμῖν δὲ διηκόνουν αὐτά, ἃ νῦν ἀνηγγέλη ὑμῖν διὰ τῶν εὐαγγελισαμένων ὑμᾶς.[48] The author's practice of reading

---

discussions in Achtemeier, *1 Peter*, 110–11; Michaels, *1 Peter*, 44–5; Selwyn, *Epistle*, 136, cf. 300–3. Hort's contention (*Epistle*, 54) that the εἰς here "is substantially the same" as that in 1:10 (τῆς εἰς ὑμᾶς χάριτος; "the grace that should come to you," KJV) is persuasive. Beare (*Epistle*, 92) contends that these two εἰς phrases are "constructed in careful parallelism ... thus emphasizing the two themes of prophetic utterance—the manifestation of Christ in humiliation and in glory, and the gifts bestowed upon [Christians]." With Schutter (*Hermeneutic and Composition in 1 Peter*, 107–8), however, I see no reason to make these mutually exclusive options, especially in a letter that upholds Christ as an "example" in whose steps his disciples must follow (2:21). Hort (*Epistle*, 55) is likewise open to this possibility. On the related theme of messianic woes, see Dubis, *Messianic Woes in First Peter*, 110–17.

47. The genitive Χριστοῦ can still be understood in a variety of ways. The Spirit may be "of Christ" in the sense that it foretold Christ's suffering and glorification to the prophets of old. This reading fits well with the author's elaboration that this Spirit bore witness to τὰ εἰς Χριστὸν παθήματα καὶ τὰς μετὰ ταῦτα δόξας (1:11). Alternatively, τὸ ... πνεῦμα Χριστοῦ can refer to the Spirit which belongs to the person of Christ or originates from him in some way—options made possible by the author's conviction that he existed even before the creation of the world (1:20). These interpretive possibilities also allow for the Spirit to be the pre incarnate Christ himself, i.e. his spirit form prior to his bodily existence in history. It appears difficult to nail down one clear reading of this particular construction, and the diversity of conclusions among commentators reflects this ambiguity: see, e.g., Elliott, *1 Peter*, 346; Achtemeier, *1 Peter*, 109–10; Michaels, *1 Peter*, 44; Brox, *Der erste Petrusbrief*, 69–70; Schlosser, *Épître*, 79; Davids, *Epistle*, 62.

48. The letter's emphasis on readers as the "target audience" of God's salvific action (e.g., εἰς ὑμᾶς in 1:4, 10, 25) has led Elliott (*1 Peter*, 336, 353) to speak of the "for-you-ness" of its presentation of the gospel.

Christ and the Christian community back into Israel's scriptures and history corroborates with the practice seen in other New Testament writings (e.g., 1 Cor. 10:4; Col. 1:15–17), and is probably reflective of a shared set of hermeneutical principles in early Christian exegesis. Indeed, he may well have agreed with Paul's conviction that the scriptures "were written down to instruct us, on whom the ends of the ages have come" (1 Cor. 10:11).[49]

As an index of the author's conception of the past and its relationship to the present, his reading of Isaianic texts is perhaps most paradigmatic.[50] The eternally-enduring "word of the Lord" promised by the prophet is the good news about Jesus Christ announced to the Anatolian readers (1:25; cf. Isa. 40:8).[51] Jesus' passion and glorification, from the author's perspective, identifies him both as the Isaianic cornerstone chosen by God but rejected by the builders (2:4–7; cf. Isa. 28:16) and as the "stone of stumbling" (2:8, KJV; cf. Isa. 8:14). Christ is also the well-known suffering Servant of YHWH (2:22–24; cf. Isa. 53:5–7, 9, 12), so prominent in Deutero-Isaiah, whose crushing brings redemption to many. Once again, the author's reading of these texts reflects his conviction that, like the other prophets, Isaiah directly bore witness to Christ's suffering and glorification.

Yet the author's exegesis of Isaiah is not only Christological but also ecclesiological in tone. By this I mean that the prophecies are applied directly to the praxis of the communities to whom 1 Peter is addressed. The "word of the Lord" spoken of by Isaiah is not only identified as the gospel concerning Jesus: it is the same good news that has been proclaimed to readers (τὸ ῥῆμα τὸ εὐαγγελισθὲν εἰς ὑμᾶς) and has become the source of their spiritual rebirth (1:23–25), beckoning them to live in accordance with their new identity in Christ (2:1–3). Likewise, Isaiah's oracle of the cornerstone bears immediate relevance to his readers and their circumstances. On the one hand, it calls the readers to be built into a spiritual house[52] and exercise their holy priesthood through the offering of spiritual sacrifices (2:5), but it also serves as an explanation for the predestined disobedience of those who reject the gospel (2:7–8). The prophecies concerning the suffering Servant of YHWH, moreover, were not only fulfilled in Christ, but through this very fulfillment they provide Christians, especially Christian slaves, with an "example" (ὑπογραμμός) so that they might imitate Jesus' endurance in suffering

---

49. On Paul's practice of "ecclesiocentric hermeneutics," see Richard B. Hays, *Echoes of Scripture in the Letters of Paul* (New Haven, CT: Yale University Press, 1993), 84–121.

50. For more detailed discussions of 1 Peter's Christological exegesis of the following Isaianic texts, see Moyise, "Isaiah in 1 Peter," 178–83; Horrell, "Jesus Remembered?"

51. The author's modification here, replacing τὸ . . . ῥῆμα κυρίου for τὸ . . . ῥῆμα τοῦ θεοῦ ἡμῶν (LXX Isa. 40:8, reflecting the MT's וּדְבַר־אֱלֹהֵינוּ), most likely indicates that he intends this construction as an objective genitive ("the word concerning the Lord [i.e. Jesus]") rather than a subjective genitive ("the word spoken by the Lord"). "From [the author's] perspective, the word that endures forever is the word about Jesus Christ, his suffering and glorification" (Elliott, *1 Peter*, 391). Cf. Moyise, "Isaiah in 1 Peter," 177; Achtemeier, *1 Peter*, 142.

52. On which, see Section 6.2 below.

(2:21). Summing up the intertextual dynamics between 1 Peter and Isaiah, Moyise states: "[The author's] indebtedness to Isaiah is clear and goes beyond mere prooftexting. It is a word that speaks to his reader's circumstances."[53]

The author's exegesis of Isaiah illustrates *in nuce* his twofold conviction, expressed in 1:10–12, that the prophets pointed forward to Christ's suffering and glorification, and that they addressed directly the announcement of the gospel to his first-century readers. This perspective on history engenders a paradox of continuity and discontinuity. On the one hand, it forges links between the past and the "now" of the readers by pointing to the prophets of Israel who prophesied of the gospel now made known to them—who "were serving not themselves but you." On the other hand, that past is also regarded as radically discontinuous with the present on account of what has been revealed. The prophets could only search and inquire in vision and oracle; it is only those living in the present who have truly experienced what they foresaw. The tension of this paradox is then drawn upon by the author to launch into exhortation: "Therefore, gird up . . ." (Διὸ ἀναζωσάμενοι, 1:13). The aspect of continuity highlights the duration of God's plan and preparation, while the aspect of discontinuity underscores the privileged position of the recipients above the prophets and even the angels (1:12). Because both aspects are true, they must now lay hold of the present and not look back to their former desires stoked by ignorance (1:14). The past, like the present, generates a moral imperative of its own.

The past in 1 Peter is neither dead nor immobile but alive, urging itself upon the present. It does so through Jesus of Nazareth, who by his suffering and glorification has transposed his followers into the unfolding story of Israel. Israel's story has become their story. For this reason, in his exegesis of prophetic texts the author of 1 Peter makes no attempt to build a bridge between an "original context" and the situation of his readers, as a modern expositor might do. For him, there is no "bridge" as such, because that "original context" *is* the present in which he and his readers were living. Isaiah's word, stone, and servant have no meaning apart from Christ and those who follow him. The past is charged with the "now" of Jesus Christ, and has broken into the eschatological present.

4.3.2 *The Contest for History and the Politics of Identity*

In the way it reads the sacred texts of Israel, 1 Peter participates alongside other schools of Jewish exegesis of the time in a discursive contest of meaning concerning the scripturized past.[54] The author's aim is not merely to provide a "correct" reading of scripture, but rather to root his readers in a past out of which they emerge as the fulfillment of God's blueprint for history. They are drawn into a narrative that

---

53. Moyise, "Isaiah in 1 Peter," 188.

54. This is the overarching thesis of Schutter, *Hermeneutic and Composition in 1 Peter*, though the attention there is largely focused on parallels between 1 Peter and exegesis at Qumran.

begins, in effect, even before creation (1:20), embracing Noah (3:20), Sarah and other "holy women" of long ago (3:5–6), and, last but not least, Abraham (3:6), the paradigmatic alien and sojourner (πάροικος καὶ παρεπίδημος, LXX Gen. 23:4; cf. 2:11).[55] These men and women of old have truly become forerunners whose lives and experiences, as recorded in scriptural testimony, both prefigure the readers' struggle and furnish them with models for doing God's will in the world. In summoning these forerunners, the author situates his readers in a genealogy based on spiritual kinship into which they are incorporated by virtue of their new birth.

This accounts for why he no longer thinks of them as Gentiles and repeatedly contrasts the gospel's demands with the misbehaving of "the nations" (2:12; 4:3), and also why he applies to his readers the call to holiness issued in the Torah without mediation (1:15–16; cf. Lev. 11:44). Similarly, the Psalms and Proverbs are deployed as injunctions that are immediately relevant for their struggles (e.g., 3:10–12 citing Ps. 34:12–16; and 5:5 citing Prov. 3.34). The readers do not merely belong to the new family in some vague or analogous sense. They have been ransomed from the futile ways of their Gentile ancestors and have truly become members of God's own family: "once you were not a people, but now you are God's people" (2:10; cf. Hos. 1:6). Such unqualified application of language that was in former times exclusively reserved for the tribes of Israel is, as Achtemeier points out, "more than simply illustrative—it is foundational and constitutive for the Christian community in a way that has not always been recognized by those who have studied this epistle."[56] The interpretation of scripture in 1 Peter thus lays claim to Israel's scripturized past in a particular way and, by means of this, fashions out of it a narrative of Christian identity for its readers.

What is most salient to our examination of the letter's construction of time, however, is not simply that 1 Peter reads scriptural texts in a Christological way, but rather that it construes *history*—and time as a whole—in a Christological way. As I mentioned earlier, the author interprets scripture Christologically because time is itself Christological. His biblical hermeneutic is, in other words, grounded in metaphysics—in a cosmology centered on the events of Jesus' death and resurrection. To return to his point regarding the prophets of old (1:10–12): their ministry was not for themselves—nor, presumably, for their contemporaries—but for those who live in the age of Christ's manifestation. The past only has meaning relative to the present, illumined as it were by Christ's entrance into the world.

Construals of the past are nothing short of political, and can even be aggressive in their own way. As I have shown in Section 1.3.1, the reconstruction of the past—that is, its selective retrieval, evocation, or "use" in the present—is an ideological process conditioned by power relations. Malaysian historian Farish Noor writes

---

55. Liebengood (*Eschatology*, see esp. 175–214) proposes that the unifying narrative substructure at work in 1 Peter is provided by Zech. 9–14. See Section 1.1.2 above for a brief discussion of this option.

56. Achtemeier, *1 Peter*, 69.

that "[t]he recounting of the past and the act of remembering our manifold histories are as much a psycho-social endeavour as they are political and politicised ones."[57] The act of remembering is not innocent. It is molded (or re-molded) within an individual's or a community's experience, interests, and interpretation of concrete, material conditions. As such, the past is not "homogeneous, empty time, but time filled by the presence of the now [*Jetztzeit*]."[58]

In the way it reads Israel's scripture—and thus its history—1 Peter enters the realm of identity politics, wielding what we might regard as a form of "revisionism" that recuperates the past at the service of the gospel and those who believe. Contest for the meaning of Israel's past and its politics of identity was, of course, by no means foreign to Jewish and Christian groups in the first century AD. We find ample evidence for such phenomena in Second-Temple Jewish and Christian literature, from Qumran to the later New Testament writings.[59] Yet, for life in the shadow of the Roman Empire, these competing identity narratives cannot be safely relegated to the realm of differing ideas. They acquire varying degrees of potential as forms of counter-discourse to imperial politics, depending on the extent to which they resist or absorb the identities inculcated by Rome's imperial discourse.

David Novitz points out that, because the way in which humans see themselves shapes the way they behave toward themselves and toward others, the narration of identity becomes a quintessentially political process—one in which the state has great stakes.

> The State invariably assumes a proprietorial interest in our individual identities, and is concerned to see them develop in certain ways rather than others. Schools,

---

57. Farish A. Noor, "History, and the Toys That Fascists Play With," in *What Your Teacher Didn't Tell You: The Annexe Lectures, Vol. 1* (Petaling Jaya, Malaysia: Matahari Books, 2009), 9.

58. Walter Benjamin, *Illuminations: Essays and Reflections*, ed. Hannah Arendt, trans. Harry Zohn (New York, NY: Schocken Books, 1969), 261.

59. One of the most provocative examples of this in the New Testament is Jn 8:31–59, in which the Johannine Jesus effectively cuts off his opponents from Abrahamic patrimony—and, consequently, an entire past—with the shocking pronouncement: "You are from your father the devil" (8:44). Elsewhere in the Fourth Gospel, concern with questions of identity is also evident in passages such as 1:47 and 4:9, 22. The scholarly debate over the referents of οἱ Ἰουδαῖοι in John points to the complex ways in which this text approached the question of identity in the nascent days of Christianity. Cf. Daniel Boyarin, *Border Lines: The Partition of Judaeo-Christianity* (Philadelphia, PA: University of Pennsylvania Press, 2004), esp. 87–147.

For a study of construal of the past and its relationship to communal identity at Qumran, see Maxine L. Grossman, *Reading for History in the Damascus Document: A Methodological Study*, vol. XLV, Studies on the Texts of the Desert of Judah (Leiden, Boston, and Cologne: Brill, 2002). Also worth mentioning here is a work in Pauline Studies that has generated much discussion: Daniel Boyarin, *A Radical Jew: Paul and the Politics of Identity* (Berkeley, CA: University of California, 1994).

the media, and religion are only some of the institutions which are used to convey narrative structures in terms of which we are encouraged to see ourselves. They offer ideals of personhood—whether in history lessons, deportment manuals, or popular magazines.... They do this precisely because those who are dominant within the State often wish to prevent people from adopting damaging or potentially dangerous narrative identities.[60]

Novitz's key insight here is that the narration of the past is crucial to political life, being one of the means by which a shared identity and solidarity are created. Any political community, whether a village, a nation-state, or an empire, has a vested interest in how its past is constructed and memorialized.

The practices of the imperial cults in ritual, iconography, and architecture, though by no means homogeneous, served to legitimize and normalize the presence of Rome in Anatolia. From the perspective of statecraft, the cults can be thought of as apparatuses that narrated identity in a specific way for the inhabitants of Asia Minor—chiefly, that of the Anatolian body as the rightful object of Roman power. In the Asian decree of 9 BC and in the myth of perpetual empire, the construction of this identity takes explicit narrative form: history unfolds in a pre-determined way such that the proper response to Rome is submission. By means of the imperial festivals, events in the lives of the emperors and their families are narrated via ritual and celebration into the daily grind of local communities, promoting and securing their sociopolitical dependence on the imperial center. The "ideal personhood" instilled here is clear: the Anatolian body defined as dependent, imperial subject—in Foucault's terms, a "docile body."[61]

Once we consider the inherently political nature of identity-making, the self-understanding of the Christian community constructed by 1 Peter's retelling of the past becomes more electric. In its departures from the "story" told in the imperial cults, the Petrine narrative must be evaluated in terms of its destabilizing potential. "To challenge ... narrative structures [fostered by the State] is, of course, to act politically; so that the politics of narrative identity can easily reach into the core of State politics."[62] The recollection of the past in 1 Peter locates the unfolding of history in the hands of the one true God and reconstitutes the letter's readers, regardless of their ethnic and national origins, into one "holy nation" of "God's

---

60. David Novitz, "Art, Narrative, and Human Nature," in *Memory, Identity, Community: The Idea of Narrative in the Human Sciences*, ed. Lewis P. Hinchman and Sandra Hinchman (Albany, NY: State University of New York Press, 1997), 153.

61. "A body is docile that may be subjected, used, transformed and improved" (Michel Foucault, *Discipline and Punish: The Birth of the Prison*, trans. Alan Sheridan [Harmondsworth: Penguin, 1979], 136). It should be noted, however, that Foucault was chiefly concerned with regulation by means of physical coercion.

62. Novitz, "Art, Narrative, and Human Nature," 153.

people," situating them in a temporal schema that lays aside the Empire's view of itself as the apex of human achievement. Seen in these terms, the identity which the author narrates is fundamentally political in nature. In 1 Peter there is no past of cosmic self-destruction from which Augustus and his successors rescued Anatolian civilization. There is only that past in which God in his supreme foreknowledge directed the world toward "the end of all things," the manifestation of Christ. That past was dark not because of any political chaos but because of the readers' captivity to the useless practices of their ancestors (1:18) and their consequent alienation from the true God (2:10; 4:3). In that same past, however, the Spirit of Christ was already at work in prophet, vision, and oracle, announcing beforehand the culmination of history in the messianic age. It is only by adhering to the gospel and the life of discipleship it demands that humans can see the past for what it is—not a record of the triumph of imperial machinations, but the execution of the divine blueprint of redemption.

In 1 Peter's retelling of history, imperial accomplishments are provincialized, and the self-understanding of entire groups within Anatolian society radically reconfigured. The mechanisms of empire are to be honored (2:13–17), it is true, but what is said in this instance only amplifies what is left unsaid: the historical self-representation of the Empire as the architect of peace (see Section 1.3.1 above) is passed over in silence. If the council of Asia summed up its past with the word "war," the author reduces that same past to ignorance of God (1:14). Rome is, if anything, not so much the pacifier of peoples as the entity that must be pacified with diplomatic obedience "for the Lord's sake" (2:13), even if its flawed judicial systems are entirely capable of punishing the innocent (3:17; 4:16). The Petrine vision of the past places God and Christ at the center, decentering the history of Roman power in Anatolia and writing the Empire out of history.

4.4 The Future in 1 Peter: Complicating the Things to Come

In 1 Peter, the future, like the past, flows (back) into the present. The author places it in front of his readers and draws from it as the basis of ethical instruction—for example, in encouraging them to persevere amid trials (1:6–8; 5:10), or exhorting them to persevere in a way of life that puts them at odds with wider society (2:12). Living at the inauguration of the last age, his eschatological vision embraces the future as the era of the fullness of salvation and glory (5:1), marked by the reappearance of Christ in history (5:4). The eschatological intensity he feels in the present is in part formed by his vision of the future. This present-focus, in turn, projects into that future a world which, as I will show below, challenges the Roman Empire's narration of the future in significant ways.

Let us begin by looking at a sketch of the author's construal of the future. He anticipates the reappearance of Christ in the world (1:7, 13; 4:13) and the glory that will be revealed at his return (5:1, 4; cf. 4:14). Although divine judgment has already begun within the house of God (4:17a), the coming "day of visitation" (2:12) will be one on which both the living and the dead will be brought to divine judgment (4:5).[63] God will judge all impartially, according to the deeds of each (1:17), meting out vindication for the faithful (5:6, 10) and chastisement for those who disobey the gospel, "the ungodly and the sinners" (4:17b–18). The righteous deeds of Christians in this life will, on that day, draw praise, glory, and honor to God even from non-believers (2:12; cf. 1:7). In that final appointed moment (ἐν καιρῷ ἐσχάτῳ, 1:5), the imperishable, undefiled, and unfading inheritance kept in heaven for them will finally be revealed (1:4).[64] Given all this, the proper orientation of the Christian toward the future is for good reason captured in the expression, "living hope" (ἐλπίδα ζῶσαν, 1:3).[65] Followers of Christ must let the prospect of final reward fuel their joy in

---

63. On "the day of visitation," see n. 33 above.

64. For a very different reading of these passages, see Parker, "The Eschatology of 1 Peter." Passages regarded by most scholars as pertaining to the final advent of Christ (1:4–5, 7, 13; 2:12; 4:13; 5:1) are consistently interpreted by Parker as referring instead to the first advent of Christ in history. "[The Petrine author's] concern is not with what is going to happen, but with explaining for the churches of Asia what is happening, of making sense of a situation which gave him (and them?) cause for anxiety" (31). All instances of ἀποκάλυψις in the letter, Parker argues, refer not to Christ's anticipated reappearance but rather to his continuously being revealed in and through his suffering disciples (following but extrapolating Hort; see n. 21 above). While Parker's exegesis in most cases is commended by his attentiveness to possibilities in the Greek, the outcomes often fit awkwardly into the wider context. It is difficult to see, for example, how the inheritance in 1:4, in light of vv. 6–7, is not an awaited one, but rather something that is already given, as Parker argues (*idem*, 28). Similarly, the reading of ἀποκάλυψις in 4:13 as something that is already happening, i.e. Christ's revelation of glory in the present suffering of his followers (not at his own second coming), demands that they "be glad and shout for joy" at a time of tribulation when, the author says, judgment is being passed even on the household of God (4:17a), and "it is hard for the righteous to be saved" (4:18, citing Prov. 11:31). Overall, it seems to me that Parker's proposals are *possible*, but not plausible, readings.

65. Martin Williams (*The Doctrine of Salvation in the First Letter of Peter* [Cambridge: Cambridge University Press, 2011], 153–4) contends, on syntactical grounds, that the Christian's hope is "living" because it is based on the resurrection of Jesus from the dead evoked in the same verse . Concurring, Achtemeier (*1 Peter*, 95) makes the case that the use of the participial form (ζῶσαν) rules out seeing life as the object of ἐλπίς ("hope of/for life"; though 1505 1852 1 vg[mss] sy[h] bo and some patristic witnesses attest to the variant ἐλπίδα ζωῆς); rather, "living hope" here refers to hope that is not in vain (dead) but is grounded on Jesus' resurrection. Michaels (*1 Peter*, 19) links ζῶσαν instead to the new birth indicated by the preceding ἀναγεννήσας. Brox (*Der erste Petrusbrief*, 61) embraces both options: this "living hope" has for its prerequisite (*Voraussetzung*) Jesus' resurrection, through which the readers have been born anew (so Elliott, *1 Peter*, 334 and Horrell, *Epistles*, 24).

present times, even as the genuineness of their faith is tested by the fire of suffering (1:6–7).[66]

Working with this basic sketch, we can move on to the ways in which the author's construal of the future disrupts that which is, by comparison, envisioned in the imperial cults. For the purposes of the task at hand, I will focus on two aspects of his eschatological outlook: (1) the dynamics of hiddenness and revelation in the *parousia* (ἀποκάλυψις; 1:7, 13; 4:13); and (2) the emphasis on permanence as a quality of God's future.

4.4.1 Hiddenness, Revelation, and Reserve: De-Colonizing the Future

Michaels observes that although 1 Peter does not fit into the genre of "apocalypse," it "nevertheless shares with certain Jewish apocalyptic writings the notion of a Christ now hidden but waiting to be revealed."[67] What makes 1 Peter unique among contemporary apocalyptic texts such as 4 Ezra and 2 Baruch is the distinctive Christian conviction that the Messiah is Jesus of Nazareth.[68] Though conceived long ago in God's foreknowledge, he remained "hidden" until his manifestation (φανερωθέντος) in the appointed age (1:20). Jesus has, however, been "hidden" again, having gone into heaven where he is seated at God's right hand (3:22), where he is unseen even to those who believe in and love him (1:8). Thrice, the author describes his anticipated reappearance in the world as an "unveiling" or "apocalypse" (ἀποκάλυψις, 1:7; 1:13; 4:13). This is the crowning event of the letter's eschatology (5:4; cf. 5:1). The Petrine temporal schema delays God's decisive, eschatological fullness to an anticipated yet unseen future time.[69] The world is not yet as it will be.

---

66. The pronoun ᾧ in ἐν ᾧ ἀγαλλιᾶσθε (1:6) can have two possible antecedents: (1) if masculine, to καιρῷ (ἐσχάτῳ); or (2) if neuter, to the entire thought in 1:3–5. For a detailed discussion of each possibility, see Williams, *The Doctrine of Salvation*, 165. In either case, the motive for Christian joy remains eschatological—it is either the appointed time of final reward or the triad of new birth, living hope, and imperishable inheritance. There is no need, as some commentators do, to take ἀγαλλιᾶσθε as a present tense verb with a future meaning, thus deferring the act of rejoicing to the finalized eschaton itself (see the discussion in Mark Dubis, *1 Peter: A Handbook on the Greek Text* [Waco, TX: Baylor University Press, 2010], 10). Rejoicing can certainly take place in the present by way of anticipation of the eschatological reward(s), even amid suffering (4:13), especially when salvation is already experienced by way of foretaste (1:9; cf. Mt. 5:12).

67. Michaels, *1 Peter*, lxix.

68. Michaels, *1 Peter*, lxx. Along similar lines, John J. Collins (*The Apocalyptic Imagination*, 268, 278–9) states that Christian apocalypticism was distinguished from its Jewish counterpart by two characteristics: (1) a realized messianic eschatology, i.e. the belief that the Messiah had already come; and (2) the conviction that the Messiah was Jesus of Nazareth.

69. Michaels, *1 Peter*, lxx.

In the imperial cults, things are quite different. The present is hyperextended into a stable, unchanging future that remains captive to "the perpetual rule of the Romans." That future is secured in turn by at least two other ideological apparatuses discussed in the previous chapter: the myth of uninterrupted continuity in the line of succession, and unwavering confidence in Rome's divinely-ordained, unstoppable rise in history—what Price terms "the ideology of imperial victory." The temporal discourse of the imperial cults is aimed at guaranteeing the present in the future—that is, "by preventing the imagination from imagining the end of the world."[70] In her book *Time and Social Theory*, Barbara Adam, following Torsten Hägerstrand, describes such efforts as attempts to "colonize" the future.[71] This type of colonization is characterized by the endeavor to regulate and eliminate uncertainty in the future with an array of practices and institutions. In modern societies, architecture, banking, law, and insurance are targeted at "extending our present to include and secure the future as a resource *now*."[72] Insuring one's life and property, for example, protects one against the vicissitudes of a potentially dangerous and unmanageable future. In Roman Anatolia, cultic veneration of the imperial family—in ritual, image, architecture—bound the rhythms of daily life to the imperial center and propagated a world in which stability and peace were inherently linked to Roman flourishing. All these elements conveyed the assurance, "It is as it always will be." They lay siege on the future in order to legitimize and sustain domination in the present.

By contrast, the articulation of the future in 1 Peter bears marks of eschatological reserve and thus an element of instability. The Messiah is now "hidden" though he continues to reign as God's co-regent (3:22), and it is only in his second and final reappearance in the world that the definitive, eschatological state will be made known. Even for believers, the future promises no hard certitude: God will judge *all* people impartially according to their deeds (1:17)—including his own (4:17a; 5:5b–6), and so they must persevere if they want to obtain the final reward (1:7; 5:1–4, 8–9). This prospect should instill in them the attitude of reverential fear (ἐν φόβῳ, 1:17; cf. 2:17). God's future, to return to Adam's phraseology, resists colonization. It lies in the hands of the sovereign God and demands from all who subscribe to it the posture of humble expectation (5:6). Absent are human mechanisms that can tame or secure its outcomes. Humans are not, regardless of how powerful they are, the architects or rule-makers of the Petrine conceptualization of history. Here, the theocentric quality of the future negates the imperial vision, relativizing Rome's achievements and recasting its "invincibility" as sheer hubris. It is God and his Christ who reign over cosmos and time.

We judge whether or not an airplane is "on course" by gauging the extent to which it is moving toward a stipulated destination. By envisioning a different *telos* to the passage of time, 1 Peter implicated the imperial charter as "off course." Wayne

---

70. Friesen, *Imperial Cults*, 130.
71. Barbara Adam, *Time and Social Theory* (Oxford: Polity Press, 1990), 138–9.
72. Adam, *Time and Social Theory*, 139. (Emphasis in original.)

Meeks has argued that early Christian eschatologies "disestablished" the world with their alternative endings—undermining dominant cultural systems, relativizing claims to power, and providing rationales for Christian behavior that ran against the social grain.[73] They referred all of time and, indeed, life itself to the anticipated, definitive state of affairs in Christ. As far as the recipients of 1 Peter are concerned, we can already detect the beginnings of the social strain exerted by their eschatology in the references to suffering, hardship, and estrangement so prominent in the letter. For the author, if non-Christians around them could no longer understand where they were headed, it was only natural (4:4).

4.4.2 Judgment and Vindication: Relativizing Roman Justice in Anatolia

The author of 1 Peter, as I have already mentioned, does concede a basic level of confidence in the efficacy of Anatolian judicial mechanisms. The emperor and his governor can still be trusted to punish wrongdoers and reward those who do right (2:14), such that those who bring false accusations against Christians will be silenced (2:15) and put to shame (3:16). But this confidence is limited: not even Rome can guarantee justice at all times. The innocent are still vulnerable to wrongful punishment (2:17), especially believers who are charged with being Christians (4:16).[74] What, then, of Rome's pledge of *iustitia*? The Empire could, after all, turn against them.

By invoking God as "the one who stands ready to judge the living and the dead" (4:5), the author points to a more reliable source of justice for Christians living under Roman rule in Anatolia. The prospect of divine vindication in the future means that they have recourse beyond imperial mechanisms of justice. A wedge is driven between Christians and the body politic: all earthly systems of justice must be kept at arm's length and accepted only with bounded allegiance. The tables can and will be turned: if Christians have to face accusations and defend themselves in the present (cf. 3:15–16), it is their accusers who will have to face God in the impending day of judgment.[75] For now, those who suffer on account of their faith must entrust their cause to the faithful Creator (πιστῷ κτίστῃ) while persevering in doing good (4:19).

The author insists that the scope of divine judgment will encompass everyone who has ever walked the planet: ζῶντας καὶ νεκρούς—an expression which extends God's judgment to span all time.[76] The universality and absolute reliability of divine justice—the one whom Christians call Father is "the one who judges without

---

73. Wayne A. Meeks, *The Origins of Christian Morality: The First Two Centuries* (New Haven, CT/London: Yale University Press, 1993), 174–210.

74. On this, see Horrell, "The Label Χριστιανός."

75. Horrell, *Epistles*, 77; Michaels, *1 Peter*, 234.

76. On this expression Michaels (*1 Peter*, 235) comments: "The universality of the phrase is a universality of time: God is Lord and Judge not only over the present, but over the past as well."

partiality" (τὸν ἀπροσωπολήμπτως κρίνοντα, 1:17)—implies that God will bring under scrutiny even those who are guardians of civic justice in this life, including Caesar and his officials (2:13–14). The invocation of God as κτίστης in 4:19 stands in contrast to their creaturely status (cf. ἀνθρωπίνῃ κτίσει, 2:13): they, too, are subject to the one Creator and Judge of all. Before the Father's impartial eye all human beings will stand on level ground, whether emperor, governor, or the elite powerbroker who presents himself as a guarantor of justice. By absolutizing the divine justice that will be meted out "in the revelation of Jesus Christ," the Petrine vision of the future puts the emperor and his auxiliaries in their place, relativizing both their reliability and their power as arbiters of justice in this world. The fullness of *iustitia* will indeed come—but it is not yet.

4.4.3 The Rhetoric of Impermanence: Circumscribing Empire

The durability of God's redemptive work in Christ is a powerful motif in 1 Peter, and constitutes an important part of the author's construal of the future. This theme can be seen in several places throughout the letter. In 1:3–4, we read that God has given a new birth (ἀναγεννήσας, v. 3) to his readers. Two aspects of this new birth are relevant for the present consideration: (1) it has been accomplished through Jesus' resurrection from the dead (δι' ἀναστάσεως Ἰησοῦ Χριστοῦ ἐκ νεκρῶν, v. 3); and (2) it has made believers heirs of a divine inheritance, described in turn with three α-*privatum* adjectives: "imperishable," "undefiled," and "unfading" (ἄφθαρτον καὶ ἀμίαντον καὶ ἀμάραντον; 1:4).[77] The new birth is thus linked to imperishability in two ways: by its *means* (having taken place through the imperishability of Jesus in the face of death), and by its *orientation* (leading to an imperishable future inheritance).[78] This is hardly surprising, since it is the God who raised Jesus from the dead who has also "re-begotten" them; he is thus "Father" to both (1:3, 17). Quite fittingly, then, the blood of the (imperishable) sacrificial Lamb with which they have been ransomed—and with which they have been sprinkled (1:2)—is later contrasted with "perishable things, (like) silver and gold" (φθαρτοῖς, ἀργυρίῳ ἢ χρυσίῳ, 1:18; cf. 1:2). Likewise, genuine faith in Jesus survives the testing of fire because it is more precious than perishable gold (1:7). This motif of imperishability is furthered in another place, where the Christian birthright is said to originate not from perishable (human) seed but from the imperishable (divine) seed of God's word (ἀναγεγεννημένοι οὐκ ἐκ σπορᾶς φθαρτῆς ἀλλὰ ἀφθάρτου, 1:23).[79] Not coincidentally, the latter is described as "abiding" (μένοντος), that is, resisting the decaying effects of time—a point stressed again in the deployment of a text from Isaiah (μένει εἰς τὸν αἰῶνα, 1:25; cf. Isa. 40:8), where it is contrasted with the ephemerality of grass and flowers. The

---

77. For Beare (*Epistle*, 83–4), these adjectives mean that "the inheritance is untouched by death, unstained by evil, unimpaired by time."
78. On the relationship between new birth and imperishability, see n. 8 above.
79. See the discussion on the possible meanings of this "seed" in n. 7 above.

imperishable word-seed brings forth imperishable fruit: both in the heart of the believing wife (3:4) and in the unfading crown of glory promised to faithful elders (5:4).

On the basis of these texts, we can see that permanence is a signature of the divine realm and the redeemed order, whereas decay is characteristic of the unredeemed, created order. Feldmeier writes that, in 1 Peter,

> [t]he divine is characterized by its independence from what is regarded as the essence of this world, namely the maelstrom of transitoriness that appears in destruction, contamination, and aging, and destroys all beauty and goodness.[80]

One of the core soteriological convictions of the epistle is precisely that divine imperishability has broken into creation: in Christ, God has "opened up a new horizon in the middle of the perishable world."[81] It is crucial that this Petrine antinomy not be allowed to remain in the sphere of speculative metaphysics. Rather, it must be situated in the concrete historical conditions, i.e. the sociopolitical realities of empire, in which the first readers of 1 Peter lived. The tension this may have generated for the letter's original readers immediately becomes palpable.

In the Asian decree, the proconsul Maximus described a cosmos that "had deteriorated and suffered misfortune" and "would gladly have accepted its own destruction" (ἥδιστα ἂν δεξαμένωι φθοράν) had Augustus not been born to save it from wreckage. It is Caesar who, in the proper time, rescues the world by restoring its form (σχῆμα), such that the Augustan moment can be justly considered the "beginning of life and existence" (ἀρχὴν τοῦ βίου καὶ τῆς ζωῆς) for all.[82] The mythic construction of Rome's perpetual rule, built on the pillars of uninterrupted imperial succession and mystified in its ideology of inexorable victory, thus becomes key in ensuring the continuation of this revivification and life-giving schema.[83] The Roman sociopolitical order—implemented by praxes such as martial power, taxation, and conquest—is thereby naturalized, conceived as a matter of cosmic necessity. In typical fashion, hegemony "asserts as normative and universal what are in fact particular and contingent ways of perceiving the world."[84]

The manner in which Rome represented itself to its subjects can be further illuminated by Franz Rosenzweig's critique of the state. In *The Star of Redemption*, Rosenzweig argues that states secure the consent of the governed by attempting to

---

80. Feldmeier, "Salvation and Anthropology in First Peter," 210.
81. Feldmeier, "Salvation and Anthropology in First Peter," 211.
82. *OGIS* 458.6–10.
83. On the eternity of the Empire, see Section 3.3 above.
84. Portier-Young, *Apocalypse Against Empire*, 12. See also Daniel Miller, "The Limits of Dominance," in *Domination and Resistance*, ed. Daniel Miller, Michael Rowlands, and Christopher Y. Tilley, One World Archaeology, no. 3 (London and New York, NY: Routledge, 1995), 63–79.

"give to the peoples eternity in time."[85] By this he means that the state presents itself as an anchoring force in the ever-changing lives of its citizens, purporting itself to be the people's guardian against the destabilizing winds of change. This self-representation provides the rationale for its exercise of power on the bodies of its citizens, whether lawfully or by coercion. Nonetheless, change in the world, for Rosenzweig, is both inevitable and real. Because of this, the state is forced to retain power by masking social change in the rhetoric of preservation and renewal. Nevertheless, its self-conceptualization as a constant entity is illusory, and its promise of "eternity in time"—a society always stable and harmonious—entirely empty.

This promise—of the state as the preserver of order and bulwark against upheaval—was essential to Rome's self-representation to its provincials. Tacitus reports that the Roman general Quintus Petillius Cerialis used it to persuade the Gaelic tribes to submit rather than rebel:

> The good fortune and order of eight hundred years have built up this mighty fabric [i.e. the Empire] which cannot be destroyed without overwhelming its destroyers: moreover, you are in the greatest danger, for you possess gold and wealth, which are the chief causes of war. Therefore love and cherish peace and the city wherein we, conquerors and conquered alike, enjoy an equal right: be warned by the lessons of fortune both good and bad not to prefer defiance and ruin to obedience and security.[86]

Here, the Empire is the protector of its subjects' well-being. If nothing else, people should submit to Rome to protect themselves from something worse (in Cerialis' view, the barbarism of the Germanic tribes). To break away from the Empire is to choose ruin: "if the Romans are driven out—which Heaven forbid—what will follow except universal war among all peoples?"[87]

Yet, for the author of 1 Peter, decay and perishability are inevitable in the created order. In fact, these qualities precisely distinguish it from the order of redemption transformed by grace. The unspoiled inheritance prepared by God for the faithful originates from the divine realm (ἐν οὐρανοῖς, 1:4), for imperishability itself belongs to the divine. God accomplishes through his Messiah what worldly, "perishable things" (1:18) cannot—he redeems the world by granting it a new birth that orients people toward that which is everlasting. In light of this reality, all human efforts to secure existence, order, and power in perpetuity must be unmasked as vanity, if not downright folly. Such a view is by no means foreign to the Hebrew Bible. In the hymns of Israel we find this text:

---

85. Franz Rosenzweig, *The Star of Redemption*, trans. Barbara E. Galli (Madison, WI: University of Wisconsin Press, 2005), 352.
86. Tacitus, *Hist.* 4.74 (Moore trans.). Cf. Ando, *Imperial Ideology*, 66.
87. Tacitus, *Hist.* 4.74.

Do not put your trust in princes, in mortals, in whom there is no help.
When their breath departs, they return to the earth;
on that very day their plans perish.
                                                            Ps. 145:3–4, NRSV

The reign of God, by contrast, will endure forever, "for all generations" (Ps. 145:10). Perhaps not coincidentally, this juxtaposition of the fragility of earthly kingdoms against God's reign is the very same sentiment expressed in the broader context of Isa. 40:4–9, the text deployed in 1 Pet. 1:24–25. In Isaiah 40, the messenger announcing the end of Judah's chastisement under Babylon both declares the transience of human life ("All people are grass," v. 6) and heralds the rule of "the everlasting God ... [who] does not faint or grow weary" (v. 28). While we cannot be sure if the author of 1 Peter intended the political force of this specific citation, what remains certain is that he was keenly aware of the reality of imperial power (2:13–14, 17), and that he viewed the human order of things as temporary, a holding pattern that will only last "a little while" (1:6; 5:10). The readers' impending share in God's glory, on the other hand, will be eternal (τὴν αἰώνιον ... δόξαν, 5:10; cf. 5:4).

The juxtaposition of perishability and imperishability in the letter, therefore, holds robust political implications. The readers cannot, must not, subscribe to Rome's rhetoric of permanence, for the order sustained by imperial rule and its apparatuses is only temporary. In emphasizing the perishability of human life, the letter also demystifies the fortuitous births and military victories of emperors celebrated in the festivals of the imperial cults, along with their propaganda of uninterrupted successions that were so crucial to the Empire's façade of stability and impenetrability to change and defeat. In short, Rome is implicitly assigned an expiration date. In place of all this, Christians have an inheritance kept in the heavens and secured by God's enduring word which they have already heard and received. Allegiance to the emperor and his delegates must, at best, be circumscribed by the Empire's finitude in time. In the grand scheme of a totalizing empire, such conditional allegiance, as the early martyrdom literature shows, at times counted for no allegiance at all.[88]

4.5 Conclusion

In this chapter I have endeavored to construct the temporal imagination of 1 Peter by examining the view of time embedded in its conception of the world and the

---

88. Horrell ("Between Conformity and Resistance," 232–3) documents martyrdom accounts in which circumscribed allegiance ("polite [non]conformity") was deemed insufficient by imperial authorities and seen instead as a form of resistance. See also Horrell, "Honour Everyone," 200–4.

practice of Christian discipleship. A starting point is to be found in 1:20, which concisely expresses the perspective we find elsewhere in the letter—that is, of time as the divinely-guided, purposeful movement of the cosmos around a single axis: the revelation of God in Jesus of Nazareth. This view of time as the measure of God's saving activity (rather than, say, quantities of production) lay at the heart of the author's conception of the present as an eschatologically-charged moment. Through Christ's passion, death, and resurrection, God has revealed also the purpose of time. He has given them a new identity and called them to a new way of life in line with that direction. In light of this, they must reform their lives according to what God has done and is doing, and leave behind their old way of life with its ignorance and futility. Christians experience suffering and alienation because the Gentiles have not yet caught up with what has happened to the world in Christ. Nevertheless, if they bear witness patiently and accept graciously their share in Christ's sufferings, even those who oppose the gospel will experience a change of heart.

The author's theocentric, Christological, and soteriological construction of time also construes the past and the future in specific ways. The past is disclosed as the period of preparation in which the spirit of Christ was already at work, pointing the prophets toward his entrance into history. This perspective allows the author to interpret the scriptures of Israel accordingly, i.e. to read them Christologically, not as a hermeneutical exercise as such, but rather because this way of reading reflects the Christological structure of time itself. By narrating the past in this way, the author challenges in various ways the narratives of personhood we find in the practices of the imperial cults, in which both person and community are constructed as dependent subjects of the emperor and his empire. Similarly, the Petrine view of the future, which defers the fullness of cosmological meaning and social justice to *God's* future, effectively shakes it loose from imperial control, interrogating Rome's promise to secure peace and justice with its *imperium*. The motif of imperishability in the author's vision of the future further undermines Roman claims to an eternal empire. In his view, only that which is transformed by God's work in Christ is truly abiding; no human accomplishment can survive decay.

In this chapter, I have considered various ways in which this early Christian discourse of time may have pushed against that which we find in the Roman imperial cults of Anatolia. How this ideological contest played itself out for the letter's original readers, of course, remains enshrouded in history. Nonetheless, I contend that 1 Peter and the imperial cults configured time to reflect their respective—and divergent—ways of conceiving the real. Affirmation of the temporal discourse in 1 Peter was a simultaneous and firm "No" to the temporal logic of the imperial cults, for the simple fact that it could not tolerate more than one axis. By placing God, Christ, and redemption at the center of his temporal matrix, the author of 1 Peter already decentered Caesar and negated the claims made in the Asian decree and embodied in imperial-cultic praxes. My analysis assumes that no construction of time is, in the end, politically innocent. This is the case even in a text like 1 Peter, which is ostensibly more irenic than other biblical writings such as Daniel or Revelation. Its theologically-driven elucidation of time is no less socially formidable for this fact.

Whether or not the author of 1 Peter explicitly *intended* a direct confrontation, however, cannot be known without a psychologizing and thus highly-conjectural reconstruction of his intentions. We have only his public address to the Anatolian churches, not a personal journal. My point remains, however, that the letter would have generated sufficient dissonance in the Anatolian readers who regarded his words in the letter as authoritative. As such, we already have in 1 Peter a text that destabilizes Roman claims and thus can be genuinely regarded as one that poses ideological resistance to the Empire.

Chapter 5

SPACE IN THE IMPERIAL CULTS[1]

The spread of cultic veneration of the Roman emperor and his family engendered a reconfiguration of the spatial imagination in which the known world was redefined around Rome.[2] This process was a subcomponent of a broader development—the emergence of an imperial discourse of world conquest that reshaped how Roman authorities and subjects alike thought about the world.[3] The observation of Dionysius of Halicarnassus may be taken as one such example:

> But Rome rules every country that is not inaccessible or uninhabited, and she is mistress of every sea, not only of that which lies inside the Pillars of Hercules but also of the Ocean, except that part of it which is not navigable; she is the first and the only State recorded in all time that ever made the risings and the settings of the sun the boundaries of her dominion.[4]

In his last testament, Augustus boasted that he had "made the world subject to the rule of the Roman people (*orbem terrarum imperio populi Romani subiecit*)."[5] This statement reflects the profound nexus between the *orbis terrarum* and the *orbis Romanus* forged in the imperial period. Claude Nicolet speaks of an "obsession with space"[6] that characterized the Augustan period. The energetic nexus between

---

1. Some of the material in this chapter and the next first appeared in Wei Hsien Wan, "Repairing Social Vertigo: Spatial Production and Belonging in 1 Peter," in *The Urban World and the First Christians*, ed. Steve Walton, Paul Trebilco, and David W. J. Gill (Grand Rapids, MI: Eerdmans, 2017), 287–303.

2. Friesen, *Imperial Cults*, 54.

3. On the development of Roman geography in the Augustan period, see the important work of Claude Nicolet, *Space, Geography, and Politics in the Early Roman Empire* (Ann Arbor, MI: University of Michigan, 1991).

4. Ant. rom., 1.3.3 (Cary trans.).

5. Prescript to the Latin version of the *Res Gestae*. Throughout, I have used the reconstructed text and translation in Alison E. Cooley, *Res Gestae Divi Augusti: Text, Translation, and Commentary* (Cambridge: Cambridge University Press, 2009).

6. Nicolet, *Space, Geography, and Politics*, 8.

imperial politics and geography gave birth to a feverish increase in partial and global censuses and the publication of cadastral books and maps in various regions, as well as the establishing of road itineraries. The world to be conquered also had to be known, measured, and drawn.[7]

At the center of the new imperial geography lay the city of Rome, with her imperial provinces both East and West conceived as dependent peripheries, subject to varying strategies of governance as emperor and Senate saw fit.[8] John Helgeland, for example, has pointed out that the encampment practices of the Roman army essentially reproduced this Romanocentric geography.[9] Each camp was "a symbolic representation of Rome itself: the *praetorium* symbolized the capitol, the walls were the boundaries around the city, the camp was the city of Rome on the frontier."[10] This was accomplished in part by reproducing Roman time—that is, by observing the same civil calendar (with its holy days and festivals) as was kept in Rome. This gave the Roman solder a sense of belonging even if he may have felt lost in the middle of nowhere. More important, however, is the imperial geography constructed in these practices: "the military camp became a receptacle for receiving and amplifying the spiritual force of Rome all along its borders. The borders (*limes*) too were regarded as sacred and soldiers claimed that the gods watched over them. Beyond the borders was chaos, peopled by weird people living in an uncustomary way."[11] For Helgeland, this way of thinking was a "deep structure" within the Roman cultural imagination.

A crucial aspect to the Roman project of empire, this process of spatial transformation was propagated in the concrete practices of the imperial cults. This chapter will elucidate the key features of such practices. Its primary aim is not to give an account of architectural structures, although this, as will be evident, is necessary for the task. Rather, I seek to discern in material and social practice what Lefebvre called "representations of space," i.e. the ways in which (imperial) space is conceived symbolically via a range of material and social practices. The bulk of the chapter will be devoted to the most tangible of transformations initiated by the cults—that is, the introduction of cultic sites dedicated to the veneration of the imperial family. After considering their strategic positioning in Anatolian

---

7. Nicolet, *Space, Geography, and Politics*, 95.

8. Although this point will be developed in the rest of this chapter, it is interesting to note at this juncture that Nicolet (*Space, Geography, and Politics*, 9) points to a curious passage in Velleius Paterculus that is suggestive of a germinal Romanocentric geography. In *Hist.* 2.109, Roman military forces preparing for battle against Maroboduus, king of Marcomanni in Bohemia, appear to have employed north-oriented maps that measured distances from the boundaries of Italy.

9. John Helgeland, "Time and Space: Christian and Roman," in *ANRW*, vol. 23.2 (Berlin and New York, NY: Walter de Gruyter, 1980), 1285–305.

10. Helgeland, "Time and Space," 1299.

11. Helgeland, "Time and Space," 1299.

landscapes, we will consider three case studies of specific imperial temples—those in Ephesus, Aphrodisias, and Ankara. Each case study will draw out the particular way in which the cultic site reflects distinct elements of the imperial constructions of space. Following these, I will turn to the spatial incorporation of the imperial cults in sanctuaries of traditional and local deities, and then reflect on how imperial cultic practices reconfigured civic spaces throughout Anatolia.

5.1 *The Location and Prominence of Imperial Cultic Sites*

The introduction of the Roman imperial cults occurred rather dramatically in Anatolia. As I mentioned in my coverage of the evidence in Chapter 2, the rapid spread of cultic sites dedicated to the emperor and his family serves as an index of the growth of Roman power in the region.[12] The Asian provincial decree of 9 BC examined in Chapter 3 already assumed that each major city in the province had an imperial sanctuary (*Caesareum*) in which the text promulgated by the council could be proclaimed and displayed.[13] By the end of the first century AD, there were as many as thirty imperial temples and sanctuaries dedicated to the veneration of the *Sebastoi* throughout Roman Anatolia.[14]

Consistently, imperial temples and sanctuaries were built in the most prominent and prestigious locations in a city, thus emphasizing the looming and pervasive presence of Rome over the lives of the city's inhabitants and those of its dependants. At Eresos, a benefactor built an imperial temple and sanctuary (*naos*) in the most prominent part of the city's main square and another in the commercial harbor "so that no place should lack mark of his [the benefactor's] goodwill and piety towards the god [Augustus]."[15] Likewise, a temple to the Theoi Soteres Sebastoi at Sidyma, dating to the Claudian era, was built in the center, and in Cestrus two imperial temples faced each other across the main square.[16] The *Caesareum* at Laertes faced the city's main gates,[17] and in Stratonicea, the temple to the Sebastoi Autokratores was given prominence on a terrace above the local theater.[18]

In some instances, centrality of location could not be accomplished due to existing structures. The solution was to achieve visibility by other means. This was the case with Iotape, where the city center was already crammed into one arm of the bay. The Trajanic temple was, consequently, built on the opposite arm of the bay, so that it remained clearly visible from the city center.[19] Visibility also

---

12. See Section 2.1.1 above.
13. *OGIS* 458 l. 61. Cf. Section 3.1 above.
14. Price, *Rituals and Power*, 58–9.
15. Price, *Rituals and Power*, 137, 249.
16. Price, *Rituals and Power*, 137, 263, 273.
17. Price, *Rituals and Power*, 137, 273.
18. Price, *Rituals and Power*, 137, 262.
19. Price, *Rituals and Power*, 137, 273.

appeared to be a key criterion in Pergamum, where a massive substructure had to be engineered so that a temple jointly consecrated to Trajan and Zeus Philios could occupy the highest point of the acropolis. (Although the location of the Pergamene provincial temple to Roma and Augustus, the first of its kind in the province of Asia, has not been determined, it may well have been located in the city center.)[20] The imperial temple of Ankara achieved visual prominence via its location on a hill on the west bank of the river that divided the Roman city. It thus towered over buildings such as the bath-gymnasium complex and the theater, communicating imperial protection over the city's civic life.[21] The Ephesian temple to the Sebastoi was likewise calculated to visually impress. Its precincts were built on an artificially-terraced slope on Mount Koressos, with an exposed northern side rising 10.4 meters above ground and opening into a plaza below. On the northern façade of the terrace a looming three-story stoa was built, which allowed viewers in the plaza to experience the full visual impact of the edifice.[22] In clear view of anyone approaching it from the city below, this imposing structure vividly communicated to the people of Ephesus the elevated, all-embracing presence and patronage of the emperor.[23] In Pisidian Antioch, the *Augusteum* departed from the custom of east-facing sanctuaries, built to face west on the city's eastern acropolis so that its awe-inspiring façade and propylon were plainly visible to the inhabitants below.[24]

The central locations and high visibility of these imperial buildings were by no means innocent criteria. Rather, the placement of these temples was part of the visual grammar of domination conveyed by Rome to its Anatolian subjects. Mitchell is thus right to observe that:

> ... imperial buildings literally took over and dominated the urban landscape, thus symbolizing unequivocally the central position that emperor worship occupied in city life, and the overwhelming manner in which the emperor dominated the world view of his subjects.[25]

Architecture was therefore placed at the service of empire. The strategic prominence of the imperial temples revealed the centrality of the body of the emperor to

---

20. Price, *Rituals and Power*, 137, 252.

21. Mitchell, *Anatolia, Vol. I*, 105.

22. "The visual impact of this architectural setting was a crucial aspect of the whole complex" (Friesen, *Twice Neokoros*, 70).

23. Friesen, *Imperial Cults*, 50–2.

24. Rubin, "(Re)presenting Empire," 59. Rubin does note that the tradition of east-facing temples is not rigidly observed in Anatolia. He cites the examples of the imperial temples in Ankara and Aphrodisias, both of which are built to face west. The point remains that in the case of Antioch, the orientation of the temple was conditioned by the need for the magnificent façade to face the city's inhabitants rather than away from them.

25. Mitchell, *Anatolia, Vol. I*, 107.

Rome's construction of Anatolian space. Power radiated, as if in concentric circles, from the body of the emperor to the bodies of his kin (fictive or real) and outward, beyond the city of Rome to the Empire's furthest-flung territories. Distance from the center did not dilute this imperial presence, for everywhere Caesar's subjects were tangibly reminded of his authority made present to them in stone—in awe-inspiring columns, façades, and plazas, whether in the heart of urban spaces or from some commanding hill. "Rome" was no longer confined to the imperial city, but every territory where the emperor's presence and power could be felt.[26] To examine this last point more closely, I turn now to the architecture of the temples themselves.

5.2 Imperial Temples: Ideology in Marble and Stone

Alongside their strategic locations, the design of the imperial temples themselves also played a crucial role in Rome's discourse of domination. To demonstrate this point, I will present in this section three case studies, each of a temple taken from a different city in Anatolia: Ephesus and Aphrodisias in Asia, and Ankara in Galatia. Since imperial temples were built under different conditions (sociopolitical, economic, topographic) that varied from province to province, there can be no such thing as a "representative temple." Nonetheless, what I wish to demonstrate here is that in each case, the structure was calculated to enforce Roman hegemony by communicating a world in the firm grasp of its empire. Of these, two were provincial capitals in the first century AD—Ephesus and Ankara—and as such were of great importance. The Aphrodisian sanctuary merits particular attention because of its distinctive way of mapping the new imperial geography, as will be shown.

5.2.1 Ephesus

An inscription discovered in Aphrodisias refers to "the temple of the Sebastoi in Ephesus that is common to Asia" (ναῶι τῶι ἐν Ἐφές[ωι] τῶν Σεβαστῶν κοινῶι τῆς Ἀσί[ας]).[27] The provincial temple in Ephesus, most likely dating to the reign of

---

26. On the remarkable shift of cultic focus from the city of Rome and its boundaries to the (mobile) personage of the emperor in the Augustan era, see Eric M. Orlin, "Augustan Religion: From Locative to Utopian," in *Rome and Religion: A Cross-Disciplinary Dialogue on the Imperial Cult*, ed. Jeffrey Brodd and Jonathan L. Reed (Atlanta, GA: Society of Biblical Literature, 2011), 49–59. Cf. S. R. F. Price, "The Place of Religion: Rome in the Early Empire," in *The Cambridge Ancient History, Vol. X: The Augustan Empire: 43 B.C. to A.D. 69*, ed. Alan K. Bowman, Edward Champlin, and Andrew Lintott, 2nd ed. (Cambridge: Cambridge University Press, 1996), 812–47.

27. IEph 2.223. For the full original text and translation, see Friesen, *Twice Neokoros*, 32–3.

Domitian, was different from its counterparts in Pergamum and Smyrna in that it was not jointly dedicated to Roma or the Roman Senate, but rather to the collective Sebastoi. Along with the Aphrodisian inscription, twelve others commemorating the temple's dedication have been found in cities throughout the province. From his close study of these inscriptions, Friesen concludes that their structure and content disclose a clear geopolitical pecking order for the province: the Sebastoi at the top, followed by free cities whose autonomies stemmed from the grace (χάρις) of the Sebastoi, and finally, subject cities, who were in turn subsidiaries of the free cities.[28] This "diffusion model" of power affirms in its own way a spatial imagination in which power radiated from the center of the Empire—not from the city of Rome *per se*, but rather from the bodies of the Sebastoi, the imperial clan.

The Sebastoi quite literally had an imposing presence in this provincial temple. Excavators have found the remains of statuary of colossal proportions: a head measuring 1.18m high, most likely that of Titus, and a left forearm 1.8m long from elbow to knuckles.[29] This scale was quite evidently calculated to awe—and perhaps even intimidate—the viewer into subordination. When considered in light of other kinds of statues found in the temple, their size acquires even further significance. The second story of the northern façade of the temple was ornamented with engaged figures, two of which have been identified as the eastern divinities Isis and Attis. This strongly suggests that the entire second story of the stoa was lined with statues of the traditional gods, with thirty-five to forty such statues on the northern façade alone.[30] Compared to these statues, those of the imperial dynasty were clearly much larger. Moreover, the imperial temple itself would have dwarfed the gods depicted on the comparatively lower stoa surrounding it. This proportionality did not necessarily mean that the Sebastoi were more important than or ontologically superior to the gods, but simply that this particular space was dedicated to them, and they were thus "hosts" to the traditional gods in the temple. Nonetheless, this maneuver was a crucial one. It conveyed very specific ideas about the relationship between the gods and the Sebastoi:

> The message [of the Ephesian temple] was clear: the gods and goddesses of the peoples supported the emperors; and, conversely, the cult of the emperors united the cultic systems, and the peoples, of the empire. The emperors were not a threat to the worship of the diverse deities of the empire; rather, the emperors joined the ranks of the divine and played their own particular role in that realm.[31]

28. Friesen, *Twice Neokoros*, 37–41; *Imperial Cults*, 46–7.
29. Friesen, *Twice Neokoros*, 60–3, with illustrations.
30. Friesen, *Twice Neokoros*, 71–2, with illustrations.
31. Friesen, *Twice Neokoros*, 75. Earlier, Simon Price (*Rituals and Power*, 147, 231–2) had insisted that the imperial cults always distinguished the ontologically-superior gods from the emperors as lesser beings, while admittedly placing them more or less on the same plane. This opinion, as Friesen points out, cannot be sustained by the proportions of the Ephesian temple, which placed the imperial family at the front and center of cultic activity, with the traditional pantheon playing the role of supporters.

The architectural situating of the Sebastoi within the other cults of the gods was not simply a matter of integrating the Caesars into a metaphysical scheme. The provincial temple of Ephesus constructed a world in which Roman rule over the peripheries not only received divine support, but also integrated its diverse subjects in social harmony.

This last point is made even more vivid by the placement of the provincial temple within the city itself. It was located on the west side of the upper agora of Ephesus, an area that contained a complex of buildings that were key to the life of the city: a basilica, a prytaneion, a possible bouleuterion, and an agora temple, most likely dedicated to Augustus. The three-aisled basilica dating to AD 11–13 lines the northern side of the agora and is the largest building in the upper city, running 167.7 meters long and 16.3 meters wide. Inscriptional evidence shows that it was dedicated to the Ephesian Artemis; Emperor Caesar Augustus, son of god; Tiberius Caesar, son of Augustus; and the demos of the Ephesians.[32] The prytaneion, also dating to the Augustan period, was reserved for the official duties of the *prytanis*, a civic official whose responsibilities in Ephesus were fourfold: (1) maintain the cult of Hestia and the eternal fire; (2) receive official guests of the city by hosting dinner parties; (3) oversee the mysteries of Artemis celebrated annually on the goddess' birthday; and (4) oversee the official cycle of 365 sacrifices throughout the city to various gods.[33]

The identification of the bouleuterion and Augusteion are more speculative. A large, semi-circular building east of the prytaneion has been identified as the city's bouleuterion on the following bases: (1) surrounding buildings seem to have civic or administrative functions; (2) absence of scene building (depictions of scenes or objects), suggesting that the building was constructed for deliberation rather than entertainment; and (3) use of imperial letters on the backdrop of the theater stage (*scenae frons*).[34] Though no dedicatory inscriptions have survived for the small temple excavated in the middle of the agora, what inscriptional evidence has survived in the area speaks of a statue of Augustus dedicated in the agora itself, as well as the mending of "the damaged wall surrounding the Augusteion."[35] That it was dedicated to Augustus is, on these grounds, the best guess.

The positioning of the provincial temple within this complex of buildings cannot be overlooked. Even if the semi-circular building and smaller temple cannot be identified with confidence, what remains certain is that the agora complex would have been frequented by the people and visitors of Ephesus for both civic and cultic purposes. Opening into this complex from the west and built on an elevated terrace, the provincial temple to the Sebastoi made present the reach of Roman power that enshrouded civic life in the provincial capital and

---

32. Friesen, *Imperial Cults*, 95.
33. Friesen, *Imperial Cults*, 97–8.
34. Friesen, *Imperial Cults*, 99.
35. Friesen, *Imperial Cults*, 100–1.

through this capital to the entire province. In the agora, under its shadow, inhabitants and visitors shared in and witnessed the vicissitudes of common life: buying and selling, conversation and debate, festal processions, diplomatic visits, sacrifices. Leisure, commerce, politics, cult—all these took place under the watchful eyes and umbrage of the imperial family. The cosmo-political order borne out in the thirteen dedicatory inscriptions was in this way materialized in sacred architecture.

5.2.2 Aphrodisias

Aphrodisias in eastern Caria was already an important cultic site in the Persian and Hellenistic periods. Though not fully urbanized during the Roman period, it nonetheless developed a strong relationship to Rome in the Augustan age. Not only was Augustus favorably disposed to the Aphrodisians for their support during civil wars, but he also possessed kinship ties to the city by way of mythic descent: his adoptive father, Julius Caesar, was believed to be a descendant of the city's patron goddess Aphrodite through her son, Aeneas. Upon becoming emperor in 27 BC, Augustus bequeathed to the city free and allied status, which rendered it independent of the Province of Asia and shielded its citizens from heavy taxation, thus facilitating economic growth.[36]

To reciprocate, the Aphrodisians built a sanctuary dedicated to the imperial family, most likely begun during the reign of Tiberius and finished during that of Nero.[37] The temple now thought to be that very Sebasteion contains an inscription in the propylon indicating that it was dedicated "to Aphrodite, the *Theoi Sebastoi*, and the *Demos*." The complex consists of four sections: the propylon; two three-story porticoes reaching 12 meters high each; and a Corinthian-style temple. The remains are among the most well-preserved in Roman Asia Minor and offer a rich trove for analysis. Since I have already focused on the ideology of location in my discussion of the temple in Ephesus, I will here focus specifically on the spatial ideology conveyed by the relief work on the porticoes. (Of these, the depictions of Claudius with Britannia and of the Pirousthae have already been discussed in Chapter 3.) Both the north and south porticoes are of an unusually great height (12 meters) and consist of three stories: two levels of marble reliefs supported by a level of columns. This design, uncommon in both Roman and Greek temple architecture, would have undoubtedly dwarfed the viewer and, combined with the narrowness of the site, intensified the experience of verticality.[38]

---

36. R. R. R. Smith, "The Imperial Reliefs from the Sebasteion at Aphrodisias," *Journal of Roman Studies* 77 (November 1987): 90; cf. Rubin, "(Re)presenting Empire," 73–4.

37. For detailed discussions of the finds at Aphrodisias, see Smith, "The Imperial Reliefs"; Smith, "Simulacra Gentium"; Rubin, "(Re)presenting Empire," 72–116; Friesen, *Imperial Cults*, 77–95, 101–3.

38. Smith, "The Imperial Reliefs," 93.

The reliefs on the second and third stories can be categorized as follows. For the purposes of this study, I will consider each register in turn.

> North portico: top level – allegorical figures
>   bottom level – idealized ethnic personifications
> South portico: top level – portraits of emperors and captives
>   bottom level – scenes from Greek mythology

5.2.2.1 Allegorical Figures   Of the fifty panels on the top register of the north portico, only two have survived.[39] Both of these are allegorical personifications: Hemera (Day), depicted as a clothed female, and Okeanos (Ocean), depicted as a naked and bearded man. Given the allegorical groupings characteristic of Hellenistic art, the presence of Day and Ocean indicates that the original relief was most likely complemented with personifications of Night (Nux) or Evening (Hespera) and Earth (Gē). R. R. R. Smith speculates that this story may have consisted of Day on the east end and Evening/Night on the west end, creating "a widely-arched time bracket" across the north portico.[40] Since a set consisting exclusively of allegorical figures would have been unlikely, he further suggests the relief of the accession of Nero (featuring also his mother Agrippina), found at the back of the northeasterly corner of the same portico, may have originally belonged to the center of this composition. If we allow for this reconstruction based on Smith's scholarly deduction, we have an enthroned Nero coronated by his mother, with Day and Evening/Night as well as Ocean and Earth bearing witness to the reach of his power.[41] One could hardly have asked for a more vivid portrayal of an empire encompassing the totality of time and space.[42]

5.2.2.2 Idealized Ethnic Personifications   In contrast to the top level, the second level of the north portico is much better preserved. Each *ethnos* is idealized as an engaged statue in high relief and standing on an inscribed base.[43] Lined up like witnesses to Roman power and totaling fifty in number, they depict the various

---

39. Rubin, "(Re)presenting Empire," 77.
40. Smith, "Simulacra Gentium," 53.
41. In the engraved sardonyx known as the Gemma Augustea, a young heir (probably Tiberius) is depicted as descending from his chariot while an array of deities crown him—among which are Augustus, Ocean, Earth, and Oecumene (Ando, *Imperial Ideology*, 287). Cf. Philo's description of the Empire in *Leg.* 10: "a dominion extending ... from the rising to the setting sun both within the ocean and beyond it" (Colson trans.).
42. "If this was indeed the case [i.e. if Smith's reconstruction is accurate] ... these allegorical depictions of Day and Night imbued the *Sebasteion* and, by extension, the Roman empire itself with an aura of temporal and geographical universality" (Rubin, "[Re]presenting Empire," 78).
43. For illustrations and photographs of these, see Smith, "Simulacra Gentium," 54; Pl. I–XI.

peoples within the borders of the Roman Empire, most likely chosen to represent the conquests of Augustus.[44] Smith has noted that the peoples are generally of three categories: they are peoples whom Augustus simply defeated, defeated and added to the Empire, or regained after their unwilling secession. As such, they are a collective testament to an empire with "a spectrum of constituents, from near-equal partners to conquered subjects and neighbours."[45] This differentiated belonging can be seen in the extant sculptures, and is conveyed by variation in clothing schemes, pose and gestures, hairstyle, and typified physical features.[46]

Two other engaged statues from this series can be compared to show some crucial distinctions in the ethnic personifications.[47] The first is an unidentified *ethnos* or Greek island, depicted as a standing female figure donning a *peplos* (thick, sleeveless dress) and a short *himation*.[48] Her hair is that of the ideal hairstyle of Greek women and goddesses—gathered tightly to the back with one curl escaping onto the neck. Her raised right hand and relaxed left hand both once held objects that have not survived time. Nonetheless, this gesture, along with her clothing and hairstyle, clearly identifies her as both "Greek" and "free." Another engaged statue from the series yields a slightly but significantly different picture.[49] Like the previous statue, she is also standing with her weight on the right leg and clothed in *peplos* and *himation*, though her *peplos* has slipped off her right shoulder, partly revealing her breast. Her arms are neither raised nor relaxed at her side, but rather crossed at the waist to communicate submissiveness.[50] The segment of her hair that has survived reveals it as gathered in a loose loop—not quite the disheveled style of a barbarian, but approximating the more "civilized" tightness of Greek buns. Collectively, these features yield a figure somewhere between the dignified Pirousthae and the vanquished Britannia of the southern portico. She is standing, clothed but not fully, her arms crossed but not bound—signs of gentler but nonetheless indubitable subjugation.[51]

---

44. Smith, "Simulacra Gentium," 58. (For a map of the distribution of these peoples, see Smith, "Simulacra Gentium," 56.)

45. Smith, "Simulacra Gentium," 59.

46. Smith, "Simulacra Gentium," 60. The dignified depiction of the Pirousthae has already been discussed in Chapter 3 above (see Section 3.3).

47. In the ensuing analysis of these figures, I am primarily relying on Friesen, *Imperial Cults*, 88–90, who is in turn commenting on the data from Smith, "Simulacra Gentium," 62–6.

48. For a photo, see Smith, "Simulacra Gentium," Pl. III.

49. For a photo, see Smith, "Simulacra Gentium," Pl. II.

50. Friesen (*Imperial Cults*, 89) is no doubt right that her crossed arms do not signify captivity since they are not bound.

51. Rubin ("[Re]Presenting Empire," 78) is right, I think, to disagree with Smith ("Simulacra Gentium," 62–4), who interpreted these features as primarily signifying semi-barbarism rather than submission in the series. As he points out, if this were the case, the Pirousthae, a tribe from the outer reaches of empire, ought to have been depicted as a barbarian rather than as a "civilized" Athena-like figure, as is the case.

It is evident, then, that the idealized *ethnē* series on the northern portico was designed to highlight at least two features of the Roman Empire. First, they impressed upon the viewer the geographical extensiveness of Roman rule, spanning at least the 50 known peoples of the ancient world represented by the reliefs.[52] Summoned like a cloud of witnesses, they not only testified to the incredible political reach of the Sebastoi, but their position beneath the allegorical depictions above them in the portico also naturalized their subjugation: their position in the Empire belonged to the cosmic order of things.[53] Second, they embodied different ways of "participating" in empire. To the degree that each people voluntarily submitted to Rome, their dignity was commensurately preserved—some completely intact, like the Pirousthae; some intact-but-compromised, like the *ethnos* represented by the semi-exposed figure. The statues therefore mapped out the *oikoumenē* not only in terms of physical territory, but also in terms of each people's response to Roman power.[54] We have, in the northern portico, a sculptural cartography of the *orbis Romanus*.

5.2.2.3 Emperors and Captives The portrayals of Roman emperors and their captives on the top register of the south portico elaborate imperial geography in yet another way: expansion via conquest. The depiction of Claudius' shaming defeat of Britannia that has already been discussed in Chapter 3 may be regarded as typical of this tier in terms of its application of idealized, heroic nudity to the emperors. This strategy expressed their power in terms reminiscent of the Olympian gods, thus lending their military feats an aura of mythic invincibility.[55] The triumphant Claudius assumes the figure of an armor-clad but bare-chested general, resembling a Greek hero, while Britannia is cast as a vanquished Amazon.[56] Similarly, in another panel Nero, displaying also a hyper-masculine muscular torso, grasps Armenia from behind, dragging her away in a display of distilled dominance. The clothing and poses of Nero and Armenia have been calculated to evoke Achilles' famous defeat of Penthesilea, queen of the Amazons—not coincidentally, a scene commemorated in the lower register of this same portico (see below). Smith suggests that, though in mythological retellings Penthesilea is slain by Achilles, the relief here presents us with a scene of victory and not of slaughter, since Nero did not obliterate Armenia but rather incorporated her into the Empire.[57]

---

52. Though it is no longer extant, the temple to Caesar Augustus in Lugdunum (*c.* 20 BC) was said by Strabo to have had "a noteworthy altar, bearing an inscription of the names of the tribes [*ethnē*], sixty in number; and also images from these tribes, one from each tribe [*ethnos*], and also another large altar" (4.3.2). Cf. Ando, *Imperial Ideology*, 312–13.
53. This latter point about the relationship between the two registers of the portico seems to have escaped the studies I have relied on here.
54. Rubin, "(Re)presenting Empire," 78–9.
55. Friesen, *Imperial Cults*, 90.
56. Rubin, "(Re)presenting Empire," 76.
57. Smith, "The Imperial Reliefs," 119.

Of course, no set of images of imperial victory can be complete without Augustus. On the top register of the south portico one finds him standing accompanied by a winged Victory (Nike). The two flank a trophy (*tropaion*), beneath which is a naked captive with arms bound at the back. The remnants indicate that Augustus' right hand once bore a scepter or spear. Now gone, it leaves in full view the eagle perched at the emperor's feet, symbolizing monarchic power. Though it was not unheard of for the emperor to be portrayed in the nude, historical narrative compositions such as this would typically have clothed him more "realistically," e.g., wearing armor or in civilian dress. Augustus' heroic nudity in this instance, a notable departure from the canonical practice, indicates an allegorical emphasis (along with the lack of reference to a specific battle), pointing to the Olympian nature of his victories in general.[58]

Another panel from the top register is also of an allegorical nature. Augustus is again depicted in the nude, striding forward dramatically. This time, it is he who is flanked, with personifications of Land and Sea to his right and left respectively. Land places a cornucopia in his right hand and Sea offers him the rudder of a ship. The message is clear: Augustus' rule has brought prosperity and peace, fertility to the land, and navigability to the seas.[59] There is in this relief no mortal human enemy to be defeated. Rather, conquest penetrates deep into the cosmic realms. Under the tutelage of Augustus' power, even the terrestrial sphere is disciplined into cooperation with the economic endeavors of human beings in the harmonies of the *Pax Romana*. As with the earlier panel, this one renders the emperor's achievements in a visual language of mythic proportions, abstracting the *euangelion* of the Augustan moment from the specifics of time and space and rendering them as a trans-temporal, trans-spatial given.

5.2.2.4 Scenes from Greek Mythology The panels of the southern portico's second story are the most well attested, with all forty-five of them surviving largely or sufficiently intact for reconstruction. As a whole, the reliefs do not seem to have a unified theme, though they collectively manifest the mythical consciousness of the Hellenic world and its "international *koinē* of myth."[60] They are devoted to well-known figures and scenes from Hellenistic mythology that would, no doubt, have been familiar to the Aphrodisians: portrayals and stories involving Demeter, Pegasus, Achilles, Apollo and the Muses, Dionysus, and Heracles among them. Significantly, several of the reliefs in this section underscore the mythic foundations of Aphrodisias and Rome. One panel captures the flight of Aeneas from Troy to Rome, and another depicts the iconic foundation of Rome in the story of Romulus, Remus, and the she-wolf. The scene of Aeneas' journey is vertically aligned with the portrayal of Augustus and Nike on the upper level (discussed above)—a detail that could not have been

---

58. Smith, "The Imperial Reliefs," 103–4.
59. Smith, "The Imperial Reliefs," 104–6.
60. Smith, "The Imperial Reliefs," 97.

entirely coincidental given Aeneas' mediating role in the well-known mythic genealogy linking the city's patron, Aphrodite, to Augustus.[61] Emphasis on Aphrodisias' ties to Rome becomes most explicit in the panel in which a personification of the city is coronated by the goddess Roma.[62] These elements in the series, together with their position beneath the images of victorious emperors on the top level, present us with a sculptural phenomenon in which the cultural vocabulary of the Hellenistic world was consciously drawn upon to—quite literally—support Rome's imperial rule, supplying it with mythical roots. This may well have been a sign of optimism on the part of Aphrodisian provincials regarding their relations to the imperial center.[63]

5.2.3 Ankara

The city of Ankara is the third stop in our survey of imperial cultic sites, and provides an occasion to consider in some detail both the content and materiality of that famous document, the *Res Gestae Divi Augusti*. Strategically situated along an east–west highway that ran across the central plateau of Anatolia to connect Sardis and Susa, Ankara was already home to a well-known fortress in the Republican period, belonging to a Galatian tribe known as the Tectosages.[64] At the dawn of Roman rule, Augustus himself founded the city in 25 BC, appointing Ankara the capital of the province of Galatia. Shortly thereafter it became host, accordingly, to a provincial temple to Roma and Augustus.[65]

The text of the *Res Gestae* is inscribed twice in this imperial temple, and appears to have been added to it only after the death of Augustus (AD 14), at least one decade after its consecration.[66] For the sake of this discussion, the temple provides an occasion to discuss the text in terms of (1) the spatial ideology of its content as well as (2) its material presence within the temple itself.

5.2.3.1 The Spatial Ideology of the Res Gestae   Originating from the heart of the Roman Empire, the *Res Gestae Divi Augusti* was the handiwork of Augustus himself. According to Suetonius, he had decreed that a "summary of his achievements" (*index rerum a se gestarum*) be inscribed in the columns of his mausoleum on the Field of Mars to the north of Rome.[67] Augustus specified that

---

61. Friesen, *Imperial Cults*, 90.
62. Smith, "The Imperial Reliefs," 97.
63. For a similar point, see Ando, *Imperial Ideology*, 313.
64. Strabo, *Geography* 12.5.2.
65. Rubin, "(Re)presenting Empire," 117.
66. Cooley, *Res Gestae*, 8–9.
67. Suetonius, *Aug.* 101. This was one of three documents sealed by Augustus and entrusted to the Vestal Virgins—the other two being a set of instructions for his funeral and a brief account of the whole empire (*breviarum totius imperii*). Dio Cassius (56.33.1–3) confirms this, although he adds a fourth document consisting of instructions for his heir Tiberius and the Roman people.

the *Res Gestae* be inscribed in bronze, making it equal to other official and legal Roman documents and vesting it with a sense of moral authority. The medium not only communicated durability and sanctity as aspects of his legacy, but also set him forward as a moral exemplar to the people and subjects of Rome, in keeping with his wishes.[68] The *Res Gestae* of Augustus was not alone in the mausoleum. It was also accompanied by other epigraphic tributes, also in bronze, commemorating the deeds of his (prematurely deceased) heirs—Agrippa, Drusus, Lucius, Gaius, and Germanicus among them—and for this reason should be contextualized within the wider accomplishments of the Augustan family, a kind of *Res Gestae domus Augustae*.[69] Nonetheless, its size and scope set it apart from its parallels in the Roman practice of the elegy (*elogia*), out of which it probably grew. It may have been inspired by the royal autobiographies of earlier Hellenistic and Achaemenid kings, most likely known to Augustus from his contacts with the East.[70]

Nicolet remarks that the document's careful listing of peoples, places, and distances between locations was such that it "appears almost as a commentary to a map and to require the guidance of a drawing."[71] Not coincidentally, he observes, just a few hundred meters from the mausoleum that housed the *Res Gestae* lay the portico on which was displayed the Romans' first global map of the known world, initiated by Augustus' son-in-law and co-regent Agrippa and completed by the emperor himself.[72] The proximity of these two documents, both in terms of location as well as authorial genesis, points again to the striking relationship between politics and geography in the imperial period.

To date, no known copy of the *Res Gestae* has been found in Rome. All three of its occurrences known to us are to be found in the province of Galatia—in the temples of Ankara, Pisidian Antioch, and Apollonia. In Ankara there exist two versions, in both Greek and Latin, whereas in Pisidian Antioch the inscription can be found only in Latin, and in Apollonia only in Greek. Rubin suggests that its dissemination in Galatia, given the *Res Gestae*'s likely roots in Hellenic and Achaemenid royal practices, may have been part of a broader Roman program to articulate its empire in terms familiar to the people of the region, evoking in particular a parallel between Augustus and his famous Persian predecessor, Darius the Great.[73] Greek translations of the text lend support to this thesis, pointing to the *Res Gestae* as a cultural bridge between Rome and her Greek-speaking subjects.

From the document's outset, the cosmological space constructed in the *Res Gestae* is patently centered on the Roman emperor and his empire. Its Latin heading designates itself as "a copy of the achievements of the deified Augustus, by

---

68. Cooley, *Res Gestae*, 3.
69. Cooley, *Res Gestae*, 6.
70. Nicolet, *Space, Geography, and Politics*, 20; Rubin, "(Re)presenting Empire," 129.
71. Nicolet, *Space, Geography, and Politics*, 9.
72. On Agrippa's map, see Nicolet, *Space, Geography, and Politics*, 95–122.
73. Rubin, "(Re)presenting Empire," 122.

which he made the world subject to the rule of the Roman people."[74] The text body proceeds to catalog the regions and peoples conquered or incorporated by Augustus into his empire, including fourteen major provinces and more than twenty lesser subjugated peoples, dropping some fifty-five geographical names to impress on its audience the immensity of the Empire's embrace.[75] Though the Greek version in several places softens the harsher language of domination—perhaps as a concession to make the text itself more palatable to Rome's Anatolian subjects—the theme of world conquest emerges unobscured.[76] At the beginning of the section enumerating the territories acquired in this expansionism, Augustus declares: "I enlarged the boundaries of all provinces of the Roman people, which had as neighbors peoples that were not subject to our rule" (RGDA 26.1). The ensuing numeration speaks not only of an empire extending to the ends of the known world, spanning Gaul, Spain, Germania, Ethiopia, Arabia, Egypt, and Armenia (RGDA 26-7), but also an empire which exercises influence even over areas not under its rule, such as those of Parthia (RGDA 29) and India (RGDA 31).

Not surprisingly, this construction of imperial space was, like the sculptures in the Aphrodisian temple, selective and calculated to yield the impression of a stable, worldwide dominion. The text refers, for example, to the pacification of Germania (RGDA 26.2) and diplomatic ties with the Germanic tribes (RGDA 26.4), but no mention is made of the Roman general Publius Quinctillius Varus' embarrassing loss of three legions to the Germans in the Battle of Teutoborg Forest, or the Romans' slippery hold on the region.[77] Roman presence in regions that were thought to mark the edges of the world, such as Ethiopia, Arabia, and Armenia, were marshaled as evidence that the entire world was in the imperial embrace.[78] Indeed, Augustus claims to have sailed through Ocean, the expanse of water thought to encompass the known world, to reach Cimbri (RGDA 26.4).[79] The unparalleled nature of this accomplishment is fittingly emphasized: "no Roman before this time has ever approached this area by either land or sea."

What about peoples who were not subject to Roman rule? On this question, the selectivity of the Res Gestae becomes most apparent. How is world conquest to be understood when there are yet rivals to Roman power? The text resolves this contradiction by construing these nations as client kingdoms, subject nonetheless to Augustus' will. This is perhaps most evident in the way the Res Gestae depicts the Parthians, whose kingdom constituted a constant threat to the Roman Empire.

---

74. All translations and quotations from the Latin and Greek originals of the Res Gestae (hereafter RGDA) are taken from Cooley, Res Gestae, 57–101.

75. Rubin, "(Re)presenting Empire," 131.

76. On the diminishing of the conquest motif in the Greek version, see Cooley, Res Gestae, 28–9.

77. Cooley, Res Gestae, 221.

78. Cooley, Res Gestae, 219.

79. On this point, see Cooley, Res Gestae, 221–3.

Augustus' control over this particular enemy is summed up in a single boast—the recovery of military standards lost to the Parthians under Antony and Crassus: "I compelled the Parthians to give back to me spoils and standards of three Roman armies and humbly to request the friendship of the Roman people" (*RGDA* 29.2). While one could argue that the loss of the military standards actually *underscores* the formidability of Parthia as a menace to Rome—a point easily bolstered by careful examination of the historical data[80]—in the *Res Gestae* the event is collapsed into a simple triumph construed only as a straightforward instance of imperial victory. The ongoing Roman struggle to secure its empire against Parthian incursion is entirely passed over, and the rival kingdom reduced to a vassal that was forced by Augustus "humbly to request the friendship of the Roman people" (*RGDA* 29.2). In an equally selective maneuver, the text speaks of Augustus' influence over Armenia only in terms of Roman intervention in the controversies over the kingdom's royal succession (*RGDA* 27.2)—an initiative that ultimately failed. (We therefore have more than sufficient reason to doubt Augustus' claim that he could have made Greater Armenia into a Roman province had he so wished [*RGDA* 27.2].) To the list of exotic peoples charmed by Augustan grandeur the text adds the Indians, who it says sent multiple embassies (*RGDA* 31.1), and the Scythians, who "sought [Rome's] friendship through envoys" (*RGDA* 31.2). Like the Ethiopians, these nations are purposefully name-dropped to emphasize, again and again, the universal scope of Rome's influence even on nations that, in actuality, lay outside her rule. The mention of India was also probably intended to invite comparison with Alexander the Great, who was forced to turn back at the edge of that exotic land.[81] "Embassies of kings from India were often sent to me," Augustus wrote, "such as have not ever been seen before this time in the presence of any Roman general" (31.1). Something greater than Alexander was here.

In sum, the *Res Gestae* maps a world in which the Roman Empire stretches from end to end of the known world—both over territories directly under imperial power as well as over regions beyond its discrete borders. The chief feature of its overtly political cartography is, unmistakably, a world defined only by its relations to Rome, the true *axis mundi*. From its vantage point, "the [E]mpire was a world, almost a new world which had been discovered, explored, and mastered."[82] Civilization spreads outward from its inception within the heart of the Empire, pacifying unruly foreign peoples in its path like a humanizing shockwave.[83] Its

---

80. Rubin, "(Re)presenting Empire," 132. The return of these standards is recorded in Dio Cassius, 53.33.1–2. For a detailed discussion of the rather delicate negotiations between Augustus and the Parthians that led to this recovery, see Cooley, *Res Gestae*, 242–3.

81. Cooley, *Res Gestae*, 249.

82. Nicolet, *Space, Geography, and Politics*, 24.

83. "The verb *pacare* may almost be regarded as a slogan of the [Augustan] regime . . .; together with its cognate noun *pax*, it encompasses the idea of pacification through military victory" (Cooley, *Res Gestae*, 222).

tenor is captured in the words of Pliny the Elder, who described the vocation of Rome in the following manner:

> chosen by the providence of the Gods to render even heaven itself more glorious, to unite the scattered empires of the earth, to bestow a polish upon men's manners, to unite the discordant and uncouth dialects of so many different nations by the powerful ties of one common language, to confer the enjoyments of discourse and of civilization upon mankind, to become, in short, the mother-country of all nations of the Earth.[84]

The *Res Gestae*, then, only documented the execution of this vision. Nevertheless, in the provincial imperial temple of Ankara, it did not simply serve as a passive record of deeds accomplished.

5.2.3.2 Text as Monument   In his study of the *Res Gestae* in Galatia, Benjamin Rubin points out that, until recently, epigraphists and historians have almost exclusively been concerned with the content of inscriptions rather than their materiality as such.[85] Driven by what he calls a "fetishism of the written word," much energy has been dedicated to the reconstruction of these ancient texts as literary products, while their other aspects, such as size, shape, and display context, have fallen by the wayside. Though estimating literacy rates in a collection of societies as vast, heterogeneous, and historically remote as the Roman Empire is a risky and contentious business, the scholarly consensus remains that the majority of the Empire's populace relied predominantly on oral rather than written communication, with only a minority in any given place being fully literate.[86]

Nevertheless, the questions in ongoing debates about literacy do not directly impede an evaluation of the *Res Gestae* as a visual icon of imperial authority. Commenting on an Antonine monument in Rome which listed all the Empire's legions in geographical order, Ando remarks:

> We would be grievously shortsighted if we privileged texts, and especially texts addressed from *principes* to subjects, as unique carriers of ideological content in the ancient world. Even on the most generous estimation of ancient levels of literacy, Augustus must have exercised considerably wider influence on popular

---

84. Pliny, *Nat.* 3.6 (Bostock trans.).

85. Rubin, "(Re)presenting Empire," 119.

86. The classic study on this topic remains William V. Harris, *Ancient Literacy* (Cambridge, MA: Harvard University Press, 1989). A range of responses to Harris' work (qualifying rather than overturning his conclusions) is to be found in John H. Humphrey et al., *Literacy in the Roman World*, Journal of Roman Archaeology Supplementary Series 3 (Ann Arbor, MI: Journal of Roman Archaeology, 1991). On the dissemination of official documents among the Empire's predominantly illiterate subjects, see Ando, *Imperial Ideology*, 101–17.

understanding of contemporary events through his manipulation of visual media.[87]

Ando's observation applies also to the *Res Gestae* in the Ankaran temple. Considered as a monument, its visual impact on the general population—and thus its efficacy as a vehicle of spatial ideology—must have been greater than that of its literary content.

The text of the *Res Gestae* in the temple of Ankara was, by virtue of its being engraved in so public a space, meant to be seen by as many people as possible. As mentioned earlier, the text of the *Res Gestae* was not a feature of the original construction, since it was most likely completed while Augustus was still alive. Consequently, its addition to the edifice after Augustus' death called for adjustments: details in the masonry of the temple walls had to be smoothed over to create space for the text.[88] The Latin text was inscribed in the *pronaos*, on the walls to the left and right of the entrance. Each wall contained three columns of writing, each about 1.17 m wide. The Greek version, on the other hand, was carved into the exterior of the southern *cella* wall in nineteen columns of text, spanning 20.5 meters in total. As with its Latin counterpart, the heading or preamble was engraved in extra-large letters to set it apart from the rest of the text. Red paint used to bring out the lettering of both inscriptions meant that they were still visible in many places to archeologists in the nineteenth century.[89]

These material aspects of Ankara's installation of the *Res Gestae* call for further reflection. At the risk of stating the obvious, I note that the inscription was displayed not in civic space as such but rather in a cultic site, thus linking Augustus' achievements to his status as *theos*. The placement of the Latin in the *pronaos* and the Greek on the exterior of the southern wall created a sanctuary that was enclosed by a boast of divine accomplishments. In this way, what took place within the temple precincts—and indeed, the temple's very existence in the city landscape—was justified to all who approached. It is not difficult to imagine that even those unable to read the actual text would have been able to learn, whether by rumor or by instruction, the essence of its contents.[90] Along with their strategic placement, the size and the striking color of the letters were after all designed to provoke at least curiosity, if not wonder, at their existence. Moreover, the display of a deity's mighty deeds in his or her dedicated sanctuary was not without precedent in the Greek-speaking world: according to Lactantius, whose source was Euhemerus' *Sacred Record*, the temple to Zeus in Tryphilia featured a column on which the god

---

87. Ando, *Imperial Ideology*, 152.
88. Cooley, *Res Gestae*, 9.
89. Cooley, *Res Gestae*, 9–10.
90. Even as text, the *Res Gestae* did not, strictly speaking, require the viewer to be literate before it could create an impression. What was needed was only that the viewer had access to a literate person. Cf. Ando, *Imperial Ideology*, 101, who draws this insight from the work of H. C. Youtie.

himself wrote "an account of his exploits."⁹¹ On this level alone, the display of the *Res Gestae* in the temple already recruited local Hellenistic religious practice into the service of the Roman emperor.

Literacy, therefore, was not strictly needed for one to "get" the message of the *Res Gestae* as it stood in the sanctuary of Ankara. Its impressive visual form as a monument already communicated quite amply the spirit of its content. This was, undoubtedly, one of the ways in which the *Res Gestae* transformed the urban space of Ankara and made present to its viewers, literate, illiterate, and everything in between, the authority of the emperor in the provincial capital.⁹²

5.3 The Imperial Cults and Sanctuaries of Traditional and Local Gods

The transformation of cultic spaces initiated by the imperial cults of Anatolia was not restricted to the construction of new buildings dedicated to the emperor and his family. Within the religiously diverse context of Roman Anatolia and the fluidity of indigenous pantheons, the imperial cults were "one aspect of an evolving polytheistic system."⁹³ Their incorporation into a broader body of religious practices can be seen in several ways, all of which express some relationship between the imperial family and traditional divinities.

Cults to the imperial family, in many instances, led to the introduction of new infrastructures within sanctuaries of the local gods. This was already a common feature of Hellenistic religion: cultic sites dedicated to a chief deity were often complexes that included a main shrine to the chief deity as well as a variety of buildings and monuments to other gods.⁹⁴ Thus, it is not surprising to find a temple to Augustus and other monuments dedicated to the imperial family within the precincts of the Temple of Artemis in Ephesus.⁹⁵ A provincial Caesareum lies among the archeological remains of a complex containing three other temples to traditional gods in Xanthos.⁹⁶ In the Pergamene shrine to Asclepius we find an imperial room containing a statue of Hadrian, which may well have been used for an imperial festival that, according to corroborating epigraphic evidence, was held at the sanctuary.⁹⁷

---

91. Lactantius, *Div. Inst.* 1.11.33. On other parallels made between Zeus and Augustus in the imperial period, see Cooley, *Res Gestae*, 41.

92. In a similar way, the placement of the *Res Gestae* in Augustus' mausoleum in Rome was calculated (quite literally—by astrologers) to express his significance in cosmological symbolism. On this, see Nicolet, *Space, Geography, and Politics*, 16–17.

93. Friesen, *Imperial Cults*, 122.

94. Price, *Rituals and Power*, 146.

95. Price, *Rituals and Power*, 254.

96. Price, *Rituals and Power*, 147.

97. Price, *Rituals and Power*, 148.

In addition to the introduction of imperial structures, we also find entire temples jointly dedicated to the emperor and traditional gods. The temple to Aphrodite in Adada was also dedicated to the Theoi Sebastoi and the city, and in the Lydian village of Dareioukome, we find a temple jointly dedicated to the Theoi Sebastoi, the Roman Senate, and the Roman People as well as the goddess Demeter Carpophorus.[98] Despite these common dedications, Simon Price is reluctant to interpret them as indications that the emperors were regarded as true sharers in the sacred space—noting, for example, that the Adadan shrine seems to have contained only a cult statue of Aphrodite. Nonetheless, this is at best an argument from silence. Price's proposal is further complicated by the fact that the Theoi Sebastoi were quite often identified with the traditional gods themselves. In Ephesus, for instance, one inscription informs us that the Demetriasts there venerated the twin sons of Drusus Caesar and Livilla as "the new Dioscuri" (the twin sons of Zeus), and Sebaste, the wife of Augustus, as Demeter Carpophorus.[99] A letter from the Domitian period, furthermore, explicitly refers to "mysteries and sacrifices" that were offered "to Demeter Carpophorus and Thesmophoros and the Theoi Sebastoi" in Ephesus "by initiates with great purity and lawful customs, together with the priestesses."[100] There was in this instance no tangible distinction made between the traditional gods and the imperial recipients of cult.[101]

Given both the complexity and flexibility of these local polytheisms, there is no need to deduce a single "theology" applicable to every case. For the purposes of my argument, questions as to how these joint dedications may have actually played out in the cultic rhythms of these sites or their implications for the ontological status of the Theoi Sebastoi are secondary. What remains is the fact that the sanctuaries were designated, at least *in name*, for cults to the Roman imperial family. This is true even at Rhodiapolis, where one inscription points to a temple and cult statues of Asclepius, Hygeia, the Sebastoi, and the city, and yet another speaks only of Asclepius and Hygeia. Price himself admits in this case that "it was possible for there to be different ideas about the same temple,"[102] and there is thus no good reason to diminish the significance of the first inscription, which seems to have reflected the views of at least one group of worshipers. My point is simply that the imperial cults inaugurated changes to cultic life in Anatolia that engendered a shift in the way these spaces were understood. Insofar as they can be taken as reflective of how people conceived them, such joint dedications signal an important transformation of cultic sites, even if their impact on ritual life remains obscure or uncertain to us. At the very least, they point to the forging of an unprecedented link between local gods and the imperial family, and a subsequent

---

98. Price, *Rituals and Power*, 149. Dareioukome: *TAM* V.2.1335.

99. *IEph* 4337 = *SEG* 4.515. For a discussion of this inscription and its significance, see Harland, "Imperial Cults within Local Cultural Life," 90–3.

100. *IEph* 213.

101. Harland, "Imperial Cults within Local Cultural Life," 92.

102. Price, *Rituals and Power*, 149.

change—an "imperialization," if one may call it that—in the very meaning of sacred spaces.

5.4 The Imperial Cults and the Transformation of Civic Spaces

As we have already seen in the case of Ephesus (Section 5.2.1 above), the imperial cults reconfigured civic spaces and public life according to the city's relations to the Empire's center. This reconfiguration reflected a broader pattern of change in cities under Roman rule, as Price observes:

> The rectangular space [of the upper agora of Ephesus] enclosed by porticoes on three sides, with a carefully positioned temple in the centre, contrasts very strikingly with the main square of a city in the classical period, such as Athens, where buildings and monuments were much more casually disposed. The Ephesian square in fact is an example of a tendency of the Hellenistic and Roman periods toward greater regularization and formalization of public space. For example, porticoes were increasingly employed to regulate the boundaries of squares, and streets in cities such as Ephesus and Pergamum were transformed by the addition of colonnades.[103]

These architectural alignments, Price goes on to argue, ought to be seen as reflective of greater Roman control over the Greek cities and the corresponding erosion of their autonomy. Specifically, they mirrored the consolidation of power under what was effectively monarchical rule in the imperial period. "Within this overall architectural development of the Greek city," Price concludes, "was embedded the architecture of the imperial cult"[104]—that is, a remapping of the Empire around the emperor and his family.

I have already argued above that the material structures of the imperial cults reflected a geography that reimagined the world with Rome at its center and the provinces as imperial peripheries. This way of mapping the world bears further implications once we conceive of the imperial cults not only in terms of their "static" structures (i.e. buildings) but also their more dynamic aspects—that is, the aspect of their enactment in ritual.

As discussed earlier in Chapter 3, the celebration of imperial festivals at the provincial and municipal levels, with their processions, sacrifices, and athletic contests, connected the rhythms of local Anatolian life to the events of the imperial center. Whether these festivals were organized on special occasions (e.g., the birth of heirs or to commemorate an emperor's victory in a battle), at regular intervals (e.g., the birthday of an emperor), or incorporated into festivals and feasts of traditional divinities such as local avatars of Zeus, Dionysus, and Aphrodite, they

---

103. Price, *Rituals and Power*, 145.
104. Price, *Rituals and Power*, 146.

entailed not only the Romanization of time but also of lived spaces. These cultic celebrations infused cities and surrounding areas by reproducing, in ritual and image, the presence of the emperor and his family.

This point can be easily seen when we consider the fact that the sacrifices that were so integral to imperial celebrations were not restricted to dedicated shrines and temples, but also took place in civic centers. In Miletus, for example, the courtyard of the council house was home to an imperial altar that would have been used for sacrifices on such occasions, thus transforming what was ordinarily a civic space into an imperial cultic site.[105] Likewise, these ceremonies could also take place in the theater. Local officials would, for example, offer incense from center-stage at the theater of Gytheum before the beginning of contests held as part of an imperial festival. The theater was also suitably outfitted with statues of Augustus, Livia, and Tiberius for such occasions.[106]

Public processions on the occasion of an imperial festival meant that the city itself became permeated with ritual. Xenophon of Ephesus' vivid description in *An Ephesian Tale* captures the lively spirit of a procession held in honor of Artemis:

> All the local girls had to process, richly adorned, and the young men. . . . A great crowd both of locals and of foreigners gathered for the spectacle. For it was the custom at that festival to find husbands for the girls and wives for the young men. The members of the procession filed past, first the carriers of sacred objects, torches, baskets and incense burners, then horses, dogs and hunting equipment for war and especially for peace.[107]

At Gytheum, processions held during imperial festivals were outfitted with the due symbols of empire. The procession began at the temple of Asclepius and Hygeia, progressing toward the imperial sanctuary where a bull, among other sacrifices, was offered. The procession culminated in the theater where, as mentioned above, an offering of incense preceded the start of athletic contests held in honor of the emperor.[108] Events such as this meant that public spaces, such as the city's main thoroughfares, theaters, squares, and hippodromes, became loci in which the city's dependence on Rome and her emperor was ritually enacted and thus made clear and present in a theater of power.

Imperial celebrations also drew people into the urban areas from the surrounding villages and countryside. To illustrate by way of analogy the transformation of urban landscapes on such occasions, Price uses the example of the bi-annual assizes at Apamea-Celaenae.[109] The provincial governor's arrival in

---

105. Price, *Rituals and Power*, 109.
106. Price, *Rituals and Power*, 149.
107. Xenophon of Ephesus, *An Ephesian Tale* 1.2.2–5, as translated in Price, *Rituals and Power*, 110.
108. Price, *Rituals and Power*, 111.
109. Price, *Rituals and Power*, 107.

the city for these judicial proceedings turned it into a hub of activity.[110] Dio Chrysostom writes that, when the courts are in session (every other year), "they bring together an unnumbered throng of people—litigants, jurymen, orators, princes, attendants, slaves, pimps, muleteers, hucksters, harlots, and artisans." Of particular interest to our discussion are his observations about the economic impact of this redistribution of people on the city:

> Consequently not only can those who have goods to sell obtain the highest prices, but also nothing in the city is out of work, neither the teams nor the houses nor the women. And this contributes not a little to prosperity; for wherever the greatest throng of people comes together, there necessarily we find money in greatest abundance, and it stands to reason that the place should thrive. For example, it is said, I believe, that the district in which the most flocks are quartered proves to be the best for the farmer because of the dung, and indeed many farmers entreat the shepherds to quarter their sheep on their land. So it is, you see, that the business of the courts is deemed of highest importance toward a city's strength and all men are interested in that as in nothing else.[111]

In context, Dio makes these points to show the people of Apamea-Celaenae that they are no less privileged for being an assize-center, despite the fact that they did not get to host the provincial imperial cult. Using Dio's words as a yardstick, Price surmises that the crowds drawn by provincial imperial festivals would have been even larger, noting that these would have drawn people from other provinces as well as traders attracted to the various tax exemptions granted on such occasions.[112]

We can, like Price, imagine quite easily how the celebration of an imperial festival would have similarly affected an urban center and its surrounding area. They were occasions on which people came together for sacrifices, processions, games, banquets, and gladiatorial contests. This meant, consequently, more business for local shopkeepers, more seasonal work for itinerant craftsmen, and a greater market in which farmers from nearby villages could sell their produce. Like the assizes, these festivals would have contributed "not a little to prosperity," as Dio says. What is most significant for our discussion here is that these changes in material and social practices—changes in the flow of goods and money, people, labor, etc.—are truly *spatial* transformations (Lefebvre's "conceived space").[113] While such transformations quite certainly existed prior to Roman occupation, it

---

110. Since there were no standing courts in the provinces, governors toured their respective provinces to convene judicial hearings at appointed cities, or assize-centers. These proceedings took place at stipulated intervals, usually annually, but this could vary. See Graham Burton, "Government and the Provinces," in *The Roman World, Volume 1*, ed. J. S. Wacher (London and New York, NY: Routledge, 2002), 431–2.

111. Dio Chrysostom, *Or.* 35.15–17 (Crosby trans.).

112. Price, *Rituals and Power*, 107.

113. Cf. Section 1.3.2 above.

is significant that, with the advent of the imperial cults, the ways people moved in and experienced urban spaces were now reconfigured according to a new, emergent criterion—that of the Roman emperor. If Harvey is correct that the ability to influence the social production of space translates into social power,[114] the imperial festivals were key to Roman domination. Festal conviviality, gainful employment, prosperity, awe at imperial ritual—these were the means by which the populace could see, feel, and taste the visceral effects of *Pax Romana*. That peace was not merely an idea but an aggregate of tangible, embodied experiences.

The related practice of euergetism that accompanied these festivals and made them possible also meant that cultic sites were transformed into loci of Roman benefaction. In Ankara, for example, imperial festivals were accompanied by public banquets (*demothoiniai*), thus imbuing an older Celtic tradition with a Roman tenor.[115] The distribution of grain and oil, athletic games, and gladiatorial shows accompanied the celebration of imperial sacrifices and added to their festal character, giving the people cause to rejoice in the very reality of empire. These were frequently sponsored by local elites who had been appointed to special offices and priesthoods of the imperial cults, providing them with opportunities to gain sociopolitical standing by aligning themselves to the emperor.[116] In this way, the very "stuff" of bodied life—food, drink, leisure—became concomitant with the patronage of the Roman Empire and its collaborators. By thus regulating the material context of personal and social experience of Rome's subjects, the imperial festivals contributed to the maintenance of the Empire's ideological and political hegemony.[117]

Collectively, the entire apparatus of imperial celebration transformed cities and their dependent territories into spaces that affirmed the benefits of Roman rule. These became sites in which the power of the imperial family was ritually performed, made real, and truly venerated as life-giving. The emperor provided the rationale for liturgy, the ruling elite furnished its execution, and the general public became participants and recipients of gifts. This ordo reflects the very logic of Rome's imperial cartography: it "performed" as a world in which grace shone forth from the emperor and, channeled through his collaborators, brought about what the *koinon* of Asia described as "a new appearance to the whole world."

5.5 Conclusion

One of the defining elements of the Roman occupation of Anatolia was the emergence of a new imperial geography in which the world came to be gradually defined in relation to Rome. At the heart of the Empire's spatial ideology was Rome itself—or, more specifically, the emperor. The imperial cults were an important

---

114. Harvey, *The Condition of Postmodernity*, 233.
115. Mitchell, *Anatolia, Vol. I*, 110.
116. Mitchell, *Anatolia, Vol. I*, 117.
117. Cf. Harvey, *The Condition of Postmodernity*, 226–7.

means by which the Empire strengthened its control over the production of space in Anatolia. They played a crucial role in several ways.

Cultic sites for the veneration of the emperor and the imperial family were often strategically erected in prominent locations to make visible Rome's power and importance in the life of the people. This was sometimes achieved by placing the sites in central locations in the city, or by building a temple on an elevated plane to inspire awe in its viewers. The latter was the strategy chosen for the temple to the Sebastoi in Ephesus. There also, the incorporation of local deities into the temple architecture as well as its location within a matrix of socially-significant structures (the agora and civic buildings) worked hand-in-hand to highlight the importance of the emperor for both city and province. Sculptures at the Sebasteion of Aphrodisias virtually transformed it into a catechism of imperial ideology. Its reliefs allegorized the eternity and vastness of Rome's rule, enshrouding the emperor's power in myth and asserting the Empire's awesome authority over both natural forces and the peoples of the known world. At Ankara, the *Res Gestae* of Augustus was put to good use. Written onto the walls of the imperial temple, the text boasted of the accomplishments of Augustan expansionism and constructed a world in which Rome was at the center. The visibility of the inscription—ensured by the size of its letters as well as their location on the *pronaos* and exterior wall—turned the document into a monument, a visual testament to the Empire's incredible reach. When an imperial cult did not possess an exclusive cultic site, its integration into the sanctuary of a local and/or traditional god transformed religious life by inserting into it the commemoration of the emperor and his family.

The power to regulate space is also the power to regulate the movement of bodies in that space.[118] The construction of these infrastructures required, in the first place, mobilization of economic machinery, including but not limited to material collaboration of a local ruling elite, the commandeering of skilled workers and slave labor, the supply of materials, and provisions for workers. These structures themselves "were not static," Justin Meggitt writes, "but dynamic in the consciousness of the inhabitants of the first-century world[;] they were places about which regular public rituals, processions, sacrifices, and feasts would be centred, in which all members of the community would be involved."[119] The actual celebration of imperial festivals in cultic sites entailed a broader program of processions, sacrifices, and athletic contests that drew people into the city from the surrounding countryside. These events provided new economic and social opportunities to Rome's subjects, re-configuring existing networks of social relations and the spatial practices of these communities. Changes brought about by the imperial cults had a discernible signature: the expanding presence of the emperor in Anatolian life. By this criterion, they redefined how people moved in space, as well as how they experienced and thought about space.

---

118. As Foucault (*Discipline and Punish*, 141) observes: "discipline proceeds from the distribution of individuals in space."

119. Meggitt, "Taking the Emperor's Clothes Seriously," 147.

Chapter 6

SPACE IN 1 PETER

I have, in the previous chapter, examined the imperial cults of Anatolia as agents of spatial production, illustrating the ways in which they collectively imagined a new geography in which the emperor was central. This chapter will now examine another way of looking at space—that of the author of 1 Peter who thought of spatial realities according to a different set of criteria. As was the case with his construal of time, his construal of space was the outworking of a cosmology that was recalibrated according to God's salvific work in Christ.

Before proceeding, it is necessary to revisit an important caveat I stated in Chapter 1 of this project—namely, what I termed "a stark asymmetry" in the types of evidence available (see Section 1.4). This asymmetry will become more evident as we move from talking about spatial imagination in the imperial cults to spatial imagination in 1 Peter. In the case of the former, we have both textual and non-textual evidence (i.e. archeological remains as well as inscriptions and documents) from which we can then reconstruct an imperial discourse of space. With the latter, however, I am reconstructing spatial discourse only from textual evidence, i.e. the letter itself. Strictly speaking, this is a limitation rather than an obstacle, since the scope of this project is concerned with comparing ideological productions—that is, we are concerned with discursive practices, of which texts are crucial (though not exclusive) sources. Though this means that we are working with much more limited evidence in the case of 1 Peter, what is important to bear in mind is that we are still dealing with a comparative study of spatial discourses. This seems to me worth restating as we transition from evidence that is more overtly concrete (e.g., temples) to evidence that is only discursive in nature.

This chapter will grapple with the spatial vision in 1 Peter as a two-pronged ideology. It investigates how the Petrine author engages in a spatial discourse that simultaneously dislocates his readers by legitimizing their experience of non-belonging (Section 6.1) and relocates them by envisioning for them a new way of belonging (Section 6.2). After looking at each of these strategies in turn, I evaluate this spatial discourse as a means of critiquing empire and offering ideological resistance against Roman imperial ideology (Section 6.3).

6.1 The Spatial Production of Non-Belonging

The author of 1 Peter addresses his letter to "the sojourning elect of the diaspora" (ἐκλεκτοῖς παρεπιδήμοις διασπορᾶς, 1:1).[1] In this section, I will argue that παρεπιδήμοις διασπορᾶς is a metaphorical designation deployed by the author to generate a sense of displacement in his readers right from the letter's beginning. Wherever they may be located in the Roman provinces of Anatolia, the readers of 1 Peter are immediately cast as a dispersed people whose sociopolitical ties to their localities are tenuous at best. Irrespective of their social location, they are sojourners; irrespective of their geographical location, they are "of the diaspora." As such, this opening constructs Anatolian space as the space of Christian non-belonging: Pontus, Galatia, Cappadocia, Asia, and Bithynia are negatively defined as spaces in which the disciples of the Nazarene only dwell as sojourners.

This opening is in keeping with the broader tenor of 1 Peter as a diaspora letter.[2] The trope of displacement it evokes is sustained by two other features in the text: first, by the theme of sojourning sustained elsewhere in the author's parenetic strategy (παροικία, 1:17; ὡς παροίκους καὶ παρεπιδήμους, 2:11); and second, by the naming of "Babylon" (5:13) as the site of the letter's origin. These basic observations already supply the key pieces we need to build the following framework for 1 Peter: it is (1) a letter written in and from "Babylon" (2) addressed to Christians of "the diaspora" (3) whom the author characterizes as "resident aliens and sojourners" (2:11; 1:1) and (4) whom he instructs in Christian discipleship for "the time of [their] residence as aliens" (παροικία, 1:17). To examine more closely the author's strategy and intent of creating a particular vision of space—one that, I will argue later, displaces his readers from the social rhythms of Anatolian life and is thus incompatible with that of Roman imperialism—we can begin by taking a closer

---

1. I have translated "sojourning elect" rather "elect sojourners" to reflect the possible emphasis on the election of the readers based on the syntax of the Greek (so also Hort, *Epistle*, 14–15). Michaels (*1 Peter*, 7) holds that ἐκλεκτοῖς is substantive and παρεπιδήμοις adjectival, since this foregrounding of election would then dovetail nicely with the emphasis on divine initiative elaborated in v. 2. Mark Dubis (*Handbook*, 2) argues for the reverse, though he appears to ignore the immediate context. Achtemeier (*1 Peter*, 81–2), Jobes (*1 Peter*, 75; followed by Schlosser, *Épître*, 50), and Green (*1 Peter*, 14) endorse a third option, taking these words as substantives in apposition. The ambiguity here apparently posed difficulties for some early readers as well, as suggested by the insertion of καί in ℵ* sy.

2. On the classification of 1 Peter as a Christian diaspora letter as well as its similarities with Jewish diaspora letters, see Lutz Doering, "First Peter as Early Christian Diaspora Letter," in *The Catholic Epistles and Apostolic Tradition: A New Perspective on James and the Catholic Letter Collection*, ed. Karl-Wilhelm Niebuhr and Robert W. Wall (Waco, TX: Baylor, 2009), 215–36, 441–57. An expanded version of this essay appears in his more recent book, *Ancient Jewish Letters and the Beginnings of Christian Epistolography*, WUNT 298 (Tübingen: Mohr Siebeck, 2012) (see esp. 430–52).

look at the key building blocks of this spatial vision: the terms παρεπίδημος, πάροικος, παροικία, and διασπορά as they are used in the letter.

6.1.1 Exile: παρεπίδημος, πάροικος, παροικία

In *A Home for the Homeless*, a landmark study that broke new ground in sociological exegesis of the New Testament and 1 Peter in particular, John H. Elliott aimed to provide, among other insights, a social profile of the original recipients of 1 Peter. One of the most well-known arguments staked out in that work is Elliott's literal reading of πάροικος and παρεπίδημος. For him, these terms and their cognates in 1 Peter have their normative, technical meaning as established from contemporaneous documentary and epigraphic evidence both Greco-Roman and early Jewish—namely, they are indicators of the readers' legal and sociopolitical standing rather than metaphorical descriptions of Christian life as a pilgrimage or sojourn on earth.[3] Thus, he argues, in 1 Peter as elsewhere in the New Testament, πάροικος (1:1, 2:11) denotes a "resident alien" with attendant, though curtailed, rights and civil status, and παρεπίδημος (2:11) "the transient visitor who is temporarily residing as a foreigner in a given locality."[4] He sums up his position as follows:

> In 1 Peter the terms *paroikia, paroikoi* and *parepidēmoi* identify the addressees as a combination of displaced persons who are currently *aliens permanently residing in (paroikia, paroikoi)* or *strangers temporarily visiting or passing through (parepidēmoi)* the four provinces of Asia Minor named in the salutation (1:1). These terms ... indicate not only the geographical dislocation of the recipients but also the political, legal, social and religious limitations and estrangement which such displacement entails.[5]

For Elliott, the original recipients of 1 Peter were already resident aliens and strangers even before their conversion to Christianity and "remained so after their conversion."[6] Their experience of displacement and alienation (as suggested by the tone of 1 Peter) was not the effect of their allegiance to Christianity *per se*, but rather of their sociopolitical standing as already-disenfranchised groups in Anatolian society—a predicament intensified once they became Christians. He asks us to imagine the following scenario:

> Comprising both resident aliens living in these [Anatolian] provinces for a greater period of time and visiting strangers briefly passing through, this group

---

3. Elliott, *A Home for the Homeless*, 21–58.
4. Elliott, *A Home for the Homeless*, 30.
5. Elliott, *A Home for the Homeless*, 48.
6. Elliott, *1 Peter*, 101.

of persons, as we may envision it, encountered missionaries of the messianic movement and was attracted to this new community as a way of attaining a haven of acceptance, security, and belonging in an alien and often hostile environment. It was with such persons that the messianic sect, itself a missionary religion on the move, first came into contact as it traveled along the trade routes of the [Roman] Empire.... After joining the movement, however, these Asia Minor strangers and aliens found that adherence to an exotic Israelite sect did not bring freedom from local suspicion and hostility but only exacerbated it.[7]

In 1 Peter, "the actual political and social condition of the addressees as *paroikoi* is used as an occasion to encourage their religious peculiarity and strangeness as well."[8] From this vantage point, the letter becomes a text of consolation to politically- and socially-disenfranchised Christians, written in part to convince its readers that they are not perennially homeless but in fact residents somewhere— not in wider society but in the believing community as *oikos tou theou*, the household of God.

Over the years, however, Elliott's position has gained little traction among other exegetes of 1 Peter—and for good reason.[9] First, it must be noted that Elliott himself seems to waver in his insistence that παρεπίδημος, πάροικος, and παροικία are to be understood strictly as markers of the readers' sociopolitical condition. Already in *A Home for the Homeless* Elliott states that "[t]here is neither need nor reason to postulate mutually exclusive literal/figurative options" with respect to these terms, and that these terms in 1 Peter "describe religious *as well as* social circumstances."[10] In his more recent commentary he puts it this way:

> ...[T]he condition of the actual alien status of *some* of the addressees provided the experiential basis for metaphorically portraying *all* of the recipients as

---

7. Elliott, *1 Peter*, 102.

8. Elliott, *A Home for the Homeless*, 35–6.

9. In addition to interpreters cited in the following discussion, see, e.g., Michaels, *1 Peter*, 7, 116; Achtemeier, *1 Peter*, 174–5; Torrey Seland, *Strangers in the Light: Philonic Perspectives on Christian Identity in 1 Peter*, Biblical Interpretation Series 76 (Leiden: Brill, 2005), 39–78; Williams, *Persecution in 1 Peter*, 96–128; Reinhold Feldmeier, *Die Christen als Fremde: die Metapher der Fremde in der antiken Welt, im Urchristentum und im 1. Petrusbrief*, WUNT 64 (Tübingen: Mohr Siebeck, 1992). One commentator who has sided with Elliott is Scot McKnight (*1 Peter*, The NIV Application Commentary [Grand Rapids, MI: Zondervan, 1996], 24–6, 47–52). Unfortunately, he does not seem aware of the criticisms that have been raised against Elliott's position (see 24 n. 16), and virtually accepts his arguments without question. Jobes (*1 Peter*, 24–41) has attempted to offer a more viable adaptation of Elliott's reading, although like McKnight she fails to sufficiently address historical and literary arguments to the contrary; moreover, her revised position is plagued by historical errors. See the criticism of Jobes in Horrell, "Aliens and Strangers?" 115–16.

10. Elliott, *A Home for the Homeless*, 42 (emphasis in original).

sharing the social condition but also the divine vocation of Israel's first and prototypical resident aliens [i.e. Abraham and Sarah].[11]

It is not difficult to see how these qualifications end up undermining Elliott's thesis that παρεπίδημος, πάροικος, and παροικία describe the actual political and social status of the original audience of 1 Peter—a point then put to work in his interpretation of other aspects of the letter, e.g., the predominantly rural setting of its readers. If these terms apply only to *some* of the addressees and are then generalized by the author to *all* of the recipients—and it is noteworthy that the author of 1 Peter gives no indication that he is making this generalization[12]—this *ipso facto* means that their *primary* meaning in 1 Peter is metaphorical and not literal. Even in its more tempered formulation in Elliott's *Anchor Bible* commentary quoted above, this exegetical stance is marred by fundamental self-contradiction.

More important, perhaps, is the problematic nature of Elliott's handling of the historical evidence. Steven Bechtler, citing a wealth of discussions by historians and classicists on the subject, points out that in both non-biblical literature and inscriptions of the period, πάροικος refers not to a resident alien but to one who was simply a non-citizen of the *polis*.[13] In Anatolia both before and during Roman occupation, the πάροικοι (Latin: *peregrinus*) were those who did not have rights to full participation in the civic affairs of the city. They did not only comprise resident aliens, but "a recognized social stratum *that included both native and nonnative residents* who were not full citizens and so did not possess the rights of citizenship."[14] Elliott's chief error, according to Bechtler, lies in defining πάροικος and παροικία in terms of displacement or foreignness ("the strange, the alien, the foreign, the 'other'")[15] rather than with non-citizenship.[16]

The greatest blow to Elliott's literal reading comes from the fact that the letter itself suggests that the author does not use πάροικος and παρεπίδημος in the technical sense. Two basic observations point us in this direction: (1) the readers

---

11. Elliott, *1 Peter*, 102 (emphasis in original); cf. *idem*, 481. Nonetheless, any apparent concession on his part is overridden, in the very same commentary, by unqualified insistence that "these terms indicate the actual social condition of the addressees as strangers and aliens in Asia Minor society" (313)—an idea rehashed (again, without qualification) in other key places of the work (368, 461). Given Elliott's own ambivalence, the reader can be excused, then, for being baffled by his admission that "[i]n actuality, it is neither necessary nor advisable to require an absolute distinction between literal and figurative usage with respect to these Petrine terms" (481).

12. As Paul does, for example, in 1 Cor. 6:11 when addressing smaller groups within the broader Christian communities of Corinth: "such were some of you."

13. Bechtler, *Following in His Steps*, 71–3.

14. Bechtler, *Following in His Steps*, 73 (emphasis in original).

15. Elliott, *A Home for the Homeless*, 24.

16. Bechtler, *Following in His Steps*, 74.

are collectively addressed as παρεπίδημοι in 1 Pet. 1:1, and (2) they are all said to be living in the state of παροικία in 1:17. If, as Elliott insists, the terms πάροικος and παρεπίδημος are to be accorded their literal sociopolitical meaning and designate not one but two distinct groups, i.e. resident aliens and transient strangers, then why does the author conflate these terms in the letter? This is best explained by interpreting πάροικος, παροικία, and παρεπίδημος as figurative designations rather than technical markers of their sociopolitical standing.[17] Accordingly, the author uses them interchangeably: he can call them παρεπίδημοι in 1:1, speak of their life as παροικία in 1:17, and address them as παροίκους καὶ παρεπιδήμους in 2:11.[18]

The joint use of πάροικος and παρεπίδημος to refer to the recipients at 2:11 further warrants a broader, more figurative reading of the terms. As Horrell points out, the text to which the author most likely alludes here is LXX Gen. 23:4, in which the patriarch Abraham speaks of his sojourn among the Hittites in the following manner: "Πάροικος καὶ παρεπίδημος ἐγώ εἰμι μεθ' ὑμῶν."[19] In this context, neither term was used in the technical meaning—in which case Abraham could have only been *either* πάροικος or παρεπίδημος but not both—indicating that the Petrine author uses them in a broader sense. Thus, 2:11 "appropriates the language with which Abraham voices the nature of his residence among the Hittites" so as to "convey something about the character of their experience rather than their literal socio-political status."[20] (Further examples of a similarly elastic usage in the Septuagint can be found in Lev. 25:23, Ps. 38:13 [MT: 39:12], and 1 Chron. 29:15.)[21] But what is it about the readers' experience that these terms are supposed to underscore?

At this juncture it is necessary to note that the literal-vs.-figurative dichotomization of these terms can lead to the oversight of a fundamental point: their power as metaphors in 1 Peter is precisely derived from the force of their literal-historical meaning in the sociopolitical world in which the epistle was produced.[22] As Horrell notes, a metaphorical reading must in no way obscure the

---

17. Troy Martin (*Metaphor and Composition in 1 Peter* [Atlanta, GA: Scholars Press, 1992], 191–2) tempers Elliott's position somewhat by maintaining that the terms πάροικος and παρεπίδημος each retain their distinctive, technical meaning ("resident alien" and "visiting alien" respectively), although the author uses them together in 2:11 as a hendiadys to designate a *single* concept: the non-citizen. This attempt at nuance, nonetheless, amounts to distinction without difference: it fails to explain why the readers are collectively referred to as παρεπίδημοι (1:1) and, a little later, their way of life described as παροικία.

18. Cf. Horrell, "Aliens and Strangers?" 117.

19. Horrell, "Aliens and Strangers?" 117. Likewise, Achtemeier, *1 Peter*, 174.

20. Horrell, "Aliens and Strangers?" 117.

21. Horrell, "Aliens and Strangers?" 118. In LXX Ps. 38:13 (MT: 39:12), the only other place in the LXX where πάροικος and παρεπίδημος occur together, the terms are used in poetic parallelism, and so do not bear their technical meanings.

22. For a similar point, see Joel B. Green, *1 Peter* (Grand Rapids, MI: Eerdmans, 2007), 16.

fact that these terms are used in 1 Peter "to depict a sense of social alienation, or estrangement from the world due to the hostility of the wider society."²³ This seems to be Elliott's basic point when, in his discussion of LXX Ps. 38:13 and LXX Ps. 118:9, 19, he plainly admits that πάροικος in these texts "portray in a figurative religious sense the relation of believer to God," though this "in no way precludes the actual social experience from which this metaphorical usage derives and receives its symbolic force."²⁴ What Elliott is determined to reject—and rightly, I think—is an over-spiritualized interpretation of these terms and the letter as a whole. However, in doing so he overcompensates. His insistence that παρεπίδημος, πάροικος, and παροικία hold their chief sociopolitical meaning in 1 Peter hyperextends their lexical meaning over and against the more immediate contextual cues discussed above. By all counts, the internal evidence, i.e. their use in 1 Peter, shows that the Petrine author uses παρεπίδημος, πάροικος, and παροικία more loosely than Elliott allows.

Nevertheless, their nature as metaphors should not cause us to underestimate the freight of meaning they bear and which deserves further consideration. While these terms may not possess the legal and technical meaning Elliott assigns to them, they are no less *sociological*—even though they belong to the realm of figurative speech. As a semantic constellation, these descriptors engender profound existential "homelessness" by evoking a prominent motif in the scriptures of Israel. Elliott himself notes that παροικέω and its cognates are used in the Septuagint to describe the itinerancy and estrangement that marked the lives of Abraham and his descendants in Egypt (Gen. 12:10; 15:13; 47:4, 9), Hittite territory (Gen. 23:4), and Canaan (cf. Gen. 17:8; Exod. 6:4; Ps. 104:12 [MT: 105:12]); of Moses and his family in Midian (Exod. 2:22); of the family of Elimelech, from which the Davidic line is traced (Ruth 1:1); of the patriarchs in Mesopotamia and Egypt (Jdt. 5:7, 8, 10); and more generally, of Israel in Egypt (Num. 20:15; Ps. 104:23 [MT: 105:23]; Isa. 52:4).²⁵ This theme did not go unnoticed in early Christian kerygma. Outside 1 Peter we find the patriarchs described as παρεπίδημοι (Heb. 11:13). Moses in Midian (Acts 7:29) and Israel in Egypt (Acts 7:6) are in turn called πάροικος (Israel's time in Egypt is, correspondingly, a παροικία, Acts 13:17); and παροικέω is used for Abraham's residence in Canaan (Heb. 11:9). Indeed, the expression παροίκους καὶ παρεπιδήμους in 1 Pet. 2:11, with its allusion to LXX Gen. 23:4, conjures a commanding figure so relevant to the epistle's readers: Abraham, the paradigmatic faithful one who sojourned among non-believers (Hittites) and recipient of the divine promises that lie at the heart of Israel's recurrent, dramatic narratives of exile and return to the land (cf. Gen. 12:1–3; 15:7; Ezek. 33:24; Rom. 4:13; Heb. 11:8–12).

That παρεπίδημος, πάροικος, and παροικία assume a broader, metaphorical meaning in 1 Peter does not necessarily dilute or over-spiritualize the sociopolitical

---

23. Horrell, "Aliens and Strangers?" 118.
24. Elliott, *A Home for the Homeless*, 28. Cf. Schlosser, *Épître*, 145.
25. I have adapted here the citations listed in Elliott, *A Home for the Homeless*, 27.

freight of these ancient traditions, but rather draws from it. In fact, they disclose the author's strategy of creating a sense of spatial dislocation in his readers. By describing them in terms of non-citizenship, he casts them as heirs to the existential legacy of God's elect—those who never truly belonged in the places they lived and endured a seemingly-perpetual state of dispossession. The author is thus not merely borrowing well-worn vocabulary to describe their present condition; he is giving them the hermeneutical lens with which to interpret rightly their experience of alienation and estrangement. Their spatial, bodily non-belonging, as with their being out of step with "Gentile time,"[26] is precisely what marks them out as heirs of the faith of Abraham. Evidence of this lies in the fact that the author immediately contrasts his readers' Christian identity as πάροικοι-παρεπίδημοι with that of the Gentiles (2:12).[27] Here we have the confluence of their new spatialized identity and the set of social relations it entails: the forging of their brotherhood in Christ, under God as "Father," means that they can no longer relate to Gentile bodies in the same way (cf. 1:18; 4:4). Once we think of these reconfigured social relations—with "everyone," within the brotherhood, with the emperor, with God (2:17)—as material interactions and practices between *bodies*, their spatiality virtually becomes self-evident. The Christian movement, after all, was constituted by Christian bodies *moving* in Anatolian space.

This strategy of displacing the readers by designating them as πάροικοι-παρεπίδημοι cannot be thought of as being simply *descriptive*—that is, it does not merely reflect their experience in the margins. It is, rather, *creative*—aimed at forming their identity, their self-perception, effectively dislodging them from the possibility of belonging fully within wider society, thus framing Christian identity precisely in terms of non-belonging. This becomes all the more evident when we consider another aspect of this trope of displacement: the author's representation of the text of 1 Peter as a letter written to "the diaspora" from "Babylon" (1:1; 5:13).

6.1.2 To the Diaspora, from Babylon

The prescript of 1 Peter explicitly marks it out as a diaspora letter: ἐκλεκτοῖς παρεπιδήμοις διασπορᾶς Πόντου, Γαλατίας, Καππαδοκίας, Ἀσίας καὶ Βιθυνίας (1:1). While it is clear that Pontus, Galatia, Cappadocia, Asia and Bithynia are regarded by the author as the "diaspora" and the term is thus used in the geographical sense, what exactly makes these territories so? In part because the present scholarly consensus favors a largely Gentile audience for 1 Peter, exegetes have tended to prefer understandings of the term "diaspora" beyond its stricter use in Jewish literature, in which the term typically refers to territories outside the land

---

26. See Chapter 4, esp. Section 4.2.1 above.
27. Elliott, *A Home for the Homeless*, 35, 44. It is noteworthy that, throughout the letter, the antithesis to the readers' identity as πάροικοι-παρεπίδημοι is not those who are residents, but "Gentiles," who are in turn defined not by their political status but rather by their ethical conduct (4.3).

of Israel to which God's elect have been dispersed (e.g., Deut. 28:25; 30:4; Jdt. 5:19; Jer. 41:17 [MT: 34:17]; 2 Macc. 1:27; cf. Jn 7:35). It would have been unlikely, after all, for the author to refer to his predominantly Gentile audience in Asia Minor as dispersed or exiled from the original promised homeland(s) of Israelite traditions (Jerusalem, Judea, Israel)—or, indeed, any other identifiable geographical area.[28]

Several options arise here that can more or less be grouped into two categories (though these are not mutually exclusive). Some commentators emphasize a more "spiritual" dimension of the readers' existential dislocation, understanding "diaspora" here to mean that Christians do not belong in this world because their true spiritual home lies in heaven.[29] Other exegetes emphasize "diaspora" as a marker of the readers' sociological or sociopolitical non-belonging.[30] Goppelt, for example, understands "diaspora" in 1:1 as indicative of a marginalized position in society, "of being elected and being a foreigner."[31] Given that 1 Peter remains largely reticent regarding any notion of a "home" in the hereafter (apart from its reference to heaven as the place where the divine inheritance is kept, 1:4) and is far more concerned with its readers' social relations,[32] the latter view has rightfully, I think, gained a surer footing in current exegesis.

Reading 1 Peter as a Christian diaspora letter, Lutz Doering suggests that "diaspora" ought to be understood in light of the readers' social marginalization as indicated by the author's use of παρεπίδημος, πάροικος, and παροικία. This link, he observes, is something that 1 Peter shares in common with contemporaneous Jewish traditions that similarly associate estrangement with divine election.[33] Being chosen by God (the "vertical dimension" of election) means that the chosen people must negotiate boundaries and manage difference vis-à-vis the non-elect (the "horizontal dimension" of election). The author of 1 Peter, Doering argues,

---

28. For this line of reasoning see, e.g., Kelly, *Commentary*, 4, 40; Michaels, *1 Peter*, 6, 8; Achtemeier, *1 Peter*, 82. Elliott's position on this is somewhat confused. While he insists that "diaspora" in 1:1 "has a customary literal (geographical) rather than figurative force"—apparently thinking of it as a geographical designation—he almost immediately lapses into the figurative by stating that the term "expresses simply the physically dispersed *situation* of the addressees [outside the land of Israel] ... and the *historical continuity* of the elect strangers with the frequent condition of Israel as a vulnerable minority in foreign and hostile regions" (*1 Peter*, 314; emphasis added).

29. E.g., Kelly, *Commentary*, 47, 103; Beare, *Epistle*, 75, 135; Davids, *Epistle*, 46–7; Best, *1 Peter*, 70. See also those listed in Elliott, *Homeless*, 55 n. 71. Though on the place of heaven in the letter, see Section 6.2.2 below.

30. E.g., Achtemeier, *1 Peter*, 82; Horrell, *Epistles*, 20–1; Feldmeier, *Letter*, 52–3; Elliott, *1 Peter*, 314 (though see n. 30 above).

31. Goppelt, *1 Peter*, 66.

32. Feldmeier (*Letter*, 52 n. 23) reads even this reference to the heavenly inheritance in the sociological sense: it indicates that "foreignness is indeed concretely experienced in society."

33. Doering, "Diaspora Letter," 230. So also Goppelt, *1 Peter*, 66.

draws from and creatively sharpens this perspective by making election the intrinsic reason for "diaspora" and stresses the readers' divinely-appointed otherness by casting them as aliens and strangers. This election is manifested in their new birth (1:3, 23; 2:1–3), such that Christians are those who have "entered into a Diaspora existence by their rebirth."[34] The life of social estrangement thus becomes integral to Christian identity in 1 Peter.

Whereas Doering and others have elucidated the social or sociological component of 1 Peter's use of "diaspora," scholars seem to have largely passed over an important, more overt dimension of its meaning: the spatial. In discussions of "diaspora" as a metaphor rooted in Jewish thought and experience, what has consistently escaped many scholars' attention is the fact that its deployment in 1 Peter is equally an act of *spatial production*. It is, in the plainest sense, a geographical term[35]—but one charged with social, political, and psychological implications. To label Roman Anatolia as a place of "diaspora" is not only to refract the readers' social estrangement through a distinctly Jewish narration of history,[36] but also to construct the entire region—uniformly—as a space of alienation, of strangeness, in which Christians are rightfully out of place as God's elect.

Contrast here the spatial construction embodied in the practices and infrastructures of the imperial cults discussed in the previous chapter—of Anatolia as an aggregate of peripheral territories within the *oikoumenē* to which Rome laid claim as center. In the words of Pliny the Elder, Rome was thus "the parent of all lands" and "the homeland of every people in the entire world."[37] If the imperial cults strove to forge a sense of spatial belonging—to Rome, to empire—then 1 Peter's use of "diaspora" pushes against, at least indirectly, that program. By turning Roman provincial spaces into "diaspora," the author not only rejects the imperial schema of

---

34. Doering, "Diaspora Letter," 231.

35. Martin (*Metaphor and Composition in 1 Peter*, 144–275) argues that "[t]he thematic motif of 1 Peter is provided by the overarching and controlling metaphor of the Diaspora," and that "images and concepts from the Jewish Diaspora dominate the [letter]" from start to finish (273). As intriguing as this thesis appears at first, its execution is marked by two serious flaws. First, while diaspora is an important trope in the letter (as I clearly believe), Martin's attempt to make it do *all* the work of holding the letter together overstrains the concept (e.g., it is unclear how newborn infants evoke diaspora [174–5]). Second, the launching point of his argument is an idiosyncratic definition of "diaspora" as "a road to be traveled, a journey to be undertaken" (150, 274), offered without any appeal to primary Second Temple or early Christian sources (including 1 Peter itself). "Diaspora" primarily refers to *space* or territory, however, and not a journey (though see n. 38).

36. In this sense, "diaspora" evokes a temporal or historical dimension, though here I focus only on its spatial aspect (see the caveat regarding this time–space division in Section 1.3 above). Nonetheless, the very spatiality of diaspora is dependent on the temporal sense it evokes: one can only be "in diaspora" in relation to a past—whether for having lived somewhere else previously, or feeling connected to a legacy tied to a different place.

37. *Natural History* 3.39.

center-and-periphery, but, drawing from the biblical motif and Jewish experience of exile, reimagines Anatolia as exilic space. As he did with the subject of suffering (see Section 4.2.2), he valorizes non-belonging in the name of the gospel, portraying his readers as a people who, by virtue of divine election, belong elsewhere and must therefore live accordingly—that is, as "aliens and strangers."

The deployment of "Babylon" at the end of the letter (Ἀσπάζεται ὑμᾶς ἡ ἐν Βαβυλῶνι συνεκλεκτὴ, 5:13) furthers the production of exilic space inaugurated by "diaspora" in the opening. That the mention of Babylon is likely part of an authorial strategy is suggested by the fact that various other letters of the New Testament, encyclicals or not, do not specify their place of origin[38] (thus giving birth to much curiosity and headache among modern scholars). As discussed in Chapter 2 (Section 2.2.2), the actual referent of the term "Babylon" has been subject to debate, as one would expect, though the majority of scholars lean in favor of "Babylon" here as a designation for Rome. This dominant view has at least two points to commend it: (1) "Babylon" is a common alias for Rome in Jewish and Christian literature following the Roman conquest of Judea in AD 70;[39] (2) early Christian traditions place the letter's attributed author, Peter, and Mark (mentioned in 1 Pet. 5:13) in Rome.[40]

Nevertheless, for the purposes of this study, what is of greater interest is not the actual historico-geographical referent of "Babylon" properly speaking, but rather its place in the author's spatial strategy. Michaels sees its use here as a semantic device in conjunction with "diaspora" in 1:1,[41] and Doering discerns in this pairing of "diaspora" and "Babylon" an *inclusio* around the letter. This framing, as Doering acutely observes, means that 1 Peter presents itself as a letter written *from* the diaspora *to* the diaspora.[42] The deployment of "diaspora" alongside "Babylon" constitutes a strategic move on the part of the author and cannot be attributed to sheer coincidence. We ought to bear in mind, for example, that the New Testament offers at least three other encyclical letters—Ephesians, James, and Revelation (chs 2–3) that bear no explicit indication of their provenance.

Once we think of the diaspora–Babylon construction as a part of the author's spatial strategy, we can more easily see that the traumatic narrative of Israel's captivity and exile under Babylon is used to good effect. It is engaged in the epistle to refigure all Roman-dominated space as an undifferentiated terrain of alienation and exile shared by the author and his readers, resulting in a spatial ideology that openly rejects any idea of imperial territory as "home." Every land under Roman domination, all of the *oikoumenē*, persists as "diaspora." This is why their suffering

---

38. This point is also made by Kelly, *Commentary*, 219–20.
39. See Chapter 2 n. 103.
40. See Chapter 2 n. 111.
41. Michaels, *1 Peter*, 311.
42. Doering, "Diaspora Letter," 233–4. Earlier in the same article, he refutes claims that diaspora letters must originate from Jerusalem or Judea as a criterion (see esp. 218–19, 223–4).

is nothing more than a share in the lot of the family of believers "in all the world" (ἐν [τῷ] κόσμῳ, 5:9). This staggering construction of exilic space legitimates its readers' marginalization and persecution by compelling them to interpret both space and their experience through the lens of a much older narrative: just as God's elect once suffered exile and estrangement in the hands of Babylon, so do Christians of the present day at the hands of Rome.[43]

As an act of spatial production, the diaspora–Babylon motif more evidently works on a "macro" scale—that is, it encompasses entire swathes of Roman territory, from the Anatolian provinces to its site of origin. Nonetheless, we can ask what implications it may have held on a smaller, immediate scale—in the spaces of everyday life of its original recipients. The more immediate, material consequences of this spatial construction become more evident once we bear in mind that the Christian praxis to which 1 Peter calls its readers is embodied and thus takes place precisely in specific "units" of space—in administrative and legal spaces (e.g., 2:13; 3:15–16), in households (e.g., 2:18–3:7), in their gathering places (4:8–11). Conversely, abandoning "human passions" (4:2), if it were to remain something other than abstract moral injunction, means that the readers must also bar themselves from activity spaces in which "licentiousness, passions, drunkenness, revels, carousing, and lawless idolatry" (4:3) take place. To think of themselves as aliens and strangers in diaspora means to accept their out-of-place-ness in these spaces as normative. The experience of difference and the negotiation of the identities of past and present ("the futile ways inherited from your ancestors," 1:18) occur precisely in the sociality of specific material spaces, all of which the author subsumes under the blanket term "diaspora." What the term normalizes, therefore, is not a general case of non-descript *Weltschmerz* or homelessness in the largeness of the cosmos, but the very specific experience of displacement in particular places—the very places one lives life itself: in *polis* and countryside, the town hall, the marketplace, the *oikos*; whether poor or rich, freeperson or house-slave, female or male.

Just as the festivals of the imperial cults drew inhabitants of both city and countryside into Roman imagination of space by means of embodied practices that confirmed that spatiality—processions; sacrifices in temple and shrines and at altars; gladiator performances and athletic contests in stadiums—so we must think of the diaspora–Babylon construct in 1 Peter as an equally concrete act of configuring space, and thus a competitor to the Empire's spatial ideology. The deployment of this trope challenges Rome's imperial geography with an alternative construal of spatiality—one that decenters the Empire both in time and space by evoking a powerful Jewish narrative of violence, subjugation, and exile. By means of a temporal as well as spatial typology, the *oikoumenē* is reimagined as "diaspora"

---

43. This is another example in which the author's construction of space is dependent upon a temporal framework—in this case, a narrative. The dimensions of time and space are interlinked sociopsychologically, just as they are mathematically.

and Rome as Babylon, the archetypal aggressor of God's elect. The social existence of Christians in Anatolia is, correspondingly, a time of exile (1:17)—one of displacement, of non-belonging—the trauma and experience of which looms so large in the scriptures of Israel. And so, for the Petrine author, it is as it once was: in Babylon and Rome, history finds a rhyme. Had Qoheleth read our text, he might have chimed laconically, "What has been is what will be, and what has been done is what will be done; there is nothing new under the sun" (Qoh. 1:9).

6.2 The Spatial Production of Belonging

If 1 Peter dislocates its readers by casting Anatolia and imperial territories as a whole as exilic or alienating space, does the letter tell its readers where they might, in fact, belong? To put this in social terms: if true Christian existence were marked by non-belonging within society at large, could Christians find belonging anywhere at all?

6.2.1 The οἶκος πνευματικός (2:5): Household or Temple?

The author's response to this question is, I believe, in the affirmative, and lies in another trope deployed in his text. In the catena of "stone" passages of 1 Pet. 2:4–8, he states that Christians are "being built into a spiritual house to be a holy priesthood, to offer spiritual sacrifices acceptable to God through Jesus Christ" (2:5). Various exegetes have dedicated their energies to the range of meanings possible for the "spiritual house" (οἶκος πνευματικός) here.[44] The apparent ambiguity arises in large part because of the interpretive options in οἶκος, a word that can refer to both a group of people (household) or a physical edifice or building.[45] Similarly, the adjectival πνευματικός can be understood in various ways, designating that which is "spiritual" as distinguished from the physical or fleshly (ψυχικός; e.g., 1 Cor. 15:44, 46), as well as that which pertains to the realm of the human spirit (e.g., 1 Cor. 14:14–16) or the spirit of God (e.g., 1 Cor. 2:14; 12:1; 14:1).[46] While the expression οἶκος πνευματικός is complicated by the semantic range of its components, several contextual cues serve to allow us to elucidate more precisely its meaning—or, at the very least, its range of meaning.

---

44. E.g., Beare, *Epistle*, 122; Kelly, *Commentary*, 89–90; Goppelt, *1 Peter*, 139–41; Michaels, *1 Peter*, 99–101; Elliott, *1 Peter*, 414–18; Achtemeier, *1 Peter*, 154–9; Jobes, *1 Peter*, 150.

45. "οἶκος," *LSJ*, 1205. Spicq (*Saint Pierre*, 84) notes that in contemporaneous inscriptions, οἶκος sometimes designates the place of worship, and other times the worshiping community.

46. For a detailed discussion of πνευματικός in 1 Peter as well as the NT in general, see Selwyn, *Epistle*, 281–5.

It is helpful to begin with the observation that this passage occurs within a series of statements regarding the readers' Christian identity: as newborn infants (2:2), a spiritual priesthood (2:5), and, famously, "a chosen race, a royal priesthood, a holy nation, God's own people" (2:9). The words οἶκος πνευματικός thus occur within a discussion about people—specifically, believers. It is also clear that the "stones" mentioned in this passage are persons. Christ is described as "a living stone, though rejected by mortals yet chosen and precious in God's sight," (2:4)—specifically, a cornerstone (ἀκρογωνιαῖος, 2:6)—and the readers are themselves "living stones" (λίθοι ζῶντες, 2:5). If the "stones" that make up the οἶκος are people, it would seem that the *primary* sense of οἶκος πνευματικός is, correspondingly, a community of people. But is it therefore necessary to conclude that this community is, specifically, a household?

To draw such a conclusion would be hasty and would impoverish the rich dynamics of the "stone" metaphor. The repeated references to stones—five times in 2:4-8, and seven if one includes the cornerstone (ἀκρογωνιαῖος, 2:6; κεφαλὴν γωνίας, 2:7)—yield an architectural density to the passage and foreground the structural aspect of this οἶκος. This is further augmented by the verb οἰκοδομεῖσθε, which denotes the process of construction.[47] What we have here is precisely a play on the semantic flexibility of οἶκος as meaning both household and building. The two senses are not mutually exclusive but rather dependent on each other.[48] As a collective, the readers' integrity as a community in Christ depends on their being fitted together like the stones that make up a single edifice: they are a building of people dependent on Christ as the cornerstone. The corporate (and corporal) sense of οἶκος is therefore derived from its spatial sense. Any attempt to reduce it to only one of these defuses its imagistic power and impoverishes the dimensions of the text. Furthermore, as I shall argue below, the structure signified by οἶκος in 2:5 is not just any building, but specifically a temple.

On this point, Elliott has been famously insistent that οἶκος in 1 Pet. 2:5 carries only the sense of "household."[49] This position stems largely from the fact that he views οἶκος here as anticipating (and thus parallel in meaning to) βασίλειον in 2:9, which he takes as a substantive, meaning "royal residence" or "house of the king."[50] Moreover, he argues, as an appositive to ἱεράτευμα ἅγιον which follows it, οἶκος

---

47. Cf. Selwyn, *Epistle*, 160; Achtemeier, *1 Peter*, 155-6, 158-9; Jobes, *1 Peter*, 150. Though it does not directly affect my argument here, οἰκοδομεῖσθε can be taken as an indicative or an imperative, and in the passive or middle voice; see Hort, *Epistle*, 109; Dubis, *Handbook*, 47-8.

48. For a similar position, see Jobes (*1 Peter*, 150), who extends this versatility in meaning to the use of οἶκος in 4:17.

49. John H. Elliott, *The Elect and the Holy: An Exegetical Examination of 1 Peter 2, 4-10 and the Phrase Basileion Hierateuma*, Novum Testamentum 12 (Leiden: Brill, 1966), 148-98; *A Home for the Homeless*, 168-70; *1 Peter*, 414-18.

50. Elliott, *A Home for the Homeless*, 169; *1 Peter*, 417. On βασίλειον as "royal residence," see Elliott, *1 Peter*, 435-7; *The Elect and the Holy*, 50-128.

makes better sense if understood as referring to a group of people, i.e. a household of (priestly) people.[51] For him, the οἶκος πνευματικός in 2:5 is identical to the οἶκος τοῦ θεοῦ in 4:17, where it clearly refers to the Christian community as God's household, and not to any structural edifice as such.[52] Elliott therefore maintains that οἶκος in 2:5 can only refer to a group of people (Christians), and cannot carry the spatial sense of "temple."[53]

I deem this position indefensible for several reasons. To begin with, given its semantic range, there is no definitive reason to suppose that οἶκος in 2:5 merely anticipates and is parallel to βασίλειον in 2:9,[54] or even that it is used in the exact same sense as in 4:17. The immediate context of its use ought to be accorded more weight than Elliott allows. Second, while it is true that οἶκος *can* function as an apposition to ἱεράτευμα which follows,[55] it is first and foremost syntactically linked to the preceding images of "living stones" and construction: "καὶ αὐτοὶ ὡς λίθοι ζῶντες οἰκοδομεῖσθε οἶκος πνευματικός..." (2:5). This safeguards the sense of οἶκος as being, at the very least, a building. Third, Elliott's reading does not sufficiently take into consideration the collective impact of the "stone" texts in 2:4–8. The scriptural texts quoted in this section—Isa. 28:16; Ps. 118:22; and Isa. 8:14–15—are, in their original context, references not to just any building, but to a very specific material edifice: the temple in Jerusalem. Finally, the occurrence of οἶκος within a verbal constellation that includes "priesthood" and "sacrifices" (ἱεράτευμα ... θυσίας, 2:5) is too laden with cultic overtones, leading the majority of interpreters to conclude, not only that the Petrine author has a physical structure in mind, but that it is a temple.[56]

---

51. Elliott, *1 Peter*, 417.

52. Elliott, *A Home for the Homeless*, 243. Even at 4:17, however, the connotation of a temple cannot be completely ruled out once it is admitted as a possibility in 2:5 (cf. LXX Ezek. 9:6; so Selwyn, *Epistle*, 226, 299–300; Michaels, *1 Peter*, 271; Achtemeier, *1 Peter*, 315–16; Goppelt, *1 Peter*, 329). Moreover, this verse occurs in the context of believers being described in language reminiscent of the temple (ὁ τῆς δόξης καὶ τὸ τοῦ θεοῦ πνεῦμα ἐφ' ὑμᾶς ἀναπαύεται, 4:14)—especially so if τῆς δόξης here refers to the *Shekinah*, as suggested by Selwyn, *Epistle*, 222–4.

53. Elliott's dismissal of the οἶκος-as-temple view is really quite sweeping: "temple, priesthood and cult play no central role in 1 Peter" (*A Home for the Homeless*, 242). Earlier in the same work, he insists that even ἱεράτευμα in 2:5 "has not been employed to describe the community in cultic terms" (168) despite the explicitly liturgical words that follow it (ἀνενέγκαι πνευματικὰς θυσίας εὐπροσδέκτους [τῷ] θεῷ).

54. As Michaels (*1 Peter*, 100–1) and Achtemeier (*1 Peter*, 159) both point out, the relationship between 2:5 and 2:9 is not as straightforward as Elliott contends.

55. Although this is not necessary, since the εἰς in 2:5 can also be read as purposive to yield the reading: "a spiritual house *for* (the ministry of) a holy priesthood." On this, see Hort, *Epistle*, 109; Michaels, *1 Peter*, 100.

56. Representative are Best, *1 Peter*, 101–2; Selwyn, *Epistle*, 159–60; Kelly, *Commentary*, 89; Goppelt, *1 Peter*, 140; Achtemeier, *1 Peter*, 156. Cf. Elliott, *A Home for the Homeless*, 241–3. See also the criticisms of Elliott's position in Feldmeier, *Die Christen als Fremde*, 203–10.

Even Michaels, who leans in favor of Elliott's "house"/"household" reading, concedes that "it is difficult to imagine a house intended for priesthood as being anything other than a temple of some sort."[57]

That the οἶκος of 2:5 refers to a temple is reinforced by its pairing with πνευματικός. The broader context suggests that this οἶκος is πνευματικός or "spiritual" not in the sense that it is invisible or non-material (no cues in the context warrant this contrast), but rather that it is "of the spirit (of God)"—that is, "caused by or filled with the (divine) spirit."[58] This sense is brought out both by the fact that (1) οἶκος πνευματικός occurs in a section dedicated to the believers' identity (cf. 2:1–10 as a whole, but especially vv. 9–10); and (2) immediately following the explication of this identity, the author urges them to abstain from carnal desires (ἀπέχεσθαι τῶν σαρκικῶν ἐπιθυμιῶν) that wage war against their soul (2:11), reflecting the spiritual–carnal antithesis we find elsewhere in the New Testament (e.g., Jn 3:5–6; 1 Cor. 3:1). This statement regarding the readers' spiritual identity develops the author's initial description of them as those who have been made holy by God's spirit (1:2) and are called to be holy as God is holy (1:16). Not surprisingly, the author later refers to them as people on whom the divine Spirit of glory rests (τὸ τῆς δόξης καὶ τὸ τοῦ θεοῦ πνεῦμα, 4:14), a description again redolent of a temple (cf. Eph. 2:21–22; 2 Cor. 6:16).[59]

We may thus conclude that οἶκος πνευματικός in 2:5 means "a spiritual house" in the sense of an edifice that stands in a particular relationship to God's Spirit. It is, as Horrell posits, "a building which belongs to God and where the Spirit is to be found."[60] More specifically, as the liturgically-saturated vocabulary of the verse indicates, it is a temple whose constitutive building blocks ("living stones") are "quickened and governed by the Spirit of God,"[61] with Jesus as the living cornerstone (2:7). This temple is the locus of the offering of spiritual sacrifices, since the community constitutes not only the temple itself but also the holy priesthood that serves within it (2:5, 9).[62] In the words of Selwyn, "[t]he house

---

57. Michaels, *1 Peter*, 100. So also Horrell, *Epistles*, 40.

58. "πνευματικός," *BDAG* 678 (§2). Achtemeier (*1 Peter*, 155–6): "The adjective πνευματικός ("spiritual") is not so much symbolic or metaphoric as it is intended to indicate its nature [i.e. that of the "house"]: it is the place where the Spirit is to be found." See also Kelly, *Commentary*, 90–1; Selwyn, *Epistle*, 160, 291; Feldmeier, *Letter*, 136. Elliott agrees with taking the genitive πνευματικός in this way ("controlled and animated by God's sanctifying spirit"; *1 Peter*, 418), although, as shown above, he does not allow for the house to be a temple (cf. *A Home for the Homeless*, 168).

59. See n. 54 above.

60. Horrell, *Epistles*, 40. Similarly, Achtemeier, *1 Peter*, 155–6.

61. Selwyn, *Epistle*, 283.

62. The early Christians were not alone in envisioning themselves as a temple. The Qumran community conceived of themselves likewise (1QS 8.5–8; 9.5–6), and spoke of the prayers they offered as sacrifices (1QS 9.3–5). Cf. Andrew M. Mbuvi, *Temple, Exile and Identity in 1 Peter*, LNTS 345 (London and New York, NY: T&T Clark, 2007), 92–4.

is spiritual, because it consists of spiritual persons and exists for spiritual purposes."[63]

6.2.2 The Locus of Belonging: οἶκος πνευματικός (2:5) as Spatial Production

Although exegesis of 1 Peter has been dedicated to the range of meanings possible for this οἶκος πνευματικός—with the consensus leaning in favor of understanding it as a reference to God's temple—scholars have as a whole yet to tease out the spatial implications of this image. How does οἶκος πνευματικός fit into the author's spatial strategy, his construction of space, in the letter as a whole? The answer lies in taking more seriously the spatiality inherent in the very meaning of οἶκος πνευματικός itself.

The author sets before us the image of a temple made up of "living stones"—that is, Christians and Christ himself (*the* paradigmatic living stone and cornerstone). What we are confronted with is a way of envisioning Christian solidarity: a temple made up of material bodies, both those of believers and of the vindicated Jesus, who has now become its cornerstone (2:7). To read οἶκος πνευματικός in this way is not to take the expression in a wooden or hyper-literal sense, but rather to think of it as robustly material, spatial, and imaginative. It tells us that Christian bodies, spread throughout the Anatolian terrain in their respective communities, are simultaneously asked to conceive of themselves as a single, trans-spatial temple joined in Christ and animated by God's spirit. While the corporate nature of this temple-image is often appreciated by interpreters, its *corporeal* character has been less so. Yet the οἶκος πνευματικός is made up of actual, material, living bodies joined in solidarity with the once-broken, now-glorified body of Jesus. The architect of solidarity is none other than God, who is also the builder of this temple (the implied performer of οἰκοδομεῖσθε, 2:5). The bonds forged by this divine construction project are, I argue, as real in the author's mind as the mystical kinship invoked elsewhere in the letter: God is the Father (1:2, 3) over the household of believers (4:17) made up of siblings scattered throughout not only Asia Minor but also "the world" (2:17, 5:9; cf. 5:12: Silvanus as "brother").

The readers of 1 Peter, therefore, are not *only* to be thought of as aliens and sojourners. Their existence in the world is marked by estrangement, yes—but there is also a place where they belong: in the imagined but no-less-real οἶκος

---

63. Selwyn, *Epistle*, 284–5. Tempting though it may be to speculate as to where this temple stands in relation to the Jerusalem Temple, any proposals must remain tenuous. Is the spiritual house he envisions simply an alternative temple, a more authentic temple, or, indeed, a *replacement* for the temple destroyed in the Jewish–Roman war? The author's silence on this matter is palpable, and is part of a broader exegetical mystery—that of Christians' relationship to Israel in the letter (cf. the discussion in Achtemeier, *1 Peter*, 69–72 and notes there). Mbuvi's supersessionist reading of 2:4–10 (*Temple, Exile and Identity*, 90–102) as a passage that contrasts "the 'new Israel'—the new 'Temple-Community'—and the Israel of old with its physical temple" (91) ultimately reads into this silence.

πνευματικός made up of their bodies and constituted as a divine collective. Scattered throughout Anatolia as dispersed communities, they are nonetheless united by one Father, one Lord, and one sanctifying Spirit (1:2). Already in the letter's opening we are presented with a paradox: the spatial dispersion of the recipients across the vastness of Roman Anatolia ("diaspora"), counterbalanced by their solidarity effected by divine election. The author underscores this paradox again toward the end of the letter, speaking of a family (ἀδελφότης, lit. "brotherhood") scattered throughout the world that is yet united in their share of Christ's sufferings (5:9; cf. 4:13). To paraphrase Paul, the temple is one and made up of many living stones, and all the living stones, though many, are one temple in Christ (1 Cor. 3:16, 12:12).

This temple of living stones is in fact very "this-worldly"—present in the here and now because of the believers who comprise it. That they live as aliens and sojourners in society need not necessarily imply that their only true home is in heaven—an inference Elliott was so careful to guard against. Indeed, it is precisely the temple's "this-worldliness" that causes their experience of disjuncture from the non-Christian bodies that inhabit shared spaces. Christian non-belonging is tied to the liminal nature of the readers' existence: they are a community unto themselves, moving amid communities regulated according to a different logic (or, more probably, different logics). Despite this difference, their corporate identity as God's spiritual house does not change the fact that they continue to live in spheres governed by the dictates of the *status quo*. As the author's parenetic concerns in the letter (esp. 2:11–3:7) indicate, Christians remain subject to regulations set by civic authorities, Christian slaves continue to be subject to the authority of their non-Christian masters, and Christian wives to that of their non-Christian husbands. What they must negotiate is how to live Christianly while remaining bound in daily practice and duty to non-Christian bodies—and this is precisely what the author sets out to help them do: to live out their exilic life (παροικία) in the fear of God (cf. 1:17; 2:12, 17).

Before proceeding to the next section, a caveat is in order. In balance to Elliott's caution and given the "this-worldly" focus of my discussion above, I should add that we must not overlook the spatial importance of heaven in the letter. This οὐρανός is where the Christian inheritance is kept (1:4), the locus from which the Spirit is sent to proclaim the good news (1:12), and, perhaps most importantly, where the victorious Christ is presently located (3:22) and from which, we can infer, he will come again (cf. 5:4). While the author does not make any explicit reference to heaven as a sort of homeland or a place to which Christians ultimately belong, it is indeed curious that οὐρανός in 1 Peter is a space which "things" not so much "enter into" as "come out of"—the inheritance, the Spirit, the returning Messiah. Rather crucially, these "things" are those which, in the letter, legitimize the recipients' non-belonging in some way: the imperishable inheritance that gives meaning to their "various trials" (1:6), the Spirit who rests on them even as they are reviled for Christ's sake (4:14), and, of course, the same Christ whose suffering serves as a model for their own (2:21). As such, heaven figures in the letter as a place with which the readers of 1 Peter are invited to identify in significant ways.⁶⁴ Given that it plays a role in legitimizing and—we should add—valorizing the experience of marginalization, the Petrine οὐρανός, like the temple in our preceding analysis, should also be counted as a space of resistance.

6.3 Spatial Imagination, Belonging, Resistance

If the imperial cults filled spaces with symbols and structures of Roman power radiating from a center, 1 Peter disputed that spatial imagination by asserting an alternative view. Just as Caesar's power was not limited to the boundaries of the city of Rome but was to be venerated in satellites of cult, the collective body of believers transcended discrete boundaries by virtue of their divine election in and through Christ. Bound up with their identity as God's elect is also their identity as aliens and strangers, inhabitants of the social margins.

We must bear in mind that both the Roman and Petrine ways of imagining space were operative concurrently, on the same bodies, and in the same space—Roman Anatolia. Each in its own right is an attempt to shape spatial, embodied practice—to modify how space is both conceived and lived in and through the body. The Roman "units" of spatial imagination—that is, the provinces that make up the imperial body politic—are acknowledged in 1 Peter (1:1), along with their mechanics of governance (e.g., governors as representatives of the emperor, 2:17f.), demonstrating the author's awareness of their existence. Yet it is precisely this awareness of them that brings into sharper focus the distinctive features of his alternative spatial imagination—one that cuts across the boundaries imposed by the Empire's geography of power and redefines space in terms of life and solidarity in Christ. As such, the configuration of space in 1 Peter must be regarded as an act of resistance, a genuine challenge to Roman hegemony because it imagined that shared space—and indeed the world—very differently.

The space produced in 1 Peter, therefore, simultaneously dislocates and relocates. It dislocates the readers by rendering them aliens and sojourners, inhabitants of a diaspora. It relocates them—or rather, reveals their true location—within a spiritual house, situated not in another plane of existence or a more-distant one, but in the very same spaces of their dislocation.⁶⁵ Where is this "spiritual house" in which they serve as priests, offering spiritual sacrifices? It is everywhere they are—in the very spaces of the daily grind occupied by their bodies and transformed by their activities. This is not simply a matter of adjusting their perspective, of looking at things differently as it were, but a material, even metaphysical, renovation of spatial practice as real as their new birth in Christ (cf. 1:3, 23). In fact, it is bound up with that new existence. Not surprisingly, the author's

---

64. On "identifying with" a place, in contrast to "identifying against" and "not identifying" with a place, see in particular Rose, "Place and Identity," 89–92.

65. For a similar point, though based on a different passage (1:3–2:10), see Horrell, "Between Conformity and Resistance," 229.

exhortation that they, like newborn infants, "grow into salvation" (2:2) is immediately followed by his injunction that they approach the living stone that is also the cornerstone of the spiritual house (2:4). The temple comes into being not simply because the readers are asked to think of space in a novel way, but because God is already at work in them, building them into a dwelling place for his Spirit of glory (cf. 4:14). This is the truth they must acknowledge and by which they must live. Little doubt that such a transformation of spatial praxis must be accompanied by an overhaul in their spatial imagination—indeed, in their understanding of the world. In the author's words, they must begin by "girding up the loins of [their] mind" (1:13).

Earlier in this chapter, I argued that the trope of diaspora ought to be seen as an act of spatial production, as a part of the author's strategy of crafting an identity of homelessness for his readers. Having discussed how he also creates a space of belonging for them, we are now in a position to consider more deeply the relationship between diaspora and belonging. In his essay, "New Cultures for Old," Stuart Hall examines two possible meanings of the term "diaspora."[66] "Diaspora" can, he states, first of all be used to describe the state of people who have been displaced from their places of origin but who nonetheless maintain their links to their homeland in some way, often seeking to return to that place. It can also, however, carry a second meaning:

> "Diaspora" also refers to the scattering and dispersal of peoples who will *never* literally be able to return to the places from which they came; who have to make some kind of difficult "settlement" with the new, often oppressive, cultures with which they are forced into contact; and who have succeeded in remaking themselves and fashioning new kinds of cultural identity. . . .[67]

Though it does not fit them perfectly, this second sense of "diaspora" approximates the situation of the recipients of 1 Peter. They too are a dislocated people, but not by virtue of physical displacement from a homeland. Rather, they are "in diaspora" because of their identity as disciples of Jesus of Nazareth. As I underscored earlier, their social dislocation is also *spatial* insofar as social estrangement is manifested in the life of the body—ridicule from one's family and neighbors, legal proceedings, marginalization from social life, etc. Like the people Hall describes above, the readers of 1 Peter can never return to the social spaces which they have left behind, having taken on new life from divine, imperishable seed (cf. 1:23).

Rather than being forced to come to terms with a new culture, it is the "old culture"—what the author calls "the futile ways inherited from [their] ancestors" (1:18)—that they must confront as people born anew in Christ. Here, Hall's words

---

66. Stuart Hall, "New Cultures for Old," in *A Place in the World?: Places, Cultures and Globalization*, ed. Doreen B. Massey and Pat Jess (Oxford: Oxford University Press/Open University, 1995), 175–215.

67. Hall, "New Cultures for Old," 206.

regarding people who live in contemporary diasporas can aid our reflection on the struggles faced by 1 Peter's original readers:

> They are people who belong to more than one world, speak more than one language (literally and metaphorically), inhabit more than one identity, have more than one home; who have learned to negotiate and translate *between* cultures, and who, because they are irrevocably the product of several interlocking histories and cultures, have learned to live with, and indeed to speak from, *difference*.... They represent new kinds of identities—new ways of 'being someone'....[68]

It was precisely their new identity in Christ, a new way of "being someone," that cast the recipients of 1 Peter as aliens and strangers. It imbued them with an aura of strangeness, making them foreigners in the same social spaces they used to inhabit (4:4). Yet, at the same time, this new identity created for them a different way of belonging by incorporating them into a new body politic—the spiritual house built by God, which they constituted as "living stones" and in which they, as a holy priesthood, offered spiritual sacrifices. All this they were to do, 1 Peter says, while remaining a people "in diaspora."

6.4 Conclusion

In the previous chapter, I argued that the practices of the imperial cults conveyed a geography of power that centered on Rome and the emperor. This construction of space, exemplified in the *Res Gestae* of Augustus as well as in buildings such as the Sebasteion of Aphrodisias, drew a multiplicity of peoples, cultures, and languages into the shadow of empire. The reconfigurations of space reflected in the imperial cults sought to draw every body—by which I mean *all bodies*—into a relationship with the rule of the Caesars. The structures and practices of the cults, from temples to festivals and everything in between, must be seen in terms of their very material, even *visceral*, effects: namely, the regulation of the movement of imperial subjects according to dictates of Roman power. In Harvey's terms, Rome's power to control the *appropriation* of space—i.e. the manner in which space is occupied by objects (buildings, squares, streets, etc), activities (uses), and people (particular individuals, classes or groups)—amounts *de facto* to the *domination* of that space.[69]

Once the full force of this spatial imagination is appreciated, the Christian discourse of space in 1 Peter clearly emerges as its competitor. On the one hand, 1 Peter normalized—we could even say vindicated—the Christian experience of non-belonging in Roman spaces and redefined this alienation as the hallmark of

---

68. Hall, "New Cultures for Old," 206–7.
69. See Harvey, *The Condition of Postmodernity*, 122.

Christian existence. Believers were construed as aliens and sojourners in diaspora. At the same time—and just as crucially—they were living stones fitted together into a single, trans-spatial temple of cosmic "brotherhood"—a universal Christian society bound together precisely by estrangement and persecution. It was thus in their non-belonging in Roman space that they in fact belonged together. Their solidarity as one spiritual house, one temple indwelt by God's spirit, is the corollary to and counterbalances the social vertigo they experience as aliens and sojourners, as inhabitants of the social margins. They are thus at once truly "at home" and truly "homeless."

CONCLUSION: (RE)PLACING THE EMPEROR, (RE)CONFIGURING THE UNIVERSE

While he [the god-king] was in the womb . . .,
signs of his greatness were already manifest:
earthquake, plumes of smoke,
rain of ashes, thunder,
flashes of lightning in the sky.
Mount Kelud collapsed, killing evildoers,
destroying evil from the land.

—Javanese poet Prapanca, *Negarakertagama*
(fourteenth century AD; author's translation)

These people . . . have been turning the world upside-down . . .

Acts 17:6, NRSV

In an essay entitled, "Paul, Roman Religion, and the Emperor: Mapping the Point of Conflict," John Barclay writes that, in the conflict between early Christianity and wider Roman society, "the battle-line was drawn not at the imperial cult as such (or alone) but at the point of the fundamental, general Christian antagonism to the entire religious structure of the Roman world." By virtue of their singular allegiance to the one God who had revealed himself in Jesus of Nazareth, Christians broke away from the cults of all other gods on whom, as it was thought, the entire cosmos, including imperial society, depended. This was something more than a matter of creedal difference or theological dispute: it was "a fundamental clash in the construction of reality and its divine order."[1]

Just such a clash has been the subject of this book. As I showed in Chapter 1, while studies of the Pauline tradition have, in recent decades, tended to emphasize its anti-imperial elements, earlier evaluations of 1 Peter for the most part concluded that its stance was amenable to the Empire. Against this trend, Warren Carter goes

---

1. John M. G. Barclay, "Paul, Roman Religion and the Emperor: Mapping the Point of Conflict," in *Pauline Churches and Diaspora Jews*, WUNT 275 (Tübingen: Mohr Siebeck, 2011), 361.

so far (too far, I think) as to argue that the Petrine author espoused a form of dissimulative protest by instructing his readers to honor the emperor by participating in the imperial cults while at the same time maintaining in their hearts an inward allegiance to Christ as Lord (3:15). David Horrell and Travis Williams have more recently detected in the letter a more calculated, or "polite," strategy of resistance. Horrell draws attention to the ways in which the author circumscribed submission to imperial authorities by subtly subordinating them under the one God, distinguishing honor due to humans from fear due to God alone (2:17). Williams posits that the Petrine author shrewdly undermined the emperor's claims to divinity by categorizing him as a "human creature" in 2:13. While these readings have rightly disrupted older ones, they have also been confined to the ways in which 1 Peter directly addresses Roman social and political structures.

I have in this work endeavored to move beyond this cynosure by "zooming out" and reading the letter from a wider angle, examining its ideology or worldview. Using James Scott's work to think about ideological resistance as a site of protest against domination, I considered how different ways of conceptualizing time and space—the fundamental axes of our perception of reality—can yield different construals of the social order. Insofar as these divergent ideologies of time and space lead to divergent ways of envisioning social hierarchies and practices (and, indeed, the world as a whole), they acquire political valences and generate potential for conflict. This is the angle I have used to reconsider 1 Peter's stance toward the Roman Empire—by asking how its construction of time and space collides with the imperial vision.

Because "imperial ideology" cannot be studied in the abstract, I chose to study it via one of its most tangible nodes: the imperial cults. These cults provided a focal point around which inhabitants throughout the Empire could rally: the emperor himself. As I have shown in Chapter 2, cultic veneration of the emperor took on diverse forms and was incorporated into Anatolian religious practice in a variety of ways. Sometimes they were standalone cults, and at other times imperial figures shared the stage with local deities, or were directly identified with one of them. Nevertheless, this variegation in form must not obscure one plain fact: their distinctly Roman tenor. Wherever and however the emperor was placed in a pantheon, he was *there*. As Clifford Ando observes, the spread of the imperial cults "allowed the Mediterranean world to share a deity for the first time":

> A traveler could recognize at least one temple in every city he visited and would know the prayers for one divinity in every ritual he witnessed; he could identify the dates of imperial holidays in any civic calendar as shared with every municipality in the empire.[2]

It is the figure of the emperor that allows us to speak of *the imperial* cults, for whatever forms these cults took, he was present—not only as a common religious element but as a unifying symbol of the Empire, both signifying its oneness and

2. Ando, *Imperial Ideology*, 407.

constituting it. As hybrid productions, these cults rendered the power of the emperor into a local grammar, functioning as "contact zones" in which the Roman and the local could envision the world together. In the words of Simon Price, the rituals of the imperial cults constituted "a system whose structure defines the position of the emperor."[3] Again, the cults did not fulfill this function in the same way everywhere, but they did inject the Roman emperor into the cosmic order, placing him where he was not before.[4]

It is within this world, with its expanding imperial presence, that I have sought to read 1 Peter anew. Throughout this study, I deliberately avoided focusing on the author's critiques of the imperial cults, examining instead how he posits a different construction of reality and enjoins a way of life restructured according to that reality. Laying the imperial cults and the Petrine text side by side, I asked how they each constructed time (Chapters 3 and 4) and space (Chapters 5 and 6) in their own way, and how these distinct ideologies might have clashed with one another. Since the summaries of my findings have already been stated at the end of each of these chapters, and also since arguments do not in fact become truer with each incantation, I will spare the reader vain repetition. Suffice to say, however, that for me, one point has emerged clearly in the course of writing these chapters, and deserves at this juncture a more synthetic articulation.

The fundamental point of difference between the imperial cults of Anatolia and 1 Peter lies in what might be called a "cosmological criterion." What I mean by this is that each side imagined time and space—and thus the social order—using different points of reference. In the case of the imperial cults, the defining cosmological criterion was the emperor himself, commemorated in festival and coin, and honored in shrines and temples. Whether or not he was the central criterion in every instance does not alter the point I am making here: what is crucial is only that, with the arrival of Roman occupation in Anatolia, the figure of Caesar disrupted—and reconfigured—how people imagined time and space, and thus society and the cosmos itself. The nature and magnitude of this impact varied from place to place, depending on how the cultural encounter took place.

For the author of 1 Peter, Jesus Christ—or, more precisely, the revelation of God in his Christ—was *the* cosmological criterion, entirely constitutive of a new way of seeing the world. The suffering of Jesus, in the Petrine view, had transformed the meaning of suffering itself (2:21–24; 4:1); in Jesus' resurrection, Christians had been born anew (1:3) and were now called to a wholly new way of life in keeping

---

3. Price, *Rituals and Power*, 8.

4. The fact that Pliny the Younger's "test" for those charged with being Christians involved the use of statues (*simulacra*) of several gods and Trajan's image (*imago*) (*Ep.* 10.96), has been cited by biblical scholars to different effect (see, e.g., the contrasting interpretations in Carter, "Going All the Way?" 25; and Barclay, "Paul, Roman Religion and the Emperor," 360; cf. Millar, "The Imperial Cult," 152–3). One thing is undeniable, however: the letter shows that the Roman emperor had now become part of the politico-religious matrix of "Roman religion," and cultic veneration to him drawn into the conflict between Christians and the Empire.

with the "new time" and "new space" inducted by this astounding event. The eschatological "now" opened up by Christ's entrance into history has disclosed the present as "the last of the ages" (1:20) toward which time had been moving all along. The past is revealed as the time of preparation for God's plan from before the foundation of the world: the Spirit of Christ long ago anticipated this moment by disclosing it to the prophets (1:10–12). When Christ comes again from heaven where he is as yet unseen (1:8; 3:22), he will bring with him the disciples' inheritance that is kept there (1:4). The open-endedness of this future, apprehended now only by faith, destabilizes any human attempt to secure it; what is sure, however, is that its permanence will outlast the transient world as the readers know it.

In light of this temporal schema, the present world, the location of their existence, is revealed not as *patria* but as "diaspora" (1:1), the place of non-belonging, in which they are aliens and strangers living out their time of exile (1:17). Alienated from their futile past (1:18), they have now become estranged in the very places they inhabit (4:4). They have not been left homeless, however: already God is building them into a spiritual house (2:5), a temple in which his Spirit of glory rests (4:14, 17). This condition of "spatial suspension," of being simultaneously estranged and "re-homed" in the trans-spatial ἀδελφότης (5:9; 2:17), corresponds to the "temporal suspension" of 1 Peter's already-but-not-yet eschatology. Christ is the one by whom time and space is to be measured.

This difference in cosmological criteria emerges clearly when 1 Peter is examined alongside the imperial cults, but it is made starker by the fact that the emperor is not entirely *absent* from view. He is right there, on top of the list of human creatures to be obeyed for the sake of the Lord (2:13), as someone to be honored. He is not to be feared, however, since that is God's prerogative (2:17). It is precisely this presence of the emperor in 2:13–17 that makes his absence—not only from the rest of the letter but from the reconfigured time and space of 1 Peter—all the more palpable. He is "there" and "not there" at the same time—almost as a foil, a kind of ideological conceit. Concerning the new world the Petrine author is eloquent: he skillfully expounds its predestination according to the foreknowledge of God, the execution of the divine plan, and the exaltation of the Messiah who is now enthroned at God's right hand. Yet it is amid all this eloquent exposition that Caesar and his authority exist as desacralized power, almost clinically regarded, stripped of the mythological legitimations we find in the grandiloquent decree of Asia or the awe-inspiring reliefs of the Aphrodisian Sebasteion. If, as Price said, the imperial cults defined the position of the emperor, 1 Peter accomplishes the same, repositioning him at the margins of a world redrawn around Christ. This is, in James Scott's words, "ideology at work where it really counts—in the rationalization of exploitation and in the resistance to that rationalization."[5]

What we find in 1 Peter is a reconfigured universe in which God and his Christ are at the center, and the emperor put in his (proper) place. In presenting to his readers such a universe, it seems to me, the author was taking on Rome in the arena of ideological contest.

5. Scott, *Weapons of the Weak*, 204.

BIBLIOGRAPHY

Achtemeier, Paul J. *1 Peter*. Hermeneia. Minneapolis, MN: Augsburg/Fortress, 1996.
Adam, Barbara. *Time and Social Theory*. Oxford: Polity Press, 1990.
Adam, Barbara. *Timewatch: The Social Analysis of Time*. Cambridge: Polity Press, 1995.
Allison, Eric. "The Strangeways Riot: 20 Years On." *The Guardian*, March 30, 2010, sec. Society.
The Analects of Confucius: Translation and Notes. Translated by Simon Leys. New York, NY: W. W. Norton, 1997.
Ando, Clifford. *Imperial Ideology and Provincial Loyalty in the Roman Empire*. Berkeley and Los Angeles, CA: University of California Press, 2000.
Ausloos, Hans, and Bénédicte Lemmelijn. "Content-Related Criteria in Characterising the LXX Translation Technique." In *Die Septuaginta – Texte, Theologien und Einflüsse: 2. Internationale Fachtagung veranstaltet von Septuaginta Deutsch (LXX.D), Wuppertal 23.–27. Juli 2008*, edited by Wolfgang Kraus, Martin Karrer, and Martin Meiser, 357–6. WUNT 252. Tübingen: Mohr Siebeck, 2010.
Ausloos, Hans, Bénédicte Lemmelijn, and Valerie Kabergs. "The Study of Aetiological Wordplay as a Content-Related Criterion in the Characterisation of LXX Translation Technique." In *Die Septuaginta – Entstehung, Sprache, Geschichte: 3. Internationale Fachtagung veranstaltet von Septuaginta Deutsch (LXX.D), Wuppertal 22.–25. Juli 2010*, edited by Siegfried Kreuzer, Martin Meiser, and Marcus Sigismund, 273–94. WUNT 286. Tübingen: Mohr Siebeck, 2012.
Aymer, Margaret P. "Empire, Alter-Empire and the Twenty-First Century." *Union Seminary Quarterly Review* 59 (2005): 140–6.
Balch, David L. *Let Wives Be Submissive: The Domestic Code in 1 Peter*. SBL Monograph Series 26. Atlanta, GA: Scholars Press, 1981.
Banazak, Gregory Allen, and Luis Reyes Ceja. "The Challenge and Promise of Decolonial Thought to Biblical Interpretation." *Postscripts: The Journal of Sacred Texts and Contemporary Worlds* 4, no. 1 (March 27, 2010): 113–27.
Barclay, John M. G. "Paul, Roman Religion and the Emperor: Mapping the Point of Conflict." In *Pauline Churches and Diaspora Jews*, 345–62. WUNT 275. Tübingen: Mohr Siebeck, 2011.
Barclay, John M. G. "Why the Roman Empire Was Insignificant to Paul." In *Pauline Churches and Diaspora Jews*, 363–87. WUNT 275. Tübingen: Mohr Siebeck, 2011.
Bauckham, Richard. "James, 1 and 2 Peter, Jude." In *It Is Written – Scripture Citing Scripture: Essays in Honour of Barnabas Lindars, SSF*, edited by D. A. Carson and H. G. M. Williamson, 303–17. Cambridge: Cambridge, 1988.
Bauman-Martin, Betsy. "Speaking Jewish: Postcolonial Aliens and Strangers in First Peter." In *Reading First Peter with New Eyes: Methodological Reassessments of the Letter of First Peter*, edited by Robert L. Webb and Betsy Bauman-Martin, 144–77. LNTS 364. New York, NY: T&T Clark, 2007.
Beard, Mary. "A Complex of Times: No More Sheep on Romulus' Birthday." *The Cambridge Classical Journal (New Series)* 33 (1987): 1–15.
Beard, Mary, John A. North, and Simon R. F. Price. *Religions of Rome*. 2 vols. Cambridge: Cambridge, 1998.

Beare, Francis Wright. *The First Epistle of Peter: The Greek Text with Introduction and Notes*. 3rd ed. Oxford: Blackwell, 1970.
Bechtler, Steven R. *Following in His Steps: Suffering, Community and Christology in 1 Peter*. SBL Dissertation Series 162. Atlanta, GA: Scholars, 1998.
Beetham, Christopher. Review of *The Eschatology of 1 Peter: Considering the Influence of Zechariah 9–14*, by Kelly D. Liebengood. *Journal of the Evangelical Theological Society* 58.1 (2015): 197–9.
Bell, Catherine. *Ritual: Perspectives and Dimensions*. New York, NY: Oxford University Press, 1997.
Benjamin, Walter. *Illuminations: Essays and Reflections*. Edited by Hannah Arendt. Translated by Harry Zohn. New York, NY: Schocken Books, 1969.
Best, Ernest. *1 Peter*. London: Oliphants, 1971.
Bhabha, Homi K. "Signs Taken for Wonders: Questions of Ambivalence and Authority under a Tree Outside Delhi, May 1817." *Critical Inquiry* 12, no. 1 (1985): 144–65.
Bhabha, Homi K. *The Location of Culture*. London and New York, NY: Routledge, 1994.
Bickerman, Elias. "Consecratio." In *Le culte des souverains dans l'Empire romain*, edited by Willem den Boer, 145–75. Entretiens sur l'Antiquité classique 19. Geneva: Fondation Hardt, 1973.
Bigg, Charles. *A Critical and Exegetical Commentary on the Epistles of St. Peter and St. Jude*. Edinburgh: T&T Clark, 1956.
Bird, Jennifer G. *Abuse, Power and Fearful Obedience: Reconsidering 1 Peter's Commands to Wives*. LNTS 442. London and New York, NY: T&T Clark International, 2011.
Bloch, Maurice. "The Ritual of the Royal Bath in Madagascar: The Dissolution of Death, Birth, and Fertility into Authority." In *Ritual, History and Power: Selected Papers in Anthropology*, 187–211. London: Athlone, 1989.
Boring, M. E. "First Peter in Recent Study." *Word and World* 24.4 (2004): 358–67.
Boring, M. E. "Narrative Dynamics in 1 Peter: The Function of Narrative World." In *Reading First Peter with New Eyes: Methodological Reassessments of the Letter of First Peter*, edited by Robert L. Webb and Betsy Bauman-Martin, 7–40. LNTS 364. New York, NY: T&T Clark, 2007.
Bourdieu, Pierre. *Outline of a Theory of Practice*. Translated by Richard Nice. Cambridge Studies in Social Anthropology 16. Cambridge: Cambridge University Press, 1977.
Boyarin, Daniel. *A Radical Jew: Paul and the Politics of Identity*. Berkeley, CA: University of California, 1994.
Boyarin, Daniel. *Border Lines: The Partition of Judaeo-Christianity*. Philadelphia, PA: University of Pennsylvania Press, 2004.
Boyarin, Jonathan. "Space, Time, and the Politics of Memory." In *Remapping Memory: The Politics of Timespace*, edited by Jonathan Boyarin. Minneapolis, MN: University of Minnesota Press, 1994.
Brox, Norbert. *Der erste Petrusbrief*. 4th ed. Evangelisch-Katholischer Kommentar zum Neuen Testament 21. Zurich & Neukirchen-Vluyn: Benziger & Neukirchener, 1993.
Burton, Graham. "Government and the Provinces." In *The Roman World, Volume 1*, edited by J. S. Wacher. London and New York, NY: Routledge, 2002.
Butler, Katie. "Homeless Protesters Set Up New Camp on Market Street in Manchester City Centre." *Manchester Evening News*, October 22, 2015.
Carter, Warren. *Matthew and Empire: Initial Explorations*. Harrisburg, PA: Trinity, 2001.
Carter, Warren. "Going All the Way? Honoring the Emperor and Sacrificing Wives and Slaves in 1 Peter 2:13–3:6." In *A Feminist Companion to the Catholic Epistles and*

Hebrews, edited by Amy-Jill Levine, 14–33. Feminist Companion to the New Testament and Early Christian Writings 8. Cleveland, OH: Pilgrim, 2004.

Carter, Warren. *John and Empire: Initial Explorations*. New York, NY: Bloomsbury/T&T Clark, 2008.

Chakelian, Anoosh. "Nick Clegg: 'It's Not Obvious' What the UK Can Do Legally on New Terror Powers." *The New Statesman*, September 2, 2014.

Chapple, Alan. "The Appropriation of Scripture in 1 Peter." In *All That the Prophets Have Declared: The Appropriation of Scripture in the Emergence of Christianity*, edited by Matthew R. Malcolm, 155–71. Milton Keynes: Paternoster, 2015.

Charlesworth, Martin Percival. "Providentia and Aeternitas." *The Harvard Theological Review* 29, no. 2 (1936): 107–32.

Chilton, David. *The Days of Vengeance: An Exposition of the Book of Revelation*. Fort Worth, TX: Dominion Press, 1987.

Collins, John J. *The Apocalyptic Imagination: An Introduction to Jewish Apocalyptic Literature*. Grand Rapids, MI: Eerdmans, 1998.

Cooley, Alison E. *Res Gestae Divi Augusti: Text, Translation, and Commentary*. Cambridge: Cambridge University Press, 2009.

Crossan, John Dominic, and Jonathan L. Reed. *In Search of Paul: How Jesus' Apostle Opposed Rome's Empire with God's Kingdom*. New York, NY: HarperCollins, 2004.

Culpepper, R. Alan. *Anatomy of the Fourth Gospel: A Study in Literary Design*. Philadelphia, PA: Fortress, 1987.

Dalton, William J. *Christ's Proclamation to the Spirits: A Study of 1 Peter 3:18–4:6*. 2nd, fully rev. ed. Analecta Biblica 23. Rome: Editrice Pontificio Istituto Biblico, 1989 (1965).

Davids, Peter H. *The First Epistle of Peter*. 2nd ed. Grand Rapids, MI: Eerdmans, 1990.

Deissmann, Adolf. *Light from the Ancient East: The New Testament Illustrated by Recently Discovered Texts of the Graeco-Roman World*. Translated by Lionel R. M. Strachan. London: Hodder & Stoughton, 1910.

Doering, Lutz. "First Peter as Early Christian Diaspora Letter." In *The Catholic Epistles and Apostolic Tradition: A New Perspective on James and the Catholic Letter Collection*, edited by Karl-Wilhelm Niebuhr and Robert W. Wall, 215–36, 441–57. Waco, TX: Baylor, 2009.

Doering, Lutz. *Ancient Jewish Letters and the Beginnings of Christian Epistolography*. WUNT 298. Tübingen: Mohr Siebeck, 2012.

Dube, Musa. *Postcolonial Feminist Interpretation of the Bible*. St. Louis, MO: Chalice Press, 2000.

Dube, Musa. "Toward a Post-Colonial Feminist Interpretation of the Bible." In *An Eerdmans Reader in Contemporary Political Theology*, edited by William T. Cavanaugh, Jeffrey W. Bailey, and Craig Hovey, 585–99. Cambridge: Eerdmans, 2012.

Dubis, Mark. *Messianic Woes in First Peter: Suffering and Eschatology in 1 Peter 4:12–19*. New York, NY: P. Lang, 2002.

Dubis, Mark. "Research on 1 Peter: A Survey of Scholarly Literature since 1985." *Currents in Biblical Research* 4, no. 2 (2006): 199–239.

Dubis, Mark. *1 Peter: A Handbook on the Greek Text*. Waco, TX: Baylor University Press, 2010.

Dussel, Enrique. "Eurocentrism and Modernity (Introduction to the Frankfurt Lectures)." *Boundary 2* 20, no. 3 (October 1, 1993): 65–76.

Elliott, John H. *The Elect and the Holy: An Exegetical Examination of 1 Peter 2, 4–10 and the Phrase Basileion Hierateuma*. Novum Testamentum 12. Leiden: Brill, 1966.

Elliott, John H. *A Home for the Homeless: A Social-Scientific Criticism of 1 Peter, Its Situation and Strategy*. Minneapolis, MN: Fortress, 1981.

Elliott, John H. *1 Peter: A New Translation with Introduction and Commentary*. New York, NY: Doubleday, 2000.
Elliott, John H. Review of *The Eschatology of 1 Peter: Considering the Influence of Zechariah 9–14*, by Kelly D. Liebengood. *Review of Biblical Literature* 06 (2018). http://www.bookreviews.org.
Fabian, Johannes. *Time and the Other: How Anthropology Makes Its Object*. New York, NY and Chichester: Columbia University Press, 1983.
Feldmeier, Reinhard. *Die Christen als Fremde: die Metapher der Fremde in der antiken Welt, im Urchristentum und im 1. Petrusbrief*. WUNT 64. Tübingen: Mohr Siebeck, 1992.
Feldmeier, Reinhard. *The First Letter of Peter: A Commentary on the Greek Text*. Translated by Peter H. Davids. Waco, TX: Baylor, 2008.
Feldmeier, Reinhard. "Salvation and Anthropology in First Peter." In *The Catholic Epistles and Apostolic Tradition*, edited by Karl-Wilhelm Niebuhr and Robert W. Wall, 203–13, 437–41. Waco, TX: Baylor, 2009.
Fishwick, Duncan. *The Imperial Cult in the Latin West: Studies in the Ruler Cult of the Western Provinces of the Roman Empire*. Vol. 1.1. Leiden: Brill, 1987.
Fishwick, Duncan. *The Imperial Cult in the Latin West: Studies in the Ruler Cult of the Western Provinces of the Roman Empire*. Vol. 3.1. Leiden, Boston, and Cologne: Brill, 2002.
Foucault, Michel. *Discipline and Punish: The Birth of the Prison*. Translated by Alan Sheridan. Harmondsworth: Penguin, 1979.
Foucault, Michel. "Space, Knowledge, and Power." Interview by Paul Rabinow. Translated by Christian Hubert, n.d. In *The Foucault Reader*, edited by Paul Rabinow, 239–56. New York, NY: Pantheon Books, 1984.
Friesen, Steven J. *Twice Neokoros: Ephesus, Asia, and the Cult of the Flavian Imperial Family*. Leiden: Brill, 1993.
Friesen, Steven J. *Imperial Cults and the Apocalypse of John: Reading Revelation in the Ruins*. New York, NY: Oxford University Press, 2001.
Friesen, Steven J. "Normal Religion, Or, Words Fail Us: A Response to Karl Galinsky's 'The Cult of the Roman Emperor: Uniter or Divider?'" In *Rome and Religion: A Cross-Disciplinary Dialogue on the Imperial Cult*, edited by Jeffrey Brodd and Jonathan L. Reed, 23–6. Atlanta, GA: Society of Biblical Literature, 2011.
Galinsky, Karl. "In the Shadow (or Not) of the Imperial Cult: A Cooperative Agenda." In *Rome and Religion: A Cross-Disciplinary Dialogue on the Imperial Cult*, edited by Jeffrey Brodd and Jonathan L. Reed, 215–26. Atlanta, GA: Society of Biblical Literature, 2011.
Galinsky, Karl. "The Cult of the Roman Emperor: Uniter or Divider?" In *Rome and Religion: A Cross-Disciplinary Dialogue on the Imperial Cult*, edited by Jeffrey Brodd and Jonathan L. Reed, 1–21. Atlanta, GA: Society of Biblical Literature, 2011.
Gallois, William. "The War for Time in Colonial Algeria." In *Breaking up Time: Negotiating the Borders between Present, Past and Future*, edited by Chris Lorenz and Berber Bevernage, 252–73. Schriftenreihe der FRIAS School of History 7. Göttingen: Vandenhoeck & Ruprecht, 2013.
Geertz, Clifford. *Negara: The Theatre State in Nineteenth-Century Bali*. Princeton, NJ: Princeton University Press, 1980.
Gell, Alfred. *The Anthropology of Time: Cultural Constructions of Temporal Maps and Images*. Oxford: Berg, 1992.
Gentry, Kenneth L. *Before Jerusalem Fell: Dating the Book of Revelation*. Fountain Inn, SC: Victorious Hope Publishing, 2010.
Gibbon, Edward. *The History of the Decline and Fall of the Roman Empire. With Notes by H.H. Milman*. Vol. 1. 6 vols. Philadelphia, PA: Porter & Coates, 1845.

Goldstein, E. B. *Cognitive Psychology: Connecting Mind, Research and Everyday Experience.* Belmont, CA: Thomson Wadsworth, 2008.

Goppelt, Leonhard. *A Commentary on 1 Peter.* Edited by Ferdinand Hahn. Translated by John E. Alsup. Grand Rapids, MI: Eerdmans, 1993.

Gordon, Richard. "The Roman Imperial Cult and the Question of Power." In *The Religious History of the Roman Empire: Pagans, Jews, and Christians,* edited by John A. North and S. R. F. Price, 35–70. Oxford Readings in Classical Studies. Oxford: Oxford University Press, 2011.

Gradel, Ittai. *Emperor Worship and Roman Religion.* Clarendon Press, 2004.

Gramsci, Antonio. *Selections from the Prison Notebooks.* Edited by Quintin Hoare and Geoffrey Nowell-Smith. London: ElecBook, 1999.

Green, Joel B. *1 Peter.* Grand Rapids, MI: Eerdmans, 2007.

Gregory, Andrew. "1 Clement and Writings That Later Formed the New Testament." In *The Reception of the New Testament in the Apostolic Fathers,* edited by Andrew Gregory and Christopher Tuckett, 130–57. Oxford and New York: Oxford University Press, 2005.

Grossman, Maxine L. *Reading for History in the Damascus Document: A Methodological Study.* Vol. XLV. Studies on the Texts of the Desert of Judah. Leiden, Boston, and Cologne: Brill, 2002.

Hall, Stuart. "New Cultures for Old." In *A Place in the World?: Places, Cultures and Globalization,* edited by Doreen B. Massey and Pat Jess, 175–215. Oxford: Oxford University Press/Open University, 1995.

Hardin, Justin K. *Galatians and the Imperial Cult: A Critical Analysis of the First-Century Social Context of Paul's Letter.* Tübingen: Mohr Siebeck, 2008.

Harland, Philip A. "Imperial Cults within Local Cultural Life: Associations in Roman Asia." *Ancient History Bulletin/Zeitschrift für alte Geschichte,* no. 17 (2003): 85–107.

Harris, William V. *Ancient Literacy.* Cambridge, MA: Harvard University Press, 1989.

Harrison, James R. *Paul and the Imperial Authorities at Thessalonica and Rome: A Study in the Conflict of Ideology.* Tübingen: Mohr Siebeck, 2011.

Harvey, David. *The Condition of Postmodernity: An Enquiry into the Origins of Cultural Change.* Oxford/Cambridge, MA: Blackwell, 1989.

Haynes, Holly. *The History of Make-Believe: Tacitus on Imperial Rome.* Berkeley and Los Angeles, CA: University of California Press, 2003.

Hays, Richard B. *Echoes of Scripture in the Letters of Paul.* New Haven, CT: Yale University Press, 1993.

Helgeland, John. "Time and Space: Christian and Roman." In *ANRW,* 23.2:1285–1305. Berlin and New York, NY: Walter de Gruyter, 1980.

Herrmann, Peter. *Der römische Kaisereid: Untersuchungen zu seiner Herkunft und Entwicklung.* Göttingen: Vanderhoeck und Ruprecht, 1968.

Herz, Peter. "Herrscherverehrung und lokale Festkultur im Osten des römischen Reiches (Kaiser/Agone)." In *Römische Reichsreligion und Provinzialreligion,* edited by Hubert Cancik and Jörg Rüpke, 239–64. Tübingen: Mohr Siebeck, 1997.

Herz, Peter. "Emperors: Caring for the Empire and Their Successors." In *A Companion to Roman Religion,* edited by Jörg Rüpke, 304–16. Malden, MA: Blackwell, 2007.

Holmes, Michael W. "Polycarp's Letter to the Philippians and Writings That Later Formed the New Testament." In *The Reception of the New Testament in the Apostolic Fathers,* edited by Andrew Gregory and Christopher Tuckett, 187–227. Oxford and New York: Oxford University Press, 2005.

Holmes, Michael W. *The Apostolic Fathers: Greek Texts and English Translations.* Grand Rapids, MI: Baker Academic, 2007.

Hopkins, Keith. *Conquerors and Slaves*. Sociological Studies in Roman History. Cambridge/New York, NY: Cambridge University Press, 1978.

Horrell, David G. *The Epistles of Peter and Jude*. Peterborough: Epworth, 1998.

Horrell, David G. *1 Peter*. T&T Clark New Testament Guides. Edinburgh: T&T Clark, 2008.

Horrell, David G. "Aliens and Strangers? The Socio-Economic Location of the Addressees of 1 Peter." In *Becoming Christian: Essays on 1 Peter and the Making of Christian Identity*. LNTS 394. London and New York, NY: Bloomsbury T&T Clark, 2013.

Horrell, David G. "Between Conformity and Resistance: Beyond the Balch–Elliott Debate Towards a Postcolonial Reading of 1 Peter." In *Becoming Christian: Essays on 1 Peter and the Making of Christian Identity*, 211–38. London and New York, NY: Bloomsbury T&T Clark, 2013.

Horrell, David G. "The Product of a Petrine Circle?: Challenging an Emerging Consensus." In *Becoming Christian: Essays on 1 Peter and the Making of Christian Identity*, 7–44. LNTS 394. London and New York, NY: Bloomsbury T&T Clark, 2013.

Horrell, David G. "'Honour Everyone...' (1 Pet. 2.17): The Social Strategy of 1 Peter and Its Significance for the Development of Christianity." In *To Set at Liberty: Essays on Early Christianity and Its Social World in Honor of John H. Elliott*, edited by Stephen K. Black, 192–210. Sheffield: Phoenix, 2014.

Horrell, David G. "Jesus Remembered in 1 Peter? Early Jesus Traditions, Isaiah 53, and 1 Pet 2.21–25." In *Early Jesus Traditions in James and 1–2 Peter*, edited by Alicia J. Batten and John S. Kloppenborg, 123–50. LNTS 478. London and New York, NY: Bloomsbury T&T Clark, 2014.

Horrell, David G. "Re-Placing 1 Peter: Proposed Locations and Constructions of Space." In *The Urban World and the First Christians*, edited by Steve Walton, Paul Trebilco, and David W. J. Gill. Grand Rapids, MI: Eerdmans, 2017.

Horrell, David G. "The Label Χριστιανός (1 Pet. 4.16): Suffering, Conflict, and the Making of Christian Identity." In *Becoming Christian: Essays on 1 Peter and the Making of Christian Identity*, 361–81. LNTS 394. London and New York, NY: Bloomsbury T&T Clark, 2013.

Horrell, David G., Bradley Arnold, and Travis B. Williams. "Visuality, Vivid Description, and the Message of 1 Peter: The Significance of the Roaring Lion (1 Peter 5:8)." *Journal of Biblical Literature* 132, no. 3 (2013): 697–716.

Horsley, Richard A., ed. *Paul and Empire: Religion and Power in Roman Imperial Society*. Harrisburg, PA: Trinity Press International, 1997.

Horsley, Richard A., ed. *Paul and Politics: Ekklesia, Israel, Imperium, Interpretation: Essays in Honour of Krister Stendahl*. Harrisburg, PA: Trinity Press International, 2000.

Horsley, Richard A. *Jesus and Empire: The Kingdom of God and the New World Disorder*. Minneapolis, MN: Fortress Press, 2002.

Horsley, Richard A., ed. *Paul and the Roman Imperial Order*. Harrisburg, PA: Bloomsbury T&T Clark, 2004.

Hort, F. J. A. *The First Epistle of St. Peter, I.1–II.17: The Greek Text with Introductory Lecture, Commentary, and Additional Notes*. Eugene, OR: Wipf & Stock, 2005.

Howard-Brook, Wes, and Anthony Gwyther. *Unveiling Empire: Reading Revelation Then and Now*. The Bible & Liberation Series. Maryknoll, NY: Orbis Books, 1999.

Humphrey, John H., Mary Beard, Alan K. Bowman, Mireille Corbier, Tim Cornell, James L. Franklin, Jr., Ann Hanson, Keith Hopkins, and Nicholas Horsfall. *Literacy in the Roman World*. Journal of Roman Archaeology Supplementary Series 3. Ann Arbor, MI: Journal of Roman Archaeology, 1991.

Jenkins, Jack. "What The Atlantic Left Out About ISIS According To Their Own Expert." *ThinkProgress*. Accessed December 11, 2015. http://thinkprogress.org/world/2015/02/20/3625446/atlantic-left-isis-conversation-bernard-haykel/.

Jennings, Willie James. *The Christian Imagination: Theology and the Origins of Race*. New Haven, CT and London: Yale University Press, 2010.

Jobes, Karen H. "Got Milk? Septuagint Psalm 33 and the Interpretation of 1 Peter 2:1–3." *Westminster Theological Journal* 64, no. 1 (2002): 1–14.

Jobes, Karen H. *1 Peter*. Grand Rapids, MI: Baker, 2005.

Kelly, J. N. D. *A Commentary on the Epistles of Peter and of Jude*. Black's New Testament Commentaries. London: Adam & Charles Black, 1969.

Kim, Seyoon. *Christ and Caesar: The Gospel and the Roman Empire in the Writings of Paul and Luke*. Grand Rapids, MI: Eerdmans, 2008.

King, Helen. *Hippocrates' Woman: Reading the Female Body in Ancient Greece*. London and New York: Routledge, 1998.

Kitchin, Rob, and Phil Hubbard, eds. *Key Thinkers on Space and Place*. 2nd ed. London: SAGE, 2010.

Lau, D. C. *The Analects: Translated with an Introduction*. London: Penguin, 1979.

Lefebvre, Henri. *The Production of Space*. Translated by Donald Nicholson-Smith. Oxford: Blackwell, 1991.

Liebengood, Kelly D. *The Eschatology of 1 Peter: Considering the Influence of Zechariah 9–14*. Society for New Testament Studies Monograph Series. Cambridge: Cambridge University Press, 2014.

Liebengood, Kelly D. "Confronting Roman Imperial Claims: Following the Footsteps (and the Narrative) of 1 Peter's Eschatological Davidic Shepherd." Pages 255–72 in *An Introduction to Empire in the New Testament*. Edited by Adam Winn. Atlanta, GA: SBL Press, 2016.

Loomba, Ania. *Colonialism/Postcolonialism*. London: Routledge, 1998.

Lozano, Fernando. "The Creation of Imperial Gods: Not Only Imposition versus Spontaneity." In *More Than Men, Less Than Gods: Studies on Royal Cult and Imperial Worship. Proceedings of the International Colloquium Organized by the Belgian School at Athens (November 1–2, 2007)*, edited by Panagiotis P. Iossif, Andrzej Stanisław Chankowski, and Catharine C. Lorber, 475–519. Leuven: Peeters, 2011.

Magie, David. *Roman Rule in Asia Minor, to the End of the Third Century after Christ*. 2 vols. Princeton, NJ: Princeton University Press, 1975.

Maier, Harry O. "From Material Place to Imagined Space: Emergent Christian Community as Thirdspace in the Shepherd of Hermas." In *Early Christian Communities between Ideal and Reality*, edited by Mark Grundeken and Joseph Verheyden, 143–60. WUNT 342. Tübingen: Mohr Siebeck, 2015.

Malbon, Elizabeth Struthers. *Narrative Space and Mythic Meaning in Mark*. San Francisco, CA: Harper & Row, 1986.

Martin, Ralph P. "The Theology of Jude, 1 Peter, and 2 Peter." In *The Theology of the Letters of James, Peter, and Jude*, edited by Andrew Chester and Ralph P. Martin, 63–168. Cambridge: Cambridge University Press, 1994.

Martin, Troy W. *Metaphor and Composition in 1 Peter*. Atlanta, GA: Scholars Press, 1992.

Massey, Doreen B. "The Conceptualization of Place." In *A Place in the World?: Places, Cultures and Globalization*, edited by Doreen B. Massey and Pat Jess, 45–85. Oxford: Oxford University Press/Open University, 1995.

Massey, Doreen B. *For Space*. London: SAGE, 2005.

Mbuvi, Andrew M. *Temple, Exile and Identity in 1 Peter*. LNTS 345. London and New York, NY: T&T Clark, 2007.
McKnight, Scot. *1 Peter*. The NIV Application Commentary. Grand Rapids, MI: Zondervan, 1996.
McKnight, Scot, and Joseph B. Modica, eds. *Jesus Is Lord, Caesar Is Not: Evaluating Empire in New Testament Studies*. Downers Grove, IL: IVP Academic, 2013.
McLean, Bradley Hudson. *An Introduction to Greek Epigraphy of the Hellenistic and Roman Periods from Alexander the Great Down to the Reign of Constantine (323 B.C.-A.D. 337)*. Ann Arbor, MI: University of Michigan Press, 2002.
Meeks, Wayne A. *The Origins of Christian Morality: The First Two Centuries*. New Haven, CT/London: Yale University Press, 1993.
Meggitt, Justin J. "Taking the Emperor's Clothes Seriously: The New Testament and the Roman Emperor." In *The Quest for Wisdom: Essays in Honor of Philip Budd*, 143-69. Cambridge: Orchard Academic, 2002.
Metzger, Bruce M. *The Canon of the New Testament: Its Origin, Development, and Significance*. Oxford and New York: Clarendon Press, 1987.
Michaels, J. Ramsey. *1 Peter*. WBC 49. Dallas, TX: Word, 1988.
Mikalson, Jon D. "Greek Religion: Continuity and Change in the Hellenistic Period." In *The Cambridge Companion to the Hellenistic World*, edited by Glenn R. Bugh, 208-22. Cambridge: Cambridge University Press, 2006.
Millar, Fergus. "The Imperial Cult and the Persecutions." In *Le culte des souverains dans l'Empire romain*, edited by Willem den Boer, 145-75. Entretiens sur l'Antiquité classique 19. Geneva: Fondation Hardt, 1973.
Millar, Fergus. "The Impact of Monarchy." In *Caesar Augustus: Seven Aspects*, edited by Fergus Millar and Erich Segal, 37-60. Oxford: Clarendon Press, 1984.
Miller, Daniel. "The Limits of Dominance." In *Domination and Resistance*, edited by Daniel Miller, Michael Rowlands, and Christopher Y. Tilley, 63-79. One World Archaeology, no. 3. London and New York, NY: Routledge, 1995.
Mitchell, Stephen. *Anatolia: Land, Men, and Gods in Asia Minor, Volume I: The Celts and the Impact of Roman Rule*. Oxford: Clarendon, 1993.
Mitchell, Stephen. "Festivals, Games, and Civic Life in Roman Asia Minor." *Journal of Roman Studies* 80 (2012): 183-93.
Moore, F. G. "On Urbs Aeterna and Urbs Sacra." *Transactions of the American Philological Association (1869-1896)* 25 (1894): 34.
Moore, Stephen D. *Empire and Apocalypse: Postcolonialism and the New Testament*. The Bible in the Modern World 12. Sheffield: Sheffield Phoenix Press, 2006.
Moyise, Steve. "The Old Testament in 1 and 2 Peter, Jude." In *The Old Testament in the New: An Introduction*. London: T&T Clark, 2001.
Moyise, Steve. "Isaiah in 1 Peter." In *Isaiah in the New Testament*, edited by Steve Moyise and M. J. J. Menken, 175-88. New York, NY: T&T Clark, 2005.
Munn, Nancy D. "The Cultural Anthropology of Time: A Critical Essay." *Annual Review of Anthropology* 21 (1992): 93-123.
Nicolet, Claude. *Space, Geography, and Politics in the Early Roman Empire*. Ann Arbor, MI: University of Michigan, 1991.
Noor, Farish A. "History, and the Toys That Fascists Play With." In *What Your Teacher Didn't Tell You: The Annexe Lectures, Vol. 1*. Petaling Jaya, Malaysia: Matahari Books, 2009.
Novitz, David. "Art, Narrative, and Human Nature." In *Memory, Identity, Community: The Idea of Narrative in the Human Sciences*, edited by Lewis P. Hinchman and Sandra Hinchman, 143-60. Albany, NY: State University of New York Press, 1997.

Oakes, Peter. "Re-Mapping the Universe: Paul and the Emperor in 1 Thessalonians and Philippians." *Journal for the Study of the New Testament* 27, no. 3 (2005): 301–22.
Orlin, Eric M. "Augustan Religion: From Locative to Utopian." In *Rome and Religion: A Cross-Disciplinary Dialogue on the Imperial Cult*, edited by Jeffrey Brodd and Jonathan L. Reed, 49–59. Atlanta, GA: Society of Biblical Literature, 2011.
Parker, David C. "The Eschatology of 1 Peter." *Biblical Theology Bulletin: A Journal of Bible and Theology* 24, no. 1 (February 1, 1994): 27–32.
Pidd, Helen, and Aidan Balfe. "Manchester Homeless People Face Jail Over City Centre Tent Camps." *The Guardian*, September 30, 2015.
Pitre, Brant. *Jesus, the Tribulation, and the End of the Exile: Restoration Eschatology and the Origin of the Atonement*. Tübingen: Mohr Siebeck, 2005.
Portier-Young, Anathea. *Apocalypse Against Empire: Theologies of Resistance in Early Judaism*. Grand Rapids, MI; Cambridge: Eerdmans, 2011.
Pratt, Kenneth J. "Rome as Eternal." *Journal of the History of Ideas* 26, no. 1 (January 1965): 25.
Price, S. R. F. "Gods and Emperors: The Greek Language of the Roman Imperial Cult." *The Journal of Hellenic Studies* 104 (January 1, 1984): 79–95.
Price, S. R. F. *Rituals and Power: The Roman Imperial Cult in Asia Minor*. Cambridge: Cambridge University Press, 1984.
Price, S. R. F. "The Place of Religion: Rome in the Early Empire." In *The Cambridge Ancient History, Vol. X: The Augustan Empire: 43 B.C. to A.D. 69*, edited by Alan K. Bowman, Edward Champlin, and Andrew Lintott, 2nd ed., 812–47. Cambridge: Cambridge University Press, 1996.
Price, S. R. F. *Religions of the Ancient Greeks*. Cambridge: Cambridge University Press, 1999.
Punt, Jeremy. "Empire and New Testament Texts: Theorising the Imperial, in Subversion and Attraction." *Hervormde Teologiese Studies/Theological Studies* 68, no. 1 (2012): 1–11. http://dx.doi.org/10.4102/hts.v68i1.1182.
Quijano, Aníbal. "Coloniality and Modernity/Rationality." *Cultural Studies* 21, no. 2–3 (March 1, 2007): 168–78.
Riches, John K., and David C. Sim, eds. *The Gospel of Matthew in Its Roman Imperial Context*. New York, NY: T&T Clark, 2005.
Rose, Gillian. "Place and Identity: A Sense of Place." In *A Place in the World?: Places, Cultures and Globalization*, edited by Doreen B. Massey and Pat Jess, 87–132. Oxford: Oxford University Press/Open University, 1995.
Rosenzweig, Franz. *The Star of Redemption*. Translated by Barbara E. Galli. Madison, WI: University of Wisconsin Press, 2005.
Rowe, Greg. *Princes and Political Cultures: The New Tiberian Senatorial Decrees*. Ann Arbor, MI: University of Michigan Press, 2002.
Rowe, Kavin C. *World Upside Down: Reading Acts in the Graeco-Roman Age*. New York, NY: Oxford University Press, 2009.
Rubin, Benjamin B. "(Re)presenting Empire: The Roman Imperial Cult in Asia Minor, 31 BC–AD 68." PhD diss., University of Michigan, 2008.
Scheid, John. *An Introduction to Roman Religion*. Edinburgh: Edinburgh University Press, 2003.
Schlosser, Jacques. *La Première épître de Pierre*. Commentaire Biblique: Nouveau Testament 21. Paris: Les Éditions du Cerf, 2011.
Schmid, Christian. "Henri Lefebvre's Theory of the Production of Space: Towards a Three-Dimensional Dialectic." In *Space, Difference, Everyday Life: Reading Henri*

Lefebvre, edited by Kanishka Goonewardena, Stefan Kipfer, Richard Milgrom, and Christian Schmid, 27–45. New York, NY: Routledge, 2008.

Schüssler Fiorenza, Elisabeth. "The First Letter of Peter." In *A Postcolonial Commentary on the New Testament Writings*, edited by Fernando F. Segovia and R. S. Sugirtharajah, 380–403. The Bible and Postcolonialism 13. London and New York: T&T Clark, 2009.

Schutter, William L. *Hermeneutic and Composition in 1 Peter*. Tübingen: Mohr Siebeck, 1989.

Scott, James C. *Weapons of the Weak: Everyday Forms of Peasant Resistance*. New Haven: Yale University Press, 1987.

Scott, James C. *Domination and the Arts of Resistance: Hidden Transcripts*. New Haven, CT and London: Yale, 1990.

Seland, Torrey. *Strangers in the Light: Philonic Perspectives on Christian Identity in 1 Peter*. Biblical Interpretation Series 76. Leiden: Brill, 2005.

Selwyn, E. G. *The First Epistle of St. Peter: The Greek Text with Introduction, Notes and Essays*. London: Macmillan, 1946.

Sherk, Robert K. *Roman Documents from the Greek East: Senatus Consulta and Epistulae to the Age of Augustus*. Baltimore, MD: Johns Hopkins University Press, 1969.

Sleeman, Matthew. *Geography and the Ascension Narrative in Acts*. Cambridge: Cambridge University Press, 2009.

Smallwood, E. M. *Documents Illustrating the Principates of Gaius, Claudius and Nero*. Cambridge: Cambridge, 1967.

Smith, Jonathan Z. *Drudgery Divine: On the Comparison of Early Christianities and the Religions of Late Antiquity*. Jordan Lectures in Comparative Religion 14. London: School of Oriental and African Studies, University of London, 1990.

Smith, R. R. R. "The Imperial Reliefs from the Sebasteion at Aphrodisias." *Journal of Roman Studies* 77 (November 1987): 88–138.

Smith, R. R. R. "Simulacra Gentium: The Ethne from the Sebasteion at Aphrodisias." *Journal of Roman Studies* 78 (November 1988): 50–77.

Soja, Edward W. *Thirdspace: Journeys to Los Angeles and Other Real-and-Imagined Places*. Cambridge, MA: Blackwell, 1996.

Spicq, Ceslaus. *Les Epîtres de Saint Pierre*. Paris: Gabalda, 1966.

Stern, Sacha. *Calendars in Antiquity: Empires, States, and Societies*. Oxford: Oxford University Press, 2012.

Sugirtharajah, R. S. "Charting the Aftermath: A Review of Postcolonial Criticism." In *The Postcolonial Biblical Reader*, edited by R. S. Sugirtharajah, 7–32. Oxford: Blackwell, 2006.

Talbert, Charles H., ed. *Perspectives on First Peter*. Macon, GA: Mercer University Press, 1986.

Terry, John. "Why ISIS Isn't Medieval." *Slate*, February 19, 2015.

Thatcher, Tom. *Greater Than Caesar: Christology and Empire in the Fourth Gospel*. Minneapolis, MN: Fortress Press, 2009.

The Woolf Report: A Summary of the Main Findings and Recommendations of the Inquiry into Prison Disturbances. London: Prison Reform Trust, 1991.

Webster, Jane. "Ethnographic Barbarity: Colonial Discourse and 'Celtic Warrior Societies.'" In *Roman Imperialism: Post-Colonial Perspectives*, edited by Jane Webster and Nicholas J. Cooper, 111–24. Leicester Archaeological Monographs 3, 1996.

Whitlark, Jason A. *Resisting Empire: Rethinking the Purpose of the Letter to "the Hebrews."* London/New York, NY: Bloomsbury, 2014.

Williams, Jennifer. "Manchester's Homeless Protest Camp Banned from City Centre." *Manchester Evening News*, July 20, 2015.

Williams, Martin. *The Doctrine of Salvation in the First Letter of Peter*. Cambridge: Cambridge University Press, 2011.

Williams, Travis B. "Reconsidering the Imperatival Participle in 1 Peter." *Westminster Theological Journal* 73 (2011): 59–78.

Williams, Travis B. *Persecution in 1 Peter: Differentiating and Contextualizing Early Christian Suffering*. Supplements to Novum Testamentum 145. Leiden: Brill, 2012.

Williams, Travis B. "The Divinity and Humanity of Caesar in 1 Peter 2,13: Early Christian Resistance to the Emperor and His Cult." *ZNW* 105 (2014): 131–47.

Wood, Graeme. "What ISIS Really Wants." *The Atlantic*, March 2015.

Zanker, Paul. *The Power of Images in the Age of Augustus*. Translated by Alan Shapiro. Ann Arbor, MI: University of Michigan Press, 1988.

INDEX OF BIBLICAL REFERENCES

HEBREW BIBLE AND SEPTUAGINT

Genesis
12:10 (LXX)	163
15:13 (LXX)	163
17:8	163
23:4 (LXX)	116, 162, 163
47:4 (LXX)	163
47:9 (LXX)	163

Exodus
2:22 (LXX)	163
6:4 (LXX)	163
12:11	104
19:5–6	104
24:16	102

Leviticus
11:44	116
25:23 (LXX)	162

Numbers
20:15	163

Deuteronomy
28:25	165
30:4	165

Ruth
1:1	163

2 Kings
4:29 (LXX)	104
9:1 (LXX)	104
19:29	101

1 Chronicles
29:15	162

Job
38:3 (LXX)	104
40:7 (LXX)	104

Psalms
34:12–16	116
38:13 (LXX)	162, 163
39:12	162
104:12 (LXX)	163
104:23 (LXX)	163
105:12	163
105:23	163
118:9 (LXX)	163
118:19 (LXX)	163
118:22	171
145:3–4	127
145:10	127

Proverbs
3:25 (LXX)	110 n.38
3:34	116
11:31	120 n.64

Qohelet
1:9	169

Isaiah
8:4	114
8:14–15	171
10:3 (LXX)	108 n.33
11:2	110
28:16	114, 171
40:4–9	127
40:6 (LXX)	101 n.7, 127
40:8	114, 114 n.51, 124
40:28	127
42:16	99
52:4 (LXX)	163
53:5–7	114
53:9	114
53:12	114

Jeremiah
1:17 (LXX)	104
6:15 (LXX)	108 n.33
29:11	25
34:17	165
41:17 (LXX)	165

Ezekiel
9:6 (LXX)	171 n.52
33:24	163

Hosea
1:6	116

Nahum
2:1 (LXX)	104

Zechariah
9–14	16–17, 116 n.55

Judith
5:7	163
5:8	163
5:10	163
5:19	165

Wisdom
3:7–8	108 n.33
13:1	105
14:22	105

1 Maccabees
10:30	101 n.7

2 Maccabees
1:27	165

New Testament

Matthew
1:11–12	67
5:12	121 n.66
5:16	108
3:17	25
24:42	107 n.32

Mark
1:11	25
1:16	62
13:32–37	107 n.32
16:19	25

Luke
1:51–53	21
1:68	108 n.33
3:21	25
12:37	107 n.32
24	112
24:51	25

John
3:5–6	172
7:35	165
8:31–59	117 n.59
20:17	25
21:18	104

Acts
4:13	62
7:6	163
7:29	163
7:43	67
12:8	104
13:17	163
15:7	68
17:6	179
17:30	105
20:31	107 n.32

Romans
3:23–24	10
4:13	163
8:31–39	9
8:35–39	8
12:1	102 n.9
12:6	109 n.36
13:1–7	9, 18
15:7–13	7

1 Corinthians
2:6–8	8
2:14	169
3:1	172
3:16	174
6:11	161 n.12
7:31	7
10:4	114
10:11	114
12:1	169
12:4–6	109 n.36
12:12	174
14:1	169
14:14–16	169
15:3–4	10
15:24–28	8
15:44	169
15:46	169
16:13	107 n.32

2 Corinthians
5:17	10
6:16	172
11:25–26	8

Galatians
1:4	7
2:8	68
6:14–15	9, 10

Ephesians
2:21–22	172
4:18	105
6:18	106 n.28

Philippians
1:13	8
1:27–30	9
2:6–11	9
3:20	9

Colossians
1:15–17	106 n.28
4:2	114

1 Thessalonians
5:1–5	8
5:1–10	107 n.32
5:1–11	9
5:6	106

2 Timothy
4:5	106

Hebrews
1:2	99
11:8–12	163
11:9	163
11:13	163

1 Peter
1:1	62–65, 69–70, 69 n.115, 158–69, 174, 175, 182
1:2	100, 124, 172, 173, 174
1:2–12	18
1:2–2:10	108 n.34
1:3	101, 101 n.7, 102 n.8, 120, 124, 166, 173, 175, 181
1:3–4	124
1:3–5	121 n.66
1:3–12	17
1:3–2:10	175 n.65
1:4	27, 101, 102 n.8, 113 n.48, 120, 124, 126, 165, 174, 182
1:4–5	120 n.64
1:5	100, 108 n.33, 120
1:6	108, 121 n.66, 127, 174

Index of Biblical References

Reference	Pages
1:6–7	18, 111, 120–1, 120 n.64
1:6–8	100–101, 119
1:7	105 n.21, 109, 119, 120, 120 n.64, 121, 122, 124
1:8	121, 182
1:9	100, 112, 121 n.66
1:10–12	106, 111–15, 116, 182
1:12	19, 104, 105 n.21, 112 n.44, 115, 174
1:12–13	103 n.14
1:13	18, 104, 105, 106–7, 106 n.22, 109 n.36, 115, 120 n.64, 121, 176
1:14	103, 104, 105, 115, 119
1:15–16	116
1:16	172
1:17	107, 120, 122, 124, 158, 159–164, 169, 174, 182
1:18	18, 103, 119, 124, 126, 164, 168, 176, 182
1:18–23	18
1:19–20	97–100
1:20	105 n.21, 113 n.47, 116, 121, 128, 182
1:23	101, 102 n.8, 102 n.9, 124, 176
1:23–25	103, 114
1:24	101 n.7
1:24–25	127
1:25	114, 124
2:1	14, 103
2:1–3	114, 166
2:1–10	18, 172
2:2	101 n.7, 102, 102 n.9, 170, 175–6
2:4	176
2:4–8	112 n.45, 114, 169, 170, 171 173 n.63
2:4–10	114, 169–73, 173–5, 182
2:5	101
2:6–7	172, 173
2:7	114
2:8	170, 171, 172
2:9	104
2:9–10	103, 104, 116, 119
2:10	103, 105, 108, 108 n.34, 116, 158, 159–64, 162 n.17, 172
2:11	108 n.34
2:11–12	18, 108, 108 n.33, 116, 119, 120, 120 n.64, 164, 174
2:12	19, 109, 123, 124, 168, 180, 182
2:13	124, 127
2:13–14	109
2:13–15	11–16, 18, 19, 119, 182
2:13–17	108
2:13–3:12	18, 109, 123
2:14	123
2:15	102, 122, 123, 124, 164, 173, 175, 180, 182
2:17	12
2:18	109
2:18–25	67, 168
2:18–3:7	109 n.36
2:19	109 n.36
2:20	19, 109 n.36, 113 n.46, 114–115
2:21	18, 112 n.45, 181
2:21–25	14
2:22	114
2:22–24	104
2:25	12
3:1	110
3:1–6	102 n.8, 125
3:4	116
3:5–6	110 n.38, 116
3:6	116
3:10–12	18
3:13–17	110
3:14	13, 123, 168, 180
3:15	109, 110, 123, 168
3:16	19
3:16–17	14, 119
3:17	18
3:17–18	18, 110, 110 n.40, 112 n.45
3:18–22	116
3:20	104, 108
3:21	121–3, 182
3:22	107, 110
4:1	103, 168
4:2	105
4:2–3	103
4:2–4	13 n.43, 18, 103, 107,

	116, 119, 168	4:17	120, 122, 170 n.48, 171–2, 171 n.52, 173, 182	5:9	102, 168, 173, 174, 182
4:4	107, 123, 164, 177, 182			5:9–10	18
4:5	109, 120, 123	4:17–18	120, 120 n.64	5:10	107, 109 n.36, 119, 120, 127
4:7	99, 104, 106, 108 n.33	4:19 5:1	123, 124 63, 108 n.3, 111, 119, 120 n.64, 121, 164, 167–169	5:12	18, 63, 173
4:8–11	107, 168			5:12–14	18
4:10	105 n.21, 109 n.36			5:12–14	17–18
4:12	107			5:13	14, 18, 66–7, 67–9, 102, 158–9, 164, 167–9
4:12–19	14, 18	5:1–4	122		
4:13	105 n.21, 108, 108 n.33, 109 n.36, 119, 120 n.64, 121, 121 n.66, 174	5:1–5	67		
		5:4	105 n.21, 119, 121, 125, 127, 174		
				2 Peter	
				3:1	65 n.98
		5:5	12, 105 n.21, 109 n.36, 116	3:3	99
				Jude	
		5:5–6	122	18	99
4:14	18, 19, 110, 119, 171 n.52, 172, 174, 176, 182	5:6	107, 120, 122	**Revelation**	
				14:8	67 n.103
		5:8	18, 104, 106–7	16:19	67 n.103
				17:5	67 n.103
		5:8–9	122	18:2	67 n.103
4:15–16	14, 18			18:10	67 n.103
4:16	67, 119, 123			18:21	67 n.103

INDEX OF MODERN AUTHORS

Achtemeier, Paul J. 15 n.50, 63 n.87,
    68 n.114, 98 n.1, 99 n.5, 102 n.9, 104,
    105 n.19, 105 n.21, 106 n.25, 106 n.29,
    108 n.33, 108 n.34, 109 n.36, 110,
    110 n.38, 112 n.44, 112 n.45, 113 n.46,
    113 n.47, 114 n.51, 116, 120 n.65,
    158 n.1, 160 n.9, 162 n.19, 165 n.28,
    165 n.30, 169 n.44, 170 n.47, 171 n.52,
    171 n.54, 171 n.56, 172 n.58, 172 n.60,
    173 n.63
Adam, Barbara 28 n.94, 68 n.114, 122
Allison, Eric 40 n.143
Ando, Clifford 24 n.86, 31 n.105, 31 n.108,
    38, 38 n.134, 38 n.135, 38 n.136, 39,
    48 n.22, 61 n.78, 61 n.79, 126 n.86,
    139 n.41, 141 n.52, 143 n.63, 147–8,
    147 n.86, 148 n.90, 180
Arnold, Bradley 107 n.31
Ausloos, Hans 64 n.94
Aymer, Margaret P. 7

Balch, David L. 12, 14 n.45, 110 n.37,
    110 n.39
Balfe, Aidan 1 n.1
Banazak, Gregory A. 28 n.96
Barclay, John M. G. 4–5, 8–10, 17, 179,
    181 n.4,
Bauckham, Richard 65 n.95, 112 n.44
Bauman-Martin, Betsy 12 n.36, 103 n.11,
    111 n.42
Beard, Mary 52 n.35, 52 n.36, 53 n.39,
    54 n.47, 54 n.49, 54 n.50, 55, 86 n.40
Beare, Francis W. 98 n.1, 102 n.9, 106 n.29,
    108 n.33, 108 n.34, 109 n.36, 112 n.45,
    113 n.46, 124 n.77, 165 n.29, 169 n.44
Bechtler, Steven R. 12, 161
Beetham, Christopher 117 n.61
Bell, Catherine 60, 86 n.41
Benjamin, Walter 117 n.58
Best, Ernest 64 n.90, 105 n.21, 109 n.36,
    112 n.44, 165 n.29, 171 n.56

Bhabha, Homi K. 58, 59 n.72
Bickerman, Elias 54
Bigg, Charles 68 n.114, 109 n.9
Bird, Jennifer G. 12
Bloch, Maurice 94 n.84
Boring, Eugene M. 4 n.1, 103
Bourdieu, Pierre 25
Boyarin, Daniel 117 n.59
Boyarin, Jonathan 37 n.132
Brox, Norbert 105 n.21, 106, 113 n.47,
    120 n.65
Burton, Graham 153 n.110
Butler, Katie 1 n.2

Carter, Warren 6 n.10, 12–14, 179, 181 n.4
Chakelian, Anoosh 33 n.117
Chapple, Alan 65 n.95, 111 n.42, 112 n.44
Charlesworth, Martin P. 89 n.52, 90 n.66
Chilton, David 67 n.103
Collins, John J. 99 n.3, 99 n.4, 121 n.68
Cooley, Alison E. 131 n.5, 143 n.66,
    144 n.68, 144 n.69, 145 n.74, 145 n.76,
    145 n.77, 145 n.78, 145 n.79, 146 n.80,
    146 n.81, 146 n.83, 148 n.88, 148 n.89,
    149 n.91
Crossan, John D. 6 n.11
Culpepper, R. Alan 26 n.91

Dalton, William J. 110 n.40
Davids, Peter H. 68 n.114, 108 n.34,
    109 n.36, 113 n.47, 165 n.29
Deissman, Adolf 4–5
Doering, Lutz 158 n.2, 165–7
Dube, Musa 8 n.19
Dubis, Mark 99 n.3, 106 n.25, 113 n.46,
    121 n.66, 158 n.1, 170 n.47
Dussel, Enrique 28 n.96

Elliott, John H. 12, 14 n.45, 17 n.61,
    62 n.84, 63 n.87, 64 n.90, 64 n.92,
    66 n.98, 66 n.99, 67 n.104, 68 n.109,

68 n.112, 68 n.114, 70 n.118, 98 n.1,
  99 n.3, 102 n.9, 102 n.10, 103, 104 n.17,
  105 n.18, 105 n.19, 105 n.21, 106–7,
  108 n.33, 108 n.34, 109 n.36, 110 n.38,
  112 n.44, 112 n.45, 113 n.48, 114 n.51,
  120 n.65, 159–63, 164 n.27, 165 n.28,
  165 n.29, 165 n.30, 169 n.44, 170–5

Fabian, Johannes 28–30, 34
Feldmeier, Reinhard 65 n.95, 101 n.7,
  102 n.8, 108 n.34, 109 n.36, 112 n.45,
  125, 160 n.9, 165 n.30, 165 n.32,
  171 n.56, 172 n.58
Fishwick, Duncan 55–6
Foucault, Michel 35, 118, 155 n.18
Friesen, Steven J. 26 n.91, 43 n.1, 44 n.6,
  46 n.13, 49 n.26, 51–2, 52 n.38, 53 n.40,
  53 n.41, 56 n.54, 78 n.13, 82, 84–5,
  88 n.48, 91 n.70, 91 n.74, 95 n.91, 96,
  122 n.70, 131 n.2, 134 n.22, 134 n.23,
  135 n.27, 136–7, 138 n.37, 140 n.47,
  140 n.50, 141 n.55, 143 n.61, 149 n.93

Galinsky, Karl 11 n.30, 52 n.38, 53 n.43
Gallois, William 29 n.99
Geertz, Clifford 51, 86
Gell, Alfred 28 n.94
Gentry, Kenneth 67 n.103
Gibbon, Edward 56 n.56
Goldstein, E. B. 34 n.121
Goppelt, Leonhard 15 n.51, 68 n.114,
  108 n.34, 109 n.36, 112 n.45, 165,
  169 n.44, 171 n.52
Gordon, Richard 59–62, 88 n.49, 91–2
Gradel, Ittai 41
Gramsci, Antonio 20, 21 n.76
Green, Joel 158 n.1, 162 n.22
Gregory, Andrew 66 n.98, 68 n.112
Grossman, Maxine 117 n.59
Gwyther, Anthony 6 n.10

Hall, Stuart 176–7
Hardin, Justin K. 6 n.10
Harland, Philip A. 60 n.74, 76 n.8, 150 n.99
Harris, William 147 n.86
Harrison, James R. 6 n.10
Harvey, David 25–6, 35–7, 154, 177
Haynes, Holly 76 n.7
Hays, Richard B. 114 n.49

Helgeland, John 132
Herrmann, Peter 92 n.78
Herz, Peter 83 n.26, 88 n.47, 91 n.69,
  91 n.71, 92 n.77
Holmes, Michael W. 65 n.98, 66 n.101
Hopkins, Keith 61
Horrell, David G. 13–16, 18–19, 63 n.86,
  63 n.87, 64 n.90, 65 n.95, 65 n.97,
  66 n.100, 66 n.102, 68 n.112, 68 n.113,
  68 n.114, 69 n.117, 70 n.118, 73 n.1,
  102 n.9, 107 n.31, 108 n.34, 112 n.45,
  114 n.50, 120 n.65, 123 n.74, 123 n.75,
  127 n.88, 160 n.9, 162–3, 165 n.30, 172,
  175 n.65, 180
Horsley, Richard A. 5–8
Hort, F. J. A. 69 n.116, 102 n.9, 105 n.17,
  105 n.19, 105 n.21, 108 n.34, 112 n.45,
  113 n.46, 120 n.64, 158 n.1, 170 n.47,
  171 n.55
Howard-Brook, Wes 6 n.10
Hubbard, Phil 35 n.123
Humphrey, John H. 147 n.86

Jenkins, Jack 33 n.119
Jennings, Willie J. 28 n.96
Jobes, Karen H. 64 n.93, 68 n.114, 101 n.7,
  102 n.9, 158 n.1, 160 n.9, 169 n.44,
  170 n.47, 170 n.48

Kelly, J. n. D. 68 n.114, 69 n.116, 98 n.1,
  102 n.9, 104 n.16, 104 n.17, 105 n.21,
  108 n.34, 109 n.36, 110 n.38, 112 n.44,
  112 n.45, 165 n.28, 165 n.29, 167 n.38,
  169 n.44, 171 n.56, 172 n.58
Kim, Seyoon 6 n.10
King, Helen 101 n.7
Kitchin, Rob 35 n.123

Lefebvre, Henri 35–7, 39–40, 132, 153
Lau, D. C. 32 n.111, 33 n.114
Lemmelijn, Bénédicte 64 n.94
Liebengood, Kelly 16–17, 116 n.55
Loomba, Ania 21 n.76, 22 n.82, 24 n.88,
  29 n.98, 58 n.70
Lozano, Fernando 57–8

McKnight, Scot 11 n.31, 160 n.9
McLean, Bradley H. 74 n.4, 81 n.17,
  82 n.22

Index of Modern Authors

Magie, David 69 n.115, 82 n.22
Maier, Harry O. 26 n.91
Malbon, Elizabeth S. 26 n.91
Martin, Ralph P. 17 n.62, 98 n.1
Martin, Troy 162 n.17, 166 n.35
Massey, Doreen 27 n.93, 35, 37, 39 n.140, 176 n.66
Mbuvi, Andrew 172 n.62, 173 n.63
Meeks, Wayne A. 122-3
Meggitt, Justin J. 5 n.5, 5 n.6, 44 n.5, 155
Menken, M. J. J. 62 n.85
Metzger, Bruce M. 66 n.98
Michaels, J. Ramsey 11-12, 14 n.44, 63 n.89, 63 n.90, 64 n.91, 66 n.99, 68 n.114, 102 n.9, 104 n.17, 105 n.18, 105 n.20, 106 n.27, 108 n.33, 108 n.34, 109 n.35, 109 n.36, 112 n.45, 113 n.46, 120 n.65, 121, 123 n.75, 123 n.76, 158 n.1, 160 n.9, 165 n.28, 167, 169 n.44, 171 n.52, 171 n.54, 171 n.55, 172
Mikalson, Jon D. 43 n.1
Millar, Fergus 13 n.42, 44 n.5, 181 n.4
Miller, Daniel 125 n.84
Mitchell, Stephen 45, 47 n.18, 49 n.27, 50 n.28, 50 n.29, 51 n.34, 56 n.55, 61, 69 n.115, 70 n.118, 79 n.14, 80 n.15, 87 n.43, 87 n.44, 134-5, 154 n.115, 154 n.116
Modica, Joseph B. 11 n.31
Moore, F. G. 89-90
Moore, Stephen D. 5 n.7, 19 n.67, 58 n.69
Moyise, Steve 62 n.85, 114 n.50, 115
Munn, Nancy D. 28 n.94, 78, 83

Nicolet, Claude 131-2, 144, 146, 149 n.92
Noor, Farish A. 116-17
North, John A. 52 n.35, 53 n.39, 54 n.47, 54 n.49, 54 n.50, 55, 60 n.73
Novitz, David 117-18

Oakes, Peter 9-11, 17
Orlin, Eric M. 135 n.26

Parker, David C. 105 n.21, 120 n.64
Pidd, Helen 1 n.1
Pitre, Brant 99 n.3
Portier-Young, Anathea 23 n.83, 26 n.91, 99 n.3, 125 n.84

Pratt, Kenneth 89 n.52, 90 n.61
Price, S. R. F. 5, 15 n.50, 43 n.1, 44 n.2, 44 n.4, 45 n.11, 46 n.16, 47-8, 49 n.24, 49 n.26, 50 n.28, 50 n.30, 51, 52 n.35, 52 n.36, 52 n.37, 53 n.39, 53 n.43, 54 n.47, 54 n.49, 54 n.50, 55, 56 n.54, 56 n.55, 56 n.58, 57 n.62, 57 n.64, 58 n.65, 61, 67, 77 n.9, 81, 83, 84 n.32, 84 n.33, 84 n.34, 84 n.35, 86 n.39, 87 n.45, 87 n.46, 88, 91, 93 n.80, 93 n.81, 94, 122, 133, 134 n.20, 135 n.26, 136 n.31, 149, 150, 151-3, 181, 182
Punt, Jeremy 8 n.17

Quijano, Aníbal 28 n.96

Reed, Jonathan L. 6 n.11, 51 n.33, 52 n.38, 135 n.26
Reyes Ceja, Luis 28 n.96
Riches, John K. 6 n.10,
Rose, Gillian 39 n.140, 175 n.64
Rosenzweig, Franz 125-6
Rowe, Greg 46 n.14, 46 n.17, 92 n.78, 93 n.79
Rowe, Kavin C. 6 n.10
Rubin, Benjamin B. 31, 43 n.1, 54 n.48, 56 n.55, 56 n.58, 58, 94 n.86, 94 n.87, 95, 134 n.24, 138 n.36, 138 n.37, 139 n.39, 140 n.51, 141 n.54, 141 n.56, 143 n.65, 144, 145 n.75, 146 n.80, 147

Scheid, John 74 n.4
Schlosser, Jacques 112 n.45, 113 n.47, 158 n.1, 163 n.24
Schmid, Christian 36 n.126, 36 n.128
Schüssler Fiorenza, Elisabeth 5, 12
Schutter, William L. 65 n.95, 112, 113 n.46, 115 n.54
Scott, James C. 3, 15, 19-25, 41, 180, 182
Seland, Torrey 160 n.9
Selwyn, E. G. 18 n.63, 102 n.9, 105 n.21, 106 n.27, 108 n.33, 108 n.34, 112 n.44, 112 n.45, 112 n.46, 113 n.46, 169 n.46, 170 n.47, 171 n.52, 171 n.56, 172-3
Sherk, Robert K. 46 n.13, 74 n.3, 79 n.14, 81
Sim, David C. 6 n.10
Sleeman, Matthew 26 n.91, 35 n.123

Smallwood, E. M. 54 n.46
Smith, Jonathan Z. 51 n.32
Smith, R. R. R. 95 n.91, 138 n.36, 138 n.37, 138 n.38, 139–43
Soja, Edward 35, 36 n.126
Spicq, Ceslaus 68 n.114, 69 n.115, 98 n.1, 105 n.21, 112 n.45, 169 n.45
Stern, Sacha 78 n.11, 81 n.18, 81 n.21, 82 n.23, 82 n.24
Sugirtharajah, R. 5 n.7, 12 n.36

Talbert, Charles H. 14 n.45
Terry, John 34 n.120

Thatcher, Tom 6 n.10
Tuckett, Christopher 66 n.98, 68 n.112

Webster, Jane 30 n.103, 31 n.107
Whitlark, Jason A. 6 n.10, 89 n.57
Williams, Jennifer 2 n.3
Williams, Martin 101 n.6, 120 n.65, 121 n.66,
Williams, Travis B. 13, 15–17, 18 n.65, 19, 63 n.90, 66 n.99, 67 n.104, 69 n.115, 69 n.117, 70 n.118, 106 n.22, 106 n.25, 107 n.31, 109 n.35, 160 n.9, 180
Wood, Graeme 33

www.ingramcontent.com/pod-product-compliance
Lightning Source LLC
Chambersburg PA
CBHW052042300426
44117CB00012B/1937